"In what other land save this one
is the commonest form of greeting
not 'Good day,' nor 'How d'ye do,'
but 'Love'?
That greeting is 'Aloha' —
love, I love you, my love to you."

— Jack London

KAUAI TRAILBLAZER
Where to Hike, Snorkel, Bike, Paddle, Surf

Second edition, revised third printing
text by Jerry Sprout
photographs, design, production by Janine Sprout

For Cynthia, Deanne and Roger

ISBN 0-9670072-1-6
Library of Congress Catalog Card Number: 99-091787

Diamond Valley Company, Publisher
89 Lower Manzanita Drive
Markleeville, CA 96120

Find us online at: www.trailblazertravelbooks.com
Printed in the United States of America

Mahalo to: Susan Kanoho, Kauaʻi Visitors Bureau; Lani Kawahara, Hawaii State Public Library; Nalani
Kaʻauawai Brun, Office of Economic Development; Kaleo Hoʻokano, Water Safety Supervisor; Mary
A. Requilman, Kauaʻi Historical Society; Keith Nitta, County Planning Department; Linda Monroe et.
al., Oceanfront Realty; Fred and Carol Tangalin; Tarey W. Low and Sam Lee, Department of Land and
Natural Resources; Frederick Wichman, Kauaʻi Place Names; Beth Tokioka, Public Information Officer,
Mayor's Office; Keala Senkus, Hularoom; Jodi Esaki; Rudival and Jamie Niere; Edwin Hagstrom; Tebo
Booth, Na Hula O Kaohikakapulani Hula Halau; Donald Bodine, Suite Paradise; Kokeʻe State Park staff;
Diane Ferry, Kinipopo Gallery; Jessica and Tracy at KKCR; Lilian de Mello; Kapaʻa Camera Club; Phyllis
Crain, Limahuli Tropical Garden; Judy Drosd and Brenda, Kauaʻi Film Commission; Robert Sanford H&S
Publishing; Phyllis Segawa, Lee Scott Sloane, Janet Leopold, and Richard Kanahele at Allerton Gardens;
Paulette Burtner, Kokeʻe Natural History Museum; Darrell Aquino, Hyatt Resorts; Ed Sancious, Hanalei
Photo Company; the crew at Holoholo Charters; Jo Evans, Outfitters Kauai; Chris Faye, Wilfred Ibara at
Gay & Robinson; Doug and Sand McMaster at Ki Hoalu; Bill and Michelle Dick; Denise Carswell, Amy
Vanderhoop, and all at Princeville Ranch; Dawn M. Traina; Chuck and Hollis at Air Kauai; Joe and Lihue
Kinimaka-Lopez; Aunty Rose; Margaret and Dennis Daniels; Samara and Frank, Children's Discovery
Musuem; Tiane, David, and Cole Cleveland at Wailua River Kayak; Chris Porter at Kauaʻi Adventure
Activities; Titus Kinimaka; and to everyone else who shared their Kauaʻi with us. Aloha!

Proofreaders: John Manzolati, Cynthia Sprout, Greg Hayes

cover: Napali Coast

Napali Coast

KAUA'I TRAILBLAZER IS DEDICATED TO THE HAWAIIAN PEOPLE, PAST
AND PRESENT, AND TO CONSERVING THE NATURAL WONDERS, CULTURE
AND TRADITIONS OF THIS PLACE THEY CALL THE GARDEN ISLE.

Waipo'o Falls

KAUAI

Trailblazer

WHERE TO
HIKE SNORKEL BIKE PADDLE SURF

JERRY & JANINE SPROUT

DIAMOND VALLEY COMPANY
MARKLEEVILLE, CALIFORNIA
PUBLISHERS
© COPYRIGHT 2006

TABLE OF CONTENTS

INTRODUCING KAUAʻI

Covering an area of 65 million square miles, the Pacific Ocean is by far the biggest single feature on Earth—as big as the other oceans combined and easily larger than the world's land masses put together. A satellite photo over the Pacific shows nothing but blue.

In the center of these waters is the Hawaiian Archipelago, some 125 islands strung in a line for nearly two-thousand miles. All the archipelago's islands comprise the State of Hawaiʻi, except the northern-most Midway Islands which are administered by the U.S. Navy. If territorial waters are considered, Hawaii covers a far larger area than Alaska. But in terms of land mass, the state is the 47th smallest, larger only than Connecticut, Rhode Island or Delaware.

NIʻIHAU

KAUAʻI

OAHU

MOLOKAI

LANAI

MAUI

KAHOOLAWE

HAWAIʻI

THE
HAWAIIAN ISLANDS

N

The archipelago is the top of the Hawaiian Ridge, a mountain range standing in seawater about 5 miles deep. Snow gathers on its 13,000-foot peaks, though situated well south of the Tropic of Cancer. Considering its entirety, the Hawaiian Ridge is the tallest mountain range on Earth.

Almost all of the islands in the archipelago are sea-washed atolls, barely above a foaming surface and home to only birds and aquatic life. Ninety-nine percent of Hawai'i's 6,415 square miles is shared among its eight most southerly islands, and two-thirds of that area is allotted to just the Big Island of Hawai'i.

In terms of people, three-quarters of the state's 1.3 million live on Oahu, about 100 miles southeast of Kaua'i. Maui and the Big Island each have more than twice Kaua'i's 75,000 resident and visitor population.

These are the most isolated populations in the world—about 2,500 miles from San Francisco, Los Angeles and Seattle to the northeast, and the same distance from Alaska, which is due north. (Although the archipelago extends west of the Bering Sea, the principal islands of the state do not take most-westerly honors from Alaska.) Japan is almost 4,000 miles to the northwest. To the south, southeast and southwest, 2,500 miles of open sea lie between Hawai'i and other Polynesian islands of Tahiti, Tonga and the Marquesas. The largest chunk of land southward is Antarctica.

Kaua'i—Kow-WAH-ee—is the northernmost of the populated Hawaiian Islands and by far the most ancient—volcanic origins date back millions of years whereas the lava has not stopped bubbling on the Big Island 400 miles to the south.

At the center of Kaua'i is 5,148-foot Mount Waialeale—Wey-ahlee-ahlee— forming the rim of an ancient volcanic caldera that, at 60 square miles, is the largest in the Pacific. Waialeale, located nearly at the center of the world's largest body of saltwater, receives the most rainfall in the world—an average of 460 inches per year. Over the eons, the island's caldera has evolved into Alakai Swamp—lying 4,000 feet above sea-level, the highest of any swamp environment in the world. As one Kauaian saying is translated, "At the birthplace of all waters, it rains and rains, and then it pours."

Rainfall on other parts of the island is radically less. Kaua'i's arid, leeward west shore gets 15 to 30 inches per year, its windward north shore gets 60 to 90 inches on average, and parts of eastern portions of the island get 40 to 60 inches of rain per year. The rain comes in buckets, both in storms and quick showers, followed by intense tropical sunshine that extends for days. The average temperature on Kaua'i is 75 degrees, around the clock, around the calendar. The average high varies just 8 degrees from the average low, and temperatures rarely break 90 degrees and never 100.

Although weather conditions cycle over a year—primarily winter's northerly trade winds and rains give way to summer's southerly Kona winds and drier conditions—on Kaua'i it is eternal summer. Something is always in bloom. These climatic conditions led to Kaua'i's nickname of the Garden Island. Virtually everything that can grow and doesn't require a cold snap is growing here, from redwoods to pineapples. Three of the country's five National Tropical Botanical Gardens are here.

The profusion of plant life that blankets Kaua'i in many shades of green also accents its startling topography: Rain, plus millennia of trade winds and pounding surf have turned what was once a volcanic dome into a series of towering ridges radiating

Nukoli'i

out from the center of the island to the sea, ridges above valleys and canyons 3- to 4-thousand-feet deep and made of red volcanic earth held together by a tremendous root mass of tropical greenery.

These valleys yield more than a dozen rivers and large streams, the only navigable fresh water in Hawai'i. The origins of these waterways are a capillary system of streams and brooks that seep from the swamp or spring from cliff walls. Many of these contributing streams are obscured by jungle foliage, only becoming apparent after a rainstorm when dark green ridges are streaked with silvery waterfalls. Where rivers and streams meet the sea are wide slack-water lagoons extending inland from a mile to several miles before disappearing into riverbank flora or giving way to rapids and cascades. At the beach, these rivers are most often shallow, almost dammed by surf-born yellow sand. During storm conditions, the slack waters can become debris-filled torrents of destruction.

Along Kaua'i's 110-mile coast, in between the rivers and streams, are grassy, open bluffs fringed by sand and coral reef beaches. The notable exception to this landscape is Napali—The Cliffs—a 25-mile quadrant of the northwest coastline. Here ridges end in wave-battered cliffs, inaccessible by car and only partially accessible by foot. Even in Napali, however, there are little beaches with valleys that supported Hawaiian communities for centuries.

Kaua'i has the longest sand beach in the islands, as well as the longest coral reef. Many of its dozens of beaches and coves are accessible only by hikes. Generally speaking, in the winter, north side beaches near Hanalei are pounded by the trade wind's swells and the south beaches of Poipu are relatively calm. In the summer, the opposite is true, as southerly Kona winds bring bigger surf to the south and the north shore's coves become aquamarine pools. Beaches on the west and east are variable in terms of water conditions—but beach conditions everywhere can vary greatly from day to day.

Kaua'i's physical features—while perhaps beyond the scope of any engineer's or animator's imagination—are perfectly designed for recreational exploration. Roads go inland at numerous places and ancient trails rim the coast and follow ridges to dizzying heights, inviting hikers and mountain bikers. Surfing beaches are too numerous to be crowded, although on any given day the local boarders may flock to the hottest spot. Coral reefs and coves create saltwater pools—home to some 650 species of fish—made for snorkeling and swimming. River lagoons and protected bays invite kayaks and outrigger canoes. These activities combined are the only way to fully appreciate this complex island.

While ecotourism may be part of Kaua'i's future economic health, it is only a recent development. The island's powerful beauty is just a backdrop for the story of the world's least understood and perhaps most interesting human migrations. The first Polynesians, from the Marquesas, sailed here in 200 AD, followed by a second migration from Tahiti that ended in the 1400s. Polynesian life was undisturbed by any other cultural influence until Europeans and Americans arrived in the late 1700s.

Alakai Swamp, Hanalei Bay

Getting To & Driving Around Kaua‘i

Air Travel
Lihue Airport, 808-246-1440
United Airlines nonstop to Lihue from Los Angeles. Other carriers fly to Honolulu, with inter-island connections on Hawaiian Airlines or Aloha Airlines. Other mainland carriers include Delta and American Airlines, plus charters. Hawaiian Airlines offers lower rates for stays of more than 30 days, and is equipped to handle surfboards and bicycles.

Car Rentals
All major car rental agencies are available at Lihue Airport.

Public Transportation
A public bus with limited schedules is available on most parts the island. For routes and timetables call County of Kaua‘i Transportation, 808-241-6410. Buses do not allow bicycles, surfboards or luggage larger than a carry-on. The bus does not service the airport.

Drive Times
From road's end at one end of the island to road's end at the other is about a two-hour drive—part of the island's coastline is roadless. All roads are scenic, with traffic only at junctions around Lihue and Kapa‘a in the morning and evening. There are no freeways; maximum speed is 50 mph.

From Lihue to:

Nawiliwili Harbor, 2 mi., 5 min.

Kalaheo, 14 mi., 20 min.

Koloa, 11 mi., 20 min.

Poipu, 15 mi., 25 min.

Hanapepe, 19 mi., 35min.

Waimea Town, 23 mi., 40 min.

Kekaha, 27 mi., 45 min.

Barking Sands Beach, 36 mi., 60 min.

Waimea Canyon, 34 mi., 60 min.

Koke‘e State Park, 38 mi., 70 min.

From Lihue to:

Wailua, 6 mi., 15 min.

Kapa‘a, 9 mi., 20 min.

Anahola, 14 mi., 25 min.

Kilauea, 24 mi., 35 min.

Princeville, 27 mi., 40 min.

Hanalei, 31 mi., 50 min.

Haena, 38 mi., 60 min.

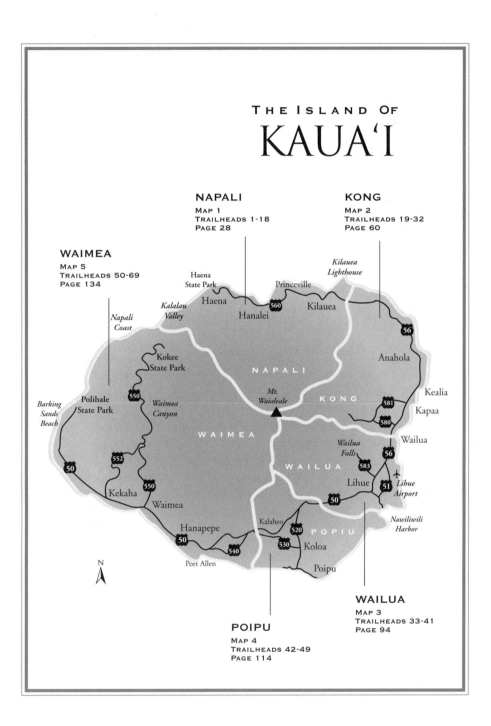

THE ISLAND OF

KAUA'I

NAPALI
MAP 1
TRAILHEADS 1-18
PAGE 28

KONG
MAP 2
TRAILHEADS 19-32
PAGE 60

WAIMEA
MAP 5
TRAILHEADS 50-69
PAGE 134

Kilauea
Lighthouse

Haena
State Park

Princeville

*Kalalau
Valley*

Haena

560

Kilauea

Hanalei

*Napali
Coast*

Kokee
State Park

N A P A L I

Anahola

56

*Mt.
Waialeale*

Kealia

*Barking
Sands
Beach*

Polihale
State Park

550

*Waimea
Canyon*

K O N G

581

Kapaa

580

Wailua

50

552

W A I M E A

*Wailua
Falls*

56

583

W A I L U A

Lihue

51

Lihue
Airport

Kekaha

550

Waimea

*Nawiliwili
Harbor*

Hanapepe

50

Kalaheo

520

530

Koloa

P O P I U

540

Port Allen

Poipu

N

POIPU
MAP 4
TRAILHEADS 42-49
PAGE 114

WAILUA
MAP 3
TRAILHEADS 33-41
PAGE 94

Key To Reading Trailhead Descriptions

23. TRAILHEAD NAME   Activities Banner
    What's Best:
    Parking:
Hike: (S A M P L E)
Snorkel, Bike, Paddle, Surf

"23." Trailhead Number: These correspond to the numbers shown on the five Trailhead Maps. There are 69 trailheads. Numbering begins on Map 1, Napali Trailheads, and numbers get bigger as you go clockwise around the island. Trailhead 69 is at the top of Waimea Canyon, on Trailhead Map 5. Within the text of the Trailhead Descriptions, numbering starts at "1." and continues sequentially.

Trailhead name: This is where you park for hiking, snorkeling and the other activities originating at this trailhead.

Activities Banner: This shows which of the five recreational activities are possible at this trailhead. Activities include one or more of the following, always listed in this order:

Hike:	Trail treks, beach walks, and around-town strolls.
Snorkel:	Both fish viewing and swimming in areas that are not in breaking surf.
Bike:	Trails, dirt roads, rural roads, and touring around town.
Paddle:	Kayaking and canoeing in rivers and streams, lagoons and bays.
Surf:	Surfing, boogie boarding, and body surfing.

What's Best: Tells you, in a nutshell, what's best about this trailhead.

Parking: Gives specific directions to the trailhead and where to park. A single trailhead may include additional parking instructions to nearby activities within the same general locale.

Abbreviations used in parking directions:

Since Kaua'i is circular, with highways around its coast, compass directions change as you drive. "Toward the mountain" and "toward the ocean" are a traditional way of giving directions in the islands.

Makai = Turn toward the ocean

Mauka = Turn toward the mountains, inland

mm. = Mile Marker. All island highways are marked at each mile, beginning at "0" where they originate. Marker signs show both the miles from the beginning and the highway you are on. For instance, mm. 6/50, is mile marker 6 on Hwy. 50. Both Hwy. 50 and Hwy. 56 originate in Lihue. Hwy. 56 goes toward Hanalei, with numbers ascending in that direction. Hwy. 50 goes to ward Polihale, with numbers ascending in that direction. Driving direction are usually given heading away from Lihue, toward the higher mile marker numbers.

HIKE: The first paragraph after the **HIKE:** symbol gives the destination of each hike for this trailhead (followed by the roundtrip distance for that destination in parentheses).

NOTE: ALL HIKING DISTANCES IN PARENTHESES ARE ROUNDTRIP.

The second and following paragraphs after the **HIKE:** symbol give details about the hike's destination, including directions. The first mention of a **Hike Destination** is boldfaced. Hike destinations are described in the same order in which they are listed in the first hiking paragraph.

SNORKEL, BIKE, PADDLE, SURF: Following the hiking descriptions are the letter symbols for the other activities that are available at this trailhead. Descriptions and details about each activity follow its symbols. The **Location** at which the activity takes place is boldfaced. Each trailhead, for example, may have several places to surf or ride a mountain bike. Directions to each activity are either the parking directions, or otherwise noted in the text.

Activities are always listed in the same order, i.e., hiking, followed by snorkeling, mountain biking, paddling and surfing. If an activity is not available at a particular trailhead, its symbol is not listed.

More Stuff: Lists secondary activities, often less popular (and less crowded) and harder to get to.

Be Aware: Notes hazards and gives safety tips.

TRAILHEAD DIRECTORY

A list of trailheads and their activities.

HIKE: HIKES & WALKS

PADDLE: KAYAKING & CANOEING

SNORKEL: SNORKELING & SWIMMING

SURF: SURFING & BOOGIE BOARDING

BIKE: MOUNTAIN AND ROAD BIKING

NAPALI

KONG

WAILUA
Map 3, Trailheads 33 through 41

POIPU
Map 4, Trailheads 42 through 49

WAIMEA
Map 5, Trailheads 50 through 69

Anahola

THE BEST OF KAUA'I

WHAT DO YOU WANT TO DO TODAY?

Best For Hikers—

Kealia Beach

Best For Hikers, cont'd—

TREES AND JUNGLE

Bamboo Forest, TH8, page 40
Sleeping Giant, TH30, page 81
Kuilau Ridge Trail, TH32, page 84
Allerton Garden, TH46, page 124
Haele'ele Ridge, TH60, page 156
Kumuwela Lookout, TH63, page 161
Nualolo Trail, TH66, page 163
Halemanu-Kokee Trail, TH67, page 165

TOWN WALKABOUTS

Hanalei, TH7, page 38
Kapa'a, TH28, page 76
Nawiliwili Harbor, TH41, page 106
Hanapepe, TH51, page 132
Waimea, TH54, page 144
Koloa, DT1, page 175

LONG-AND-SCENIC BEACHES

Kepuhi Point, TH3, page 33
Lumahai Beach, TH5, page 35
Secret Beach, TH16, page 52
Larsens Beach, TH20, page 62
Aliomanu, TH22, page 66
Nukoli'i Beach, TH35, page 100
Kekaha, TH55, page 147
Barking Sands, TH57, page 150

PEOPLE-WATCHING BEACHES

Hanalei Bay, TH7, page 37
Pu'u Poa Beach, TH9, page 43
Coconut Coast, TH29, page 78
Kalapaki Bay, TH41, page 106
Poipu Beach, TH44, page 119

HIKE-TO ONLY BEACHES

Hanakapiai Beach, TH1, page 29
Hideaways and Kenomene Beach,
    TH9, page 42
Queens Baths and Kaweonui Beach,
    TH10, page 45
Wyllies Beach, TH11, page 46
Secret Beach, TH16, page 52
Waiakalua Beach, TH19, page 61
Larsens Beach, TH20, page 62
Donkey and House Beach,
    TH26, page 72
Haula Beach, TH42, page 115
Wahiawa Bay, TH50, page 135
Pakala Beaches, TH53, page 143

**PORTS, PIERS,
JETTYS & MARINAS**

Hanalei Pier, TH7, page 37
Wailua Marina, TH33, page 95
Ahukini Landing, TH39, page 104
Nawiliwili, TH41, page 106
Kukuiula Bay, TH45, page 122
Port Allen, TH50, page 135
Waimea Pier, TH54, page 144

Hanalei Pier

Best For Snorkelers—

BEST OVERALL
Keʻe Beach, TH1, page 32
Tunnels Beach, TH2, page 33
Puʻu Poa, TH9, page 43
Anahola Bay, TH23, page 68
Lydgate Park, TH34, page 99
Poipu Beach, TH44, page 120
Prince Kuhio, TH45, page 122
Niʻihau-Lehua, TH50, page 136
Salt Pond Beach Park,
    TH52, page 141

HIKE-TO SNORKELING SPOTS
Hideaways & Kenomene,
    TH9, page 43
Kaweonui Beach, TH10, page 45
Waiakalua Beaches, TH19, page 62
Papaʻa Bay, Aliomanu Beach,
    TH22, page 63
House Beach, TH26, page 72
Wahiawa Bay, TH50, page 137

A QUIET DAY AT THE BEACH
Waikoko Beach, TH6, page 36
Anini Beach, TH13, page 49
Secret Beach, TH16, TH17, page 52
Kilauea Bay, TH18, page 54
Larsens Beach, TH20, page 63
Moloaʻa Bay, TH21, page 65
Aliomanu Beach, TH22, page 66
Queens Pond, Barking Sands,
    TH57, page 149

LOCAL-STYLE BEACHES
Kalihiwai Bay, TH14, page 50
Anahola Beach Park, TH24, page 69
Kealia Beach, TH27, page 73
Hanamaulu Bay, TH38, page 103
Lucy Wright Beach Park,
    TH54, page 146

Best For Mountain Bikers—

MOUNTAIN AND RIDGE VISTA
Powerline North, TH12, page 47
Waipaheʻe Falls, TH25, page 71
Moalepe Trail, TH31, page 83
Alexander Reservoir, TH49, page 129
Haeleʻele Ridge, TH60, page 156
Polihale Ridge, TH61, page 157
Kaʻaweiki Ridge, TH62, page 158

TROPICAL FOREST
Waialeale Basin, TH32, page 89
Halemanu Valley, TH63, page 161
Kumuwela Road, TH67, page 168
Mohihi Road, TH67, page 168

COASTAL
Kealia Beach, TH27, page 74
Kapaʻa Town, TH28, page 77
Coconut Coast, TH29, page 80
Ahukini Coast, TH40, page 106
Cane Coast Road, TH45, page 123
Salt Pond Beach Park, TH52, page 141

RIDEABOUT TOWN
Hanalei, TH7, page 39
Princeville, TH11, page 46
Kapaʻa and Coconut
  Coast, TH28-29, pages 77, 80
Nawiliwili Harbor, TH41, page 108
Waimea Town, TH54, page 146

PASTORAL ON PAVEMENT
Hanalei Wildlife Refuge, TH8, page 42
Kahiliholo Uplands, TH15, page 51
Moloaʻa Bay, TH21, page 65
Olohena Highlands, TH31, page 83
Kukuiolono Park, TH48, page 128

Best For Paddlers—

BEST OVERALL

PADDLE IN PRIVACY

Princeville Ranch

SEA VENTURES

Best For Surfers—

WINTER SURF

SUMMER SURF

ALL-YEAR POSSIBILITIES

PLACES TO WATCH SURFERS

Best Free Hula Shows—

Poipu Beach, TH44, page 119
Princeville Hotel, DT3, page 191
Coconut Marketplace, DT3, page 187
Kaua'i Marriott, DT1, page 173
Kukui Grove Shopping Center,
    DT1, page 172
Hyatt Regency, DT1, page 175

Best For A Rainy Day—

MUSEUMS AND ATTRACTIONS
Waioli Mission, DT3, page 172
Kaua'i Museum, DT1, page 172
Grove Farm, DT1, page 172
Kilohana Plantation, DT1, page 179
Waimea Sugar Museum,
    DT4, page 199
Kokee Natural History
    Museum, DT4, page 200
See Museums in Resource Links, page 226

HOTELS WITH HAWAIIANA ON DISPLAY
Princeville Resort, DT3, page 190
Kaua'i Marriott, DT1, page 173
Hyatt Regency Kaua'i, DT1, page 175
Sheraton Kaua'i Resort, DT1, page 176

WALK-AROUND SOUVENIR SHOPPING
Hanalei Town, DT3, page 92
Kapa'a Town, TH28, page 73
Coconut Marketplace, DT2, page 187
Kukui Grove, DT1, page 172
Nawiliwili Harbor, TH41, page 102
Koloa, DT1, page 175
Hanapepe, DT4, page 197

Best Local Style Eats—
see Resource Links, page 244

Aloha Diner
Duane's Ono-Char Burger
Hanamura Saimin Stand
Hanama'ulu Restaurant
Lihue Barbecue Inn
Hanalei Mixed Plate
Moloa'a Sunrise Fruit Stand
Ono Family Restaurant

Best Pacific Rim Gourmet—

A Pacific Cafe
Cafe Coco
Duke's Canoe Club
Hyatt Regency Ilima Terrace
Keoki's Paradise
Lighthouse Bistro
Mema Thai Chinese Cuisine
Princeville Hotel Cafe Hanalei

Poipu

Kalalau Trail

When the Academy Award-winning movie *South Pacific* was released in 1958, Americans were left wondering where the film's magical paradise existed in real life. They discovered that this "South Pacific" was actually on the north shore of the northernmost Hawaiian island in the north Pacific—and Kaua'i became a premier destination.

With fancifully sculpted ridges, spewing waterfalls, exotic beaches and several river lagoons, the north side of Kaua'i fits the image for most people's fantasy of what tropical splendor should be.

At road's end on the north shore is where Napali—or The Cliffs—begin. From here the notorious Kalalau Trail takes hikers on an arduous 11-mile trek along Napali to the Kalalau Valley, ducking into and out of other valleys along the way. Kalalau remains a remote and mysterious place—with stone terraces echoing an ancient Hawaiian village long since vanished, and inaccessible inlets, where many a bandito or recluse has successfully hidden out. The most famous desperado was Ko'olau the Leper, who, with his wife and young son, was able to evade a military assault by authorities trying to deport the afflicted man to Molokai. After three years, the disease finally overcame both Ko'olau and his son, leaving his courageous and loving wife to make the trek alone back to her village.

Near the Kalalau trailhead are Ke'e and Tunnels beaches, whose reef-protected waters are home to schools of colorful fish and a lure for snorkelers. Surfers ride the reef break at several places offshore of these beaches, near Haena Beach Park.

Just inland from Ke'e Beach, up Limahuli Steam, is one of Kaua'i's three National Tropical Botanical Gardens. Just around the point from Ke'e, where Bali Hai Ridge meets the ocean, is perhaps the most sacred spot in all the islands, a heiau and hula platform where cultural tradition was enacted for centuries in the form of dance and chanting. These ancient arts are still practiced there today.

Heading down the highway from Napali, several rivers and streams intersect the coast, originating in deep, steep valleys that cleave the island to its center. The Wainiha, Lumahai and Hanalei rivers are all navigable for kayakers, with a mile to several miles of still-water lagoons where fresh water meets the sea.

Wainiha River—the closest of the three to road's end—is noted for its rickety one-lane bridges. The river is framed by Wainiha Pali, a 4,000-foot high rippling green cliff that curls inland, serving as a high-altitude dam for the Alakai Swamp, which is on its other side. Wainiha Valley was home to the last of Kaua'i's original inhabitants, the Menehune people, 65 of whom were recorded as residents here by the U.S. Census in the late 1800s. Paddling the river here is one way to catch a view of this valley.

Lumahai, the next valley over from Wainiha, ends at Lumahai Beach, the poster shot for *South Pacific*. Lumahai is a huge sand beach with spectacular wave action.

The third river fanning out from Napali is the north shore's longest, the Hanalei. The river comes into Hanalei Bay through a National Wildlife Refuge, parts of which are open to hikers and cyclists. The river is also a major attraction for kayakers. The agricultural lands of Hanalei Valley are reminiscent of bygone days, when all Kauaian lands were divided into self-sufficient communities—called ahupua'a.

Hanalei Bay is a deep scoop out of the coast which today is known for several surfing beaches. The Hanalei Pier, now considered picturesque, was not all that long ago a structure vital to keeping the north shore supplied. Bowl-shaped Waioli Valley, known as the birthplace of rainbows, rises above Hanalei Town, often streaked with a half-dozen waterfalls. Joggers, hikers and cyclists will have as much fun as surfers in Hanalei, exploring not only the beach, but also the beachside neighborhood, historic church and mission, and laid-back shops.

The river-and-valley theme is less pronounced after Hanalei, as the road climbs up to the Princeville bluff. Adventure-seeking visitors may tend to overlook Princeville, with its condos and luxury hotel, but several hike-to snorkeling and surfing beaches here are among the best on the island. And inland from Princeville is Kaua'i's only trans-island trail, the Powerline, a five-star route for hikers and mountain bikers.

Kalihaiwai Stream, Hanalei River

The bluff at Princeville gives way to Anini Beach, boasting the longest coral reef in the islands. Anini is also known for its tiny seashells, as well as its snorkeling and windsurfing. A polo field and campground, set on the lawn under spreading heliotrope trees, add to the scenery that makes this beach a favorite among many visitors.

Just around the point from Anini Beach, is Kalihiwai Bay. Kalihiwai Stream—which turns heads of drivers who pass overhead on a highway bridge—is a secret among kayakers. The beach at Kalihiwai Bay is usually a safe swimming spot and also a choice for novice surfers and boogie boarders. The offshore break at Kalihiwai Bay is a sleeper surfing spot, overshadowed by nearby Hanalei Bay.

As you leave Kalihiwai, heading toward Kilauea, the river jungle lands of Kaua'i transition into open, sloping agricultural lands, fanning out above the coast and abutting ridges running parallel to the road in the distance inland. Cyclists can ride upland, through a variety of huge spreading trees, with guava, banana and papaya mixed in to add a tropical accent. Much of Kaua'i's fruit and produce is grown here.

The highway turns inland from the coast along this segment of the island, but hikers will find a number of short trails to some huge sand beaches, known for vistas and wave action. Secret Beach runs for two miles, ending at Kilauea Point under its historic lighthouse. On the other side of the point is Kilauea Bay, another mile-plus arc of fine sand. Kilauea Bay also receives Kilauea Stream, a wide lagoon sweeping inland through an open valley, itself enough to beckon paddlers to Kaua'i.

Kilauea Lighthouse, on the massive bluff between these two beaches, is the northernmost spot in Hawai'i. The lighthouse grounds are now part of the Kilauea Point National Wildlife

Refuge, and home to Laysan albatrosses, tropicbirds, boobies and a number of other exotic winged creatures. Crater Hill, above the lighthouse, is a spot not only to view birds but also the best place to take in a vista of the north coast.

Haena Beach, Hanalei Bay, Hanakapiai Falls

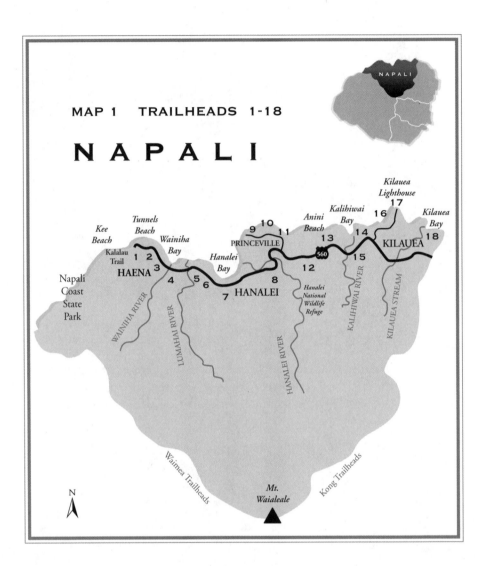

MAP 1   TRAILHEADS 1-18

NAPALI

NAPALI

Kilauea
Lighthouse
17

Kalihiwai
Bay   16   Kilauea
Bay
Tunnels   Anini   14   18
Kee   Beach   Wainha   9 10   Beach
Beach   Bay   11   KILAUEA
Kalalau   PRINCEVILLE   560 15
Trail   1 2   Hanalei   13
HAENA   3   Bay   12
Napali   4   5 6   8
Coast   7 HANALEI   Hanalei
State   National
Park   Wildlife
Refuge

WAINIHA RIVER

LUMAHAI RIVER

HANALEI RIVER

KALIHIWAI RIVER

KILAUEA STREAM

Waimea Trailheads

Kong Trailheads

N

Mt.
Waialeale

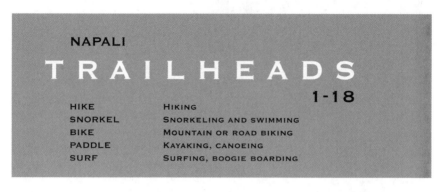

HIKE	HIKING
SNORKEL	SNORKELING AND SWIMMING
BIKE	MOUNTAIN OR ROAD BIKING
PADDLE	KAYAKING, CANOEING
SURF	SURFING, BOOGIE BOARDING

TH	TRAILHEAD
Makai	TOWARD OCEAN
Mauka	TOWARD THE MOUNTAIN, INLAND
mm.	MILE MARKER, CORRESPONDS TO HIGHWAY SIGNS

Note: All hiking distances are roundtrip unless otherwise noted.

1. KALALAU TRAIL-KEʻE BEACH HIKE, SNORKEL

WHAT'S BEST: The end of the road is the beginning of the trail for the fabulous Napali Coast—and the site of a picture-perfect snorkeling pool. This is one of Kauaʻi's headliners; get here early to avoid crowds.

PARKING: Take Hwy. 560 to its end, which is 10 mi. from the Hanalei River bridge. Overflow parking is at Haena State Park, on the right just before mm. 10/560.

HIKE: Kalalau Trail hikes: Napali view (1 mi.), Hanakapiai Beach (4 mi.), Hanakapiai Falls (8 mi.), Napali high point (6 mi.); Kauluolaka Hula Heiau (.5-mi.); Keʻe to Haena Beach (up to 2.5 mi.); Limahuli Garden (.75-mi.)

For **Kalalau Trail hikes** along the Napali Coast, begin at the trailhead kiosk on your left as you drive into the parking area. The Kalalau is a tough trail, even for seasoned hikers. Start on a sunny day, the earlier the better, as many people head up this trail, many of them ill-prepared. The trail begins steeply, climbing rocks and packed dirt, over a section that lets you know right away what you're in for. The first **Napali viewpoint** comes after just .5-mile, as the trail levels out and several wave-battered cliffs can be seen down the coast.

On the way from the viewpoint to **Hanakapiai Beach**, you'll get another good view down Napali, before dropping about 500 feet through lush foliage to the beach. You need to cross the stream at beach level, over rocks, which is not usually possible without getting your feet wet. *Be Aware:* Drownings occur at Hanakapiai—don't go near the water except on the calmest of summer days. Waves knock people down at the shoreline.

Hanakapiai Falls

To **Hanakapiai Falls**, cross the stream and look for the trail heading inland about 30 feet after the crossing. The first mile of the trail is the easiest, although often mucky. You'll pass a rain shelter and a helicopter landing site, and then enter a jungle garden of bamboo, ti, ferns, and huge mangos. The tangle of greenery hides ancient rock agricultural terraces. About halfway to the falls you cross the stream again. The trail weaves over rocks and crosses the stream two additonal times, the last one about .25-mile from the falls. (Might as well wade in your boots.) After scaling a hands-on rocky section, you reach the steep-walled amphitheater that frames Hanakapiai—a 300-foot white ribbon falling into a pool. Hanakapiai Falls gives up the big payoff, but it is a fatiguing eight miles. *Be Aware:* Steam crossings can be dangerous and should be avoided during rains and high water.

To **Napali high point**—800 feet above sea level—continue past the trail to the falls, beginning switchbacks immediately. After a mile of climbing, affording some spectacular seaward and inland views toward the falls, you reach the high point. The trail doesn't come back down to sea level until reaching the Kalalau Valley. *Be Aware:* Be careful not to step off the trail: what looks like solid ground is often matted greenery overhanging steep cliffs.

To the sublime **Kauluolaka Hula Heiau**, begin at Ke'e Beach and pick up a trail that skirts the shoreline to your left as you face the beach—this is not the Kalalau Trail. Curl around at the edge of the black rocks, losing sight of Ke'e, and then climb muddy steps, keeping left all the way. You reach the top of a series of grassy terraces, about 80 feet above the sea. Cliffs rise steeply inland and big swells crash the shore. This spot today, as it was in antiquity, is where the ancient hula and chants are performed. Below the top platform are the ruins of Kaulupaoa Heiau, which guarded the hula site. *Be Aware:* Step lightly and respect "kapu" (keep out) signs at this sacred site. You are visiting a Hawaiian cathedral.

Ke'e Beach

For **Ke'e to Haena Beach**—which is the shortcut to getting a long view down the Napali Coast—start at Ke'e Beach, and walk to your right as you face the water. Shortly into the walk, look back to see the Napali Coast, its buttresses receding in the distance. About midway on this walk you cross Limahuli Stream, inland from which was the site of Taylor Camp. Back in the hippie days—which aren't so far back on the north shore—Taylor Camp was a well-known commune. After crossing the stream, you need to negotiate the black rock shoreline around the point, or, if the surf is high, you may have to cut inland through ironwood and heliotrope trees.

Parking for **Limahuli Garden** is .25-mile before reaching road's end at Ke'e Beach; turn uphill at a signed entry. Now a National Tropical Botanical Garden, the grounds extend up lava rock terraces built by the valley's ancient dwellers. This garden is known for its native Hawaiian vegetation, as well as for plants brought here by voyaging Polynesians. The valley sits under Bali Hai. *Note:* Admission is charged for self-guided tours, which includes an informative booklet—one of the best plant books available.

SNORKEL: Ke'e Beach, when surf is breaking gently on its reef, is an ideal snorkeling pool. Keep to your right as you enter a sandy shore, swimming out along the reef, where you can take a break and sit on the ledge. The view from the water of the cliffs is a keeper. *Be Aware:* Water escapes this cove on the cliff side, so be mindful of the current. Avoid swimming here when surf is high.

2.   HAENA BEACH   HIKE, SNORKEL, SURF

WHAT'S BEST: Snorkeling, surfing and beach strolling with drop-dead views of Makana Ridge. This Kaua'i classic demands an encore.
PARKING: At Haena City Beach Park, .75-mi. after mm. 8/560, about 7 mi. from Hanalei Bay. *Note:* Different parking for the Tunnels snorkeling.

HIKE: Haena Point (2 mi.)

To rounded **Haena Point**, start up the beach to your right as you face the surf. You'll walk by Tunnels Beach, a popular snorkeling and surfing spot, on the same strip of sand from the beach park. Just beyond Tunnels is sandy Haena Point. When the surf is fairly calm, you can walk a hundred yards or so offshore in ankle-deep water; a good vantage point for photography buffs.

SNORKEL: At **Haena City Beach** are sandy places to get in and flipper around, but the real action is up the beach at Tunnels. For **Tunnels Beach** parking, look makai for a dirt drive .25-mile after mm. 8/560, past Haena Street at telephone pole #144R; it's next to a home with the address 57670. A second Tunnels Beach parking spot, usually less crowded, is .25-mile beyond the first—a dirt drive with a green chain-link fence running along both sides. It's across from telephone pole #14 and along a driveway marked by the address 57777. You'll have to step down a 6-foot rooted embankment and walk to your right. If these areas are full, park at Haena Beach. Tunnels has a generous swath of sand and a deep-water coral reef near shore that attracts a multitude of fish, as well as tourists. A bonus for Tunnels is the perfect view of Bali Hai—the name for Makana Ridge that originated from the movie, *South Pacific.* Large ironwoods at the shore cast welcome shade. *Be Aware:* Haena lifeguards normally post hazard signs when conditions are unsafe, but any time the surf is high you can count on rip current.

SURF: Surfers paddle the channel at **Tunnels Beach** to the reef break. This is a shallow break with tricky currents; ask the locals. **Cannons Beach** is on the other end of Haena City Beach Park. Scope the break—usually a left slide—from the unimproved turnouts as you leave the park headed for Ke'e. Like Tunnels, this is a reef break; watch the locals. If they're out there, consider surfing here, but it they're not, don't try it. Neither of these spots is for beginners.

Haena Beach and Makana Ridge (Bali Hai)

3. KEPUHI POINT
HIKE

WHAT'S BEST: A beach walk with Bali Hai views and solitude, even on busy days along this popular stretch of coast.
PARKING: Take the Hwy. 560 through Hanalei and continue for .5-mi. after mm. 7/560. Patrons and shoppers may park in the lot for the Hanalei Colony Resort. Parking also just past the lot; turn makai on dirt Oneone Rd.

HIKE: Haena Point (2.5 mi.)

To **Haena Point**, walk through the parking lot to a short access path between the restaurant and the resort. Head to your left when you get on the sand. Palms mingle with ironwoods among a few low-key vacation homes inland. After about .5-mile, the homes give way to open space, part of a YMCA camp, and the reef encroaches on the sandy shore. *Be Aware:* Surf and reef here can combine for dangerous swimming.

As you continue, the reef protrudes from the water, just as you reach a wide cove, noted by the half-dozen black rocks at its shore. At the far end of this cove is Haena Point, where, if conditions permit, you can walk a surprisingly far distance on a shoal. A Bali Hai view draws you along the last part of the walk. *More Stuff:* More energetic hikers can continue along the beach to Tunnels and Haena City Beach Park. Also, for a shorter version of this hike, you'll find a second beach access midway between Hanalei Colony and Tunnels. Pass the resort and turn makai on Alealea Road and look for a path that leads to the beach alongside the grounds of the YMCA camp.

WHAT'S BEST: A non-tourist bike ride, drive, or paddle up one of Hawai'i's most mysterious valleys.
PARKING: At Wainiha, a small outpost just beyond Lumahai Beach on Hwy. 560 at mm. 6/560. Park off road near the store.

BIKE: Starting in town and heading toward Haena, you immediately come to the first of two wooden, one-lane bridges, slung low across the Wainiha River. Between the first and second bridge is a dirt road upriver that you can bike about a mile, giving you a look at some dank tropical gardens and old homestead cottages. This neighborhood has been home to certain families for three centuries.

Then backtrack and cross the second bridge and head up paved Powerhouse Road, on your left. It's two miles and about a 500-foot climb to the end of the road, with most elevation gained at the beginning. Jungle flora and birds are at hand. The road opens to ridge views after about one mile. At 1.5 miles, as the road levels out, you come to a parklike homestead—palms, lawn, pond and stream cascade, all the work of a retiree who made this beautiful garden his second career. A half-mile past the homestead, the pavement ends and the dirt road is blocked by a locked gate and an assortment of "keep out" signs. As you look up the mountain, toward your right, is Wainiha Pali, the 4,000-foot cliffs which are the border of the Alakai Swamp, sitting on a plateau behind the pali. Up this river valley until the late 1800s lived a 65-person colony, the descendents of the folkloric Menehune.

PADDLE: Put in at Wainiha, in town, where the river parallels the road and a shoal separates it from the bay. The **Wainiha River** forks upstream from the bay, at the two bridges, and comes together again about a mile upstream, making a narrow island.

Lumahai Beach

Both forks can be paddled along a short stretch of navigable water, where commercial tours are not allowed, but individuals are permitted. *More Stuff:* You can access the bay at bedraggled Wainiha City Beach Park: Look makai for a dirt lane after Powerhouse Road, before the highway goes uphill.

5.   LUMAHAI BEACH   HIKE, PADDLE

> **WHAT'S BEST:** Relax where the river meets the sea, or take a walk along the crashing surf of Kaua'i's most glamorous beach.
> **PARKING:** At Lumahai City Beach Park, around the point fromHanalei Bay—.75-mi. past mm. 5/560. Unimproved parking, before the bridge.

HIKE: Lumahai Beach (2 mi.)

From the parking area at **Lumahai Beach**, which is amid an ironwood grove on the bank of the Lumahai River, walk away from the river, heading onto a mass of fine sand up to two hundred yards deep and a mile long. A little over halfway down the beach, the cliff draws nearer, and black rocks emerge from the sand, taking on the surf and creating bursts of spray. The far end of Lumahai is sometimes called Kahalahala Beach, ending at Makahoa Point, which forms the mouth of Hanalei Bay. Lumahai is the oft-photographed cover girl among Kauaian beaches, a reputation that began during the filming of *South Pacific*. *Be Aware:* Lumahai is a dangerous swimming beach. Stay clear of the shore break. Rogue waves have swept people from the shore.

More Stuff: You can get to the far end of Lumahai (Kahalahala Beach) by taking a short, trail that leads down from the road. Look for turnouts after an uphill grade and a 15 mph sign, where the highway hooks to the left. Two turnouts mark this well-used trailhead.

PADDLE: The **Lumahai River**, like the Wainiha, is a short stretch of navigable water upon which commercial outfitters are not permitted. Unlike the Wainiha, no road or dwellings are along the banks, giving paddlers a wide-open lagoon feel with jungle ridge views. Encroaching foliage blocks passage less than a mile up from the beach. Easy access is from the sandy shore described in the parking section. The Lumahai River valley, some 3,200 feet deep and 10 miles long, lies between the Hanalei and Wainiha rivers, one of three rivers flowing northward from Mount Waialeale. *Be Aware:* Keep an eye out for submerged branches, and be mindful of getting lost in tree-shrouded passageways with no exits.

6.   WAIKOKO BEACH   HIKE, SNORKEL, SURF

> **WHAT'S BEST:** A quiet beach stop on a busy road for a picnic. Float in warm water and enjoy jaw-dropping views of the Hanalei ridges.

Waikoko Beach

PARKING: Pass through Hanalei Hwy. 560. Park at turnout after crossing one-lane bridge, at mm. 4/560.

HIKE: Waikoko Beach (1 mi.)

Waikoko Beach is the continuation of Hanalei Bay beyond Waioli Stream at the edge of town. You can walk back toward town from the parking area along the beach. This beach is the homestretch for joggers who regularly run the length on Hanalei Bay, which is a little more than two miles. Smaller Waipa Stream, enters the bay up the beach from Waioli, and the sand in between is called Waipa Beach. Rocks and reef end the beach walk at the mouth of the bay, which is Makahoa Point. If you must know, this geographic feature, as seen from the other end of Hanalei Bay, forms the head of *Puff the Magic Dragon* of folk song fame. *Be Aware:* The streams can be hard to cross after rains. Your best bet is to cross where the fresh water fans out at the surf.

SNORKEL: **Waikoko Beach** is a good place to take a swim with fins and mask, although fish are not usually abundant. The entrance is sandy, into deep water, with a smaller onshore break than the rest of the bay. The view inshore from the water is portrait quality. Waikoko is protected by a coral reef, called Pohakuopio, which juts into the bay from Makahoa Point. *More Stuff:* Surfers get to a sweet beach near the point by parking at rough turnouts on the uphill grade, before getting to a highway sign that warns of curves ahead. This in a prime float-around spot in shallow water. *Be Aware:* No lifeguards serve these beaches. Watch for currents.

SURF: **Pohakuopio** reef creates an offshore break at the mouth of Hanalei Bay, especially during the winter. Locals check out the break—a left-slide that is best when wind is offshore—from turnouts along the highway as the road climbs to the bluffs toward Lumahai. Break is shallow upon the reef in places. Observe the locals and don't surf this tricky spot if no one else is out there.

7. HANALEI BAY   HIKE, SNORKEL, BIKE, PADDLE, SURF

WHAT'S BEST: Hanalei may be the best walk-around beach town in Hawaii—ringed by skyscraper ridges laced with waterfalls falling into rich farmlands, and fringed by a sandy bay and wide river.

PARKING: Take Hwy. 56 into Hanalei Valley, where it becomes Hwy. 560. Turn makai on Aku Rd., which is the first right when you enter town, past mm. 2. Continue on Aku, turn right on Weke Road, and go about .5-mi. to parking at Black Pot City Beach Park.

Note: Other beach access on Weke: Near Aku Road, which is the Hanalei City Pavilion; and, continuing on Weke, at telephone pole number 19 and at He'e Road, both within .5-mi. of the pavilion. Additional beach access, to Pine Trees at Ama'ama Road and Waioli City Beach at Anae Road, farther down Weke Rd.

HIKE: Hanalei Beach (2.5 mi.)

The **Hanalei Beach** walk begins at **Black Pot Beach**, where surfers gather, kayaks put in and Hanalei Pier affords walkers a quick trip out to the water without getting wet. The concrete pier has a covered boat house at its end, a cozy spot to make a dash for on a rainy day, or to leap from when the sun is out. You might spot a manta ray scuttling along the sandy bottom and surfers riding by on foamy waves. To the right of the pier, as you face the water, is where surfers park for the long paddle out to the offshore breaks and where the Hanalei River enters the bay—a contemplative spot.

Continuing around the bay, you'll see shore-break surfers and joggers, and pass a number of beachfront homes, some of which are historical landmarks, and bed-and-breakfast cottages—all set among palm trees and gardens. After about .5-mile on packed sand you come to the **Hanalei City Pavilion**, the main station for the Hanalei lifeguards, who are among the best-trained in the world. From the pavilion, it's about .75-mile to **Waioli Beach Park**, which ends at Waioli Stream. (You pass the picnic tables and ironwoods of Pine Trees Beach along the way.) Across the stream is called Waipa Beach, which leads to the stream of the same name. Cross Waipa Stream and you're headed for Waikoko, at the far end of the bay. Needless to say, this walk has countless options built in, starting at any of the access points described in the parking instructions, and ducking in and out from the beach to quiet roads to take in beach

Hanalei Pier

life, Hanalei style. *Be Aware:* Steep soft sand in the middle of the bay gives way to to riptide channels during high surf; watch out when wading. The streams can be difficult to cross after rains; normally, the shallow spot is where the stream meets the surf.

Walkers will also enjoy tooling around **Hanalei Town**, where exposed feet outnumber laceups ten-to-one. Explore behind the church and mission on the mountain-side at the far end of town as you head toward Haena. Behind the church are rich agricultural lands of the Waioli Valley, "the birthplace of the rainbows." After a rain, the 3,500-foot ridge above Hanalei reveals scores of ribbon waterfalls. Most of the inland is private property, but landowners usually don't mind tourists, if you ask permission.

SNORKEL: With its sandy bottom and shore break, **Hanalei Bay** is not known for snorkeling. But in calm conditions swimming is good around the pier at **Black Pot Beach**, where you'll see a few fish. Stay clear of fishing lines and surfers.

BIKE: **Hanalei** is ideal for exploring on a mountain bike. Although there is no bike path on the beach, you can get around just about everywhere—except the main road—without worrying about cars, and take in all the features mentioned in the hiking description. *Be Aware:* Riding a bicycle into Hanalei from Princeville is dangerous, particularly coming up the road from Hanalei, where there is no shoulder. Additionally, narrow Highway 560 to the end of the road is bike unfriendly.

PADDLE: At **Black Pot Beach** is a boat ramp to put in for upriver paddles or soirees into the bay and around toward Puʻu Poa Beach at Princeville Resort. To get to the ramp, got straight through the parking lot as the paved road ends. Inquire with a local outfitter before attempting an ocean paddle. The **Hanalei River** may also be accessed at one or two openings observable along the grassy bank as you drive into Hanalei after crossing the bridge. Kayak companies also provide access, including Kayak Kauai Outbound, which has its own dock. Hanalei River runs several miles into the Hanalei Valley Wildlife Refuge, below 3,500-foot tropical ridges.

SURF: For beginners and kahunas alike, the breaks at **Black Pot Beach** combine to make it one of the best and most popular spots in Hawaii. Learners and mid-level board heads like the break at the pier. The big boys and girls go for the tiers of swells rolling in a couple hundred yards offshore, beyond the mouth of the Hanalei River—called the **Queens** and **Kings**. Winter surf can top out at 40 or 50 feet. Legendary surfer Titus Kinimaka, the first person ever to ride an epic Kings break, runs a surf school at Black Pot, and he's often on hand to offer lessons or rent boards. The end of the pier is where to be for watching surfers.

For an onshore break, better for boogie boarding and in view of lifeguards, try **Hanalei City Pavilion** in the middle of the bay. The best spot for mid-level surfers is little farther down the beach, at the **Waioli Beach Park**. Between these two beaches is **Pine Trees** (look for the stand of ironwoods). *Be Aware:* Keep a lookout for flat, fothy spots in the breaking waves; these indicate channels where rip currents are going out. Pine Trees has particularly strong current.

8. HANALEI WILDLIFE REFUGE   HIKE, BIKE

WHAT'S BEST: Climb for a bird's-eye view of Hanalei Valley, or stay grounded on a hike through bamboo forest to a wild spot up the river without a paddle.
PARKING: Take Hwy. 56 toward Hanalei from Princeville and turn mauka immediately after crossing the river on the one-lane bridge. You enter the Hanalei National Wildlife Refuge, most of which is off-limits to humans.
First parking area: For the mountain hike, proceed .6-mi., passing the historic Haraguchi Rice Mill (unsigned, now refuge offices), and park on left at the improved, signed parking lot, about .25-mi. beyond the mill.

Second parking: For bamboo forest hike, proceed until pavement ends, 2 mi. in from Hwy. 560. You'll see a chain across the road and a stop sign. Park here, step over the chain and walk in straight, past the house about .1-mile—not taking the drive that goes up to the right. You immediately come to the Halelea Forest Reserve checking station. *Note:* Despite the cable, this is public access to the forest reserve. To be polite, ask permission if you see someone.

HIKE: Okolehao Trail (4.5 mi.); Bamboo forest hike to Hanalei River (2 mi.)

The splendid **Okolehao Trail** sguiggles about 1,200 feet up to the best vantage point of the Hanalei coast and valley. Cross the road to the trailhead and jog to your right on the red-dirt trail. Walk 40 or so yards on the road and turn left, uphill, on a rutted road in front of a silver gate—which leads to the historic Japanese cemetery above the old rice mill. You leave wildlife refuge lands and enter the Halelea Forest Reserve. The steep Okolehao Trail is an old road established during prohibition, when the Hawaiian liquor okolehao was being distilled from ti plants that grew along the trail. After about a mile, the road becomes a trail and footing becomes more difficult. This key juncture is marked by a huge steel power pole; cut left and head up the ridgeline.

You'll penetrate a forest of Norfolk pine and other planted trees as the trail heads inland on a series of ramps and benches. Several view knobs will entice shutterbugs to stop for a shot, but press on. One hands-on steep section heralds the end of the trail. Make sure to make the final hairpin left and walk the final several hundred feet to the top, called Kaukaopua. The summit, a flat oval adorned by ti plants, yields the satisfying 360-degree view of the Hanalei region. Wow.

Note: Before embarking on the Okolehao Trail, you may wish to take a good look at it from the scenic turnout across from the shopping center in Princeville: Kaukaopua, your destination, is the peak in the foreground above the river, down the shoulder from the double-tipped peak, that looks like Batman but is called Hihimanu. Actually named for a manta ray, this peak seems close enough to touch from the end of the maintained trail—but only fit hikers with local guides should even think about it.

More Stuff: The short but sweet walk Hanalei bird view area has been fenced off, apparently by wildlife refuge staff. Previously, after crossing the footbridge, you could take a trail that curved around to your left—passing a steep, rutted trail on the left— and come quickly to a flat grassy viewpoint, about 125 feet above the river valley. The view is across the taro field toward the Kalihiwai Ridge.

The hike through **bamboo forest** to the Hanalei River—from the second parking area—is a stomp through pig mud that is best done on a sunny day, or at least not during rain. The trail is easy to follow, but is ingrown and dark to the point of eliciting claustrophobia, if you're prone to it. After passing the house at the trailhead, you begin in a green tunnel of ferns and bamboo on a wide swath that it is not driveable,

Taro fields of Hanalei

even by the Kauaian hunters. After about .5-mile within the bamboo, the sky appears, as well as a hillock of spongy grasses too deep to trod. Then you drop down again, hearing a stream before you see it, and finally crossing it, over and under overhanging branches and roots. After this thicket—all the while the trail is plainly observable—you cross a rocky streambed, veering left, and entering the bamboo again.

After about .25-mile in this last, dark bamboo cave, you reach the riverbank. From the riverbank, you are able to walk through ferns to a better viewpoint of a sweeping turn of the river, a few hundred feet upstream. *Be Aware:* Make sure you know how to get back to the first river sighting, as the trail through the ferns is sketchy. As with all hunting trails, weekday use is best, when hunters are not present.

BIKE: Park at the start of the road into the wildlife refuge, called Ohiki Road, and take the paved road on a flat, 4-mile roundtrip cycle. On a bike is perhaps the best way to enjoy the refuge. Near the end of the road you will also see 4WD tracts that lead into the Waioli Valley inland from Hanalei town. Some of this area is private property, and other portions are difficult. The paved refuge road can be combined with a ride around Hanalei town for a full day of pleasant pedaling.

9.　PRINCEVILLE　　　　　　　　　　HIKE, SNORKEL, SURF

WHAT'S BEST: Behind sedate suburban homes and condos are showy sunset views and some of Kaua'i's best hike-to beaches with snorkeling and surfing.
PARKING: Take Hwy. 56 several miles past Kilauea to mm. 27/56. Turn makai at Princeville on Ka Haku Road, passing a large fountain, and continue 2 mi. to Princeville Hotel. Public parking is on the right, just outside hotel entrance station, or in the back rows of hotel lot.

HIKE: Fort Alexander site (.25-mi.); Pu'u Poa Beach to Hanalei River (1.25 mi.); Hideaways Beach (.5-mi.)

Fort Alexander is a stroll across the resort lawn next to the parking lot, hugging the ocean side of the grassy bluff. A pavilion on the point commemorates the Russian traders' failed attempt to gain a foothold on Kaua'i over a several-year span in the early 1800s. This is an excellent sunset spot, also used by surfers to check out the combers in Hanalei Bay and beyond. When the epic surf is up, locals flock here with binoculars. You'll also want to wander down to check out the views and sample the menu at the fabulous Princeville Resort. From the opulent lounge, a wall of towering plate glass shows off an unreal panormana.

The trail to **Hideaways Beach** is on the right, just before the hotel entrance station. Look for an eight-foot wide corridor between two chain-link fences, one of which runs along the side of tennis courts. You walk the corridor for a hundred yards, and then descend steeply, on dirt-and-wood stairs, aided initially by a sturdy pipe railing. One short section below the stairs is slick after rains. Hideaways is a cozy swath of sand, pocketed by jungled cliffs. *More Stuff:* From the far end of the beach, a hands-on trail leads over black rock and through pandanus—a 10-minute scramble—to adjacent Kenomene Beach. See *Snorkel* for a more civilized route to this pretty beach.

To **Pu'u Poa Beach**, which is the one used by the Princeville Resort and Hanalei Bay Resort, look for a beach access sign just to the left of the kiosk as you enter the Princeville Hotel driveway. Access is via a concrete ramp and stairs that run behind the hotel, skirting the drainage that separates it from the Hanalei Bay Resort. At the beach, walk to your left under spreading heliotrope trees along the shoreline. You reach black rocks, over which you scramble briefly, until getting a close-up view of Black Pot Beach at the Hanalei Bay Pier, across the river. *Note:* The asphalt path you reach at the bottom of the concrete stairs leads up to the Hanalei Bay Resort.

SNORKEL: Although small, **Pu'u Poa Beach** is one of the island's better snorkeling beaches. Expect to mingle with hotel guests on this strip of reef-protected sand. Look for a sand entry and a coral section that is perpendicular to the shoreline; you may wish to scope it out from nine stories above at the hotel's viewing patio. *Be Aware:* Water is shallow at low tide. Avoid stepping on the living coral.

Hideaways Beach, a small sand cove cupped into the bluffs, has very good snorkeling—sandy entry with clear water, coral and ample fish. Hideaways may be Kaua'i's most underrated snorkeling venue. And you won't find crowds. *Be Aware:* Be wary of high surf offshore, especially during the winter, which can cause unsafe currents, normally flowing from right to left.

As you face the water at Hideaways, **Kenomene Beach** is around the black-rock point to your right; it is the beach is straight down from the guardrail at the scenic overlook as you drive in. In low surf and tide, you can walk to this beach from Hideawys, or taked the rugged trail noted in the hiking section. But the easier access is via a concrete walkway that begins to the left as you enter the parking lot for the Pali Ke Kua condominiums next to the overlook. Once down to Kenomene Beach, look on the far end for sandy entry points among the black rocks. Snorkeling is excellent during lower surf conditions—some of the best on the island, and least used. *Be Aware:* A sign at the start of the walkway declares that access is for residents only. Use your own judgment and proceed at your own risk. Avoid swimming here during high surf.

SURF: **Hideaways** is a locals' surfing spot, with consistent offshore rollers. Driving in to the beach, stop at a scenic overlook to observe conditions—a guardrail marks the overlook. On the trail down to the beach, packing your board down the trail, you'll also come to a viewing spot, about 30 feet above the water.

Surfers also lug boards down the public access to **Pu'u Poa Beach**; under some condi-

Queen Emmas Bath

tions, it's a shorter paddle out the channel from there to catch the river mouth break off of Hanalei Bay. Novices also benefit from a beachside outfitter at Pu'u Poa, who provides lessons with board rentals.

10. QUEEN EMMAS BATHS   HIKE, SNORKEL

WHAT'S BEST: A hike-to beach and a shoreline of volcanic swimming pools, both giving a faraway feel at close-in places.

PARKING: Two different spots. For both, take Hwy. 56 past mm. 27/56 and turn into Princeville on Ka Haku Rd.

For Kaweonui Beach, go about 1 mi. and turn makai on Pepelani Loop, across from golf course lagoons and at a sign noting Sandpiper Village. Take a right off Pepelani onto Kaweonui Rd. which is past Albert St. Follow it about .5-mi., and turn right on *second* Keoniana. Park at end of cul-de-sac, being careful not to intrude on residential parking.

For Queen Emmas Baths, continue on Ka Haku past Pepelani Loop, and turn makai on Punahele Rd., about .5-mi. before reaching the Princeville Hotel. Go down Punahele about .25-mile and look for a designated, 12-car grass parking area. *Note:* During prime conditions, this lot fills up early and on-street parking is not allowed. Public officials may close this area due to safety concerns.

HIKE: Queen Emmas Baths (.5 to 1.5 mi.); Kaweonui Beach (1 mi.)

Queen Emmas Baths are a series of black-rock tidal pools and intricate reef openings named for King Kamehameha IV's Queen Emma. Steps aid on the first part of the .25-mile walk down a steep trail. At one spot near the bottom, hands may be required. Watch your footing all the way. You pass a small fresh water waterfall and pool near the bottom. Continue around to your left, walking the rocky bluffs and shoreline for about .5-mile. *Be Aware:* Observe wave action before venturing out on rocks. Use routes farther from the shoreline and avoid this area during high surf.

The access to secluded **Kaweonui Beach**, for the first few steps, is down a driveway, usually marked by orange cones, shared by a residence. From the street, look down the drive for a chain across the driveway about 50 feet away. You cross around that chain, pausing to read a number of hazard warnings posted by private owners. The first part is steeply down a wide concrete path, coming to a pump installation at the bottom, enclosed by a chain-link fence. The beach trail is behind this enclosure. It's flat for the first part, then drops down through pandanus trees on dirt-and-wood steps to the coast at a grove of ironwoods. The trail continues to your left, over roots and finally rocks before hooking into Kaweonui—a sandy nook in a black-rock cove. *Be Aware:* This trail can be slippery and you need to use your hands in a place or two

SNORKEL: On calms days the tide pools and rocky inlets of **Queen Emmas Baths** are good places to relax and enjoy a view of the endless swells rolling in from the vast Pacific. You can gear up with mask and fins, or just swim around and play in the bubbling warm water. The best pool is about .25-mile from where the trail meets the coast. *Be Aware:* Observe wave action for ten minutes before entering; people have been swept away during high surf. Baths are best at low tide.

The reef offshore of **Kaweonui Beach** limits shore break, often making for good snorkeling among a fair number of fish. You will usually find privacy at this little known cove. *Be Aware:* Privacy means you are on your own, with little chance of help should you encounter difficulty in the water. The sand slopes into deep water here.

11. WYLLIES BEACH   HIKE, SNORKEL, BIKE

WHAT'S BEST: The 'back way' to Anini Beach will be high on the beach-hike list among independent travelers. Leisure cyclists can take a spin through the green bluffs and vacationland of Princeville, or along the shores of the beach.
PARKING: Take Hwy. 56 to Princeville, just beyond mm. 27/56. Enter on the main entrance on Ka Haku Rd.
For the bike rides: Park on the right at a turnout just .1-mi. after the fountain, and just before a sign for Queen Emmas Bluffs.
For the hike or snorkel at Wyllies Beach: Continue for about .25-mi. and turn makai Wyllie Rd., also marked by a signs for the Pahia-Kaeo Kai condos. Go about .5-mi. to a cul-de-sac. Park off-road to the right of a pipe gate.

HIKE: Wyllies and Anini Beach (.5-mi. to 3 mi.)

To **Wyllies Beach**—which is actually at the far end of **Anini Beach**—walk the tree-lined path, with the golf course to your right. The wide trail descends into a shaded canopy of trees, alongside a stream. It's steep and often slippery, but not hazardous. You pop out to the beach from an umbrella of heliotrope and ironwood trees. As you begin the beach walk, look back to memorize the spot to pop back in when the time comes.

At the beach, head right and cross shallow Anini Stream, which is often blocked by a sand dam at the shoreline, and continue along the shore to Anini Beach. At one point, about .75-mile into the stroll, you need to leave the beach at a black-rock point, hopping up to the quiet road for a short distance and then back down to the beach. Anini Beach campground will be in view after the point. Windsurfers, campers, kite-boarders, and (guess what) polo players spice up the beachscape.

SNORKEL: The fresh water from the stream, in which coral cannot live, makes **Wyllies** a sandy-bottomed snorkeling area, protected by a reef farther out. Water clarity is only fair and the fish are not abundant. Wyllies is a very good spot to take a swim, which is not that easy to find during winter surf surges on the north shore. *Be Aware:* The long, shallow reef can make for a rip current in places, especially farther out.

BIKE: The **Mea Ho'ona Nea** bike trail, taking off behind the gate across the road from the fountain, is a 3-mile roundtrip, rolling ride to the Princeville Golf Club. The paved path, with blue-water views, is also a good walking and jogging path. Don't be confused by the "Walk Bike" signs on this path; they mean the path is for bikes and walking, as opposed to motorized vehicles. To continue any farther on a bike from the golf club, you need to turn right out to Hwy. 56, which does have an adequate paved shoulder. *More Stuff:* As the Mea Ho'ona Nea bike path leaves the golf course, and just before it becomes a path on a frontage road, look for a white, wooden gate on your right; the road here, at the Church of the Pacific, is directly across the highway from the road leading up past the stables to Powerline Trail north, TH12.

A good way to get a fix on the area here is to take the 6-mile **Princeville rideabout**. Cross the road from the parking area, get on the paved path, and head to your right. The path skirts the golf course before ending, where you need to use the bike shoulder on the right side of the road. At the Princeville Resort entrance station—about 2 miles from the start—walk your bike down a series of concrete steps and walkways that lead toward the beach. At the bottom of the concrete steps, take the asphalt path to your left. This very steep, short path leads to the Hanalei Bay Resort.

Bear left at the top and walk your bike to the Hanalei Bay Resort parking lot. From the big banyan at the resort's entrance, ride through a quiet residential area, with kempt gardens and shrubbery, bearing left and coming back out to the main road, Ka Haku Road. Turn right, back onto the bike path—passing Lei O Papa Road into the golf course—and turn right just beyond the golf course on Kekaulike Road, which takes you through residences to the Princeville Shopping Center.

Mountain bikers can also ride to **Anini Beach** from the parking area via the Wyllies Beach trailhead. Walk your bike down the steep part of the trail. From Wyllies Beach, you need to push the wheels across a short stretch of sand to the paved road that runs 2 miles along Anini Beach. From the far end of Anini, hardcore riders can also continue, taking Kalihiwai Road up to Highway 56, turning right, and riding about a mile to the golf club. At the entrance to the golf club, duck in and pick up the Mea Ho'ona Nea bike trail, as described above, which takes you back to the Wyllies parking area. This is about an 8-mile loop.

12. POWERLINE TRAIL NORTH   HIKE, BIKE

> **WHAT'S BEST:** Hike or pedal past the peaks and streams at the heart of Kaua'i. You begin overlooking Hanalei Valley and skirt the shoulders of Waialeale on the only cross-island trail.
> **PARKING:** Take Hwy. 56 past the Princeville Airport. Turn mauka about .4-mi. past mm. 27/56 on Kapaka St.—look for a yellow intersection sign and a sign for Princeville Ranch Stables. Go 2 mi. up to the end of the street, behind a huge concrete water tank. *Note:* Different parking for heiau hike.

HIKE, BIKE: Powerline Trail (13 mi. one-way to Keahua Arboretum, TH33. In-and-out hikes of any shorter length.); Po'oku Heiau (.5-mi.); Princeville Ranch Adventures (see *More Stuff*)

The **Powerline Trail North** is an all-day hike best attempted by prepared hikers on dry days. Cyclists and hikers alike may enjoy the route most by going in partway and seeing the other half of the trail another day from the Keahua Arboretum, TH33. In spite of its dreary name and a route following a utility easement through Kaua'i's interior, the trail offers open vistas and lush greenery that makes the power poles all but unnoticeable. Most bikers will be dismounting for ruts and puddles at numerous spots. Red-mud splotches are the badge of honor for the Powerline Trail veterans.

Kualapa Ridge, the great divide for this route, is about 7 miles in and a 1,600-foot climb, to an elevation of almost 2,000 feet—or about half as high as the other ridges of the island's interior. You encounter a number of ups and downs along the way. Just into the hike, look for a falls to the right on a shoulder jutting out from the trail. Then, about .5-mile from the trailhead, a short spur road leads to the right through ferns and trees to a good vantage point of the Hanalei Valley—river rapids below and waterfalls across the way. (The number of falls visible depends on recent rains.) Another viewpont is about 1 mile in, and a nice one is at Kapaka, nearing the 2-mile point. The best look back toward the Pacific comes near the top of Kualapa Ridge. All the while you are

*Princeville Ranch guide Amy Vanderhoop,
Kalihiwai swimming hole*

traveling above the Hanalei Valley, and you get good looks at the 3,800-foot ridge of the Halelea Forest Reserve as it rises, draped with greenery and strands of white water.

The short walk to the **Po'oku Heiau** site serves up an exquisite view of Hanalei Wildlife Refuge. Park on your right after a downhill stretch less than .5-mile from the highway, at the last heiau sign. Walk a grassy two-track to your right, which becomes a path that eventually peters out at some wicked stickers. *Note:* The overgrown heiau site is atop the hill, but the better views are from this path.

More Stuff: The Powerline Trail starts out along the border of the 2,500-acre Princeville Ranch, on which the Carswell family—stewards of this natural treasure for many generations—now operates **Princeville Ranch Adventures**. (See *Outfitters* in *Resource Links*.) You can see this stunning place on foot, by kayak, on horseback, or zinging through the air on a zipline cable that spans jungled valleys. The hike to Kalihiwai Waterfall is a thriller, and includes some plunges in fantasy-island swimmng holes. Enthusiastic and knowledgeable adventure guides will supply even Kaua'i veterans with fresh factoids on local lore and flora.

13. ANINI BEACH
HIKE, SNORKEL, BIKE, PADDLE, SURF

WHAT'S BEST: Leisurely hikes and bikes along the longest coral reef in Hawai'i, and taking a dip with the fishes. Anini has the mix for a tropical vacation, and some people never want to leave.

PARKING: Turn makai on Kalihiwai Rd. (second), which is past mm. 25/56, about 2 mi. beyond Kilauea—on an uphill grade after crossing the highway bridge over the river. Two parking areas:

For snorkeling, hiking and biking: Continue downhill, bearing left on Anini Rd., and park at the county beach park, across from the polo field, which is about 1.5 mi. from the highway.

For river kayaking: Keep right on Kalihiwai Rd. and drive down about 1 mi. to unimproved parking on left just before road's end.

HIKE: Anini Beach (up to 3 mi.)

The road to **Anini Beach** reaches sea level after about .5-mile from the highway, and then runs about 2 miles along the shore before ending at Anini Stream. The beach park area covers a .75-mile segment in the middle. The best walk starts at the beach park, where windsurfers and high-flying kite-boarders provide entertainment at Kaua'i's best spot for these sports. Head left as you face the water. The sand is coarse and the park grounds are carpeted with heliotrope leaves and sharp ironwood cones.

The coral reef, hundreds of feet offshore, makes for a wave-free coast, and trees provide pockets of shade. You leave the park after about .5-mile and walk the road a bit, around Honono Point, which is marked by a telephone pole on the ocean side of the road. After the point, you enter a tropical nook and sandy cove where Anini Stream enters the sea. This trail connects with Wyllies Beach, TH11.

SNORKEL: With its fabled reef, the snorkeling at **Anini Beach** is good, but shallow water, strong current, and coarse sand keep it from getting the highest marks. Even so, many claim this golden beach with big turquoise views as their favorite. The best snorkeling is at the camping section of the beach park, just after crossing a little bridge. *Be Aware:* At Anini, surf surge escapes through a channel between the windsurfing area and the camping area described above. Look for a series of pipes leading from near the shore out to the reef—they mark the channel. You want to enter the water to the left of that. Currents can be swift in the shallow waters near the channel.

You'll also find snorkeling at sandy nooks with turnouts just as you drop down to sea level from the highway—at a spot called **Hanapai Beach**. Water can be choppy, amid black rocks. Also, at the other end of Anini—around Honono Point—is a safe swimming spot. Look for **Baby Beach**, a sandy pool near the road, protected by its own small crescent of black rocks. As noted in TH11, swimming is good at the end of the road, although the incursion of fresh water means little reef life.

BIKE: **Anini Beach**, a four-mile rideabout, is a flat pedal along which you can check out the windsurfing or catch a polo match at the field across from the beach park. From a bicycle is a good way to pick and choose among the many beach access places along the road. Adventurous cyclists can connect with **Princeville** via Wyllies, as de-

Anini Beach

scribed in TH11. Or, going the other way, you can pedal up and out of Anini, and then down the river access road—which is second Kalihiwai Road. Once at the bottom, carry your bike across the shallow river at the sand bridge where the river meets the surf; not recommended during the winter rains. Once across, you connect with **Kalihiwai Bay**, TH14. This route is part of a way to get from Princeville almost to Kilauea without having to be on the highway.

PADDLE: The reef far offshore of **Anini Beach** makes for a safe and scenic lagoon for salt-water paddling—the best on Kauaʻi—especially beyond the beach park at road's end. Put in near the stream and work your way back toward park. The **Kalihiwai River** paddle, is the same as described in TH14.

SURF: Anini Beach is not known for surfing; but during winter surf, good board-heads try the reef break, which slides both right and left. Windsurfing and kite-boarding are the things to do at Anini, with beachside rentals and instruction available. These sports are limited to certains times and locations, as noted by signs.

14. KALIHIWAI BAY   BIKE, PADDLE, SURF

WHAT'S BEST: Surfing a deep-water break, taking a paddle up a lesser-known exotic river, and playing in the waves at a locals' beach. Get out of the car and hang around for a while.

PARKING: Take Hwy. 56 past Kilauea. At about .75-mi. past mm. 23/56, turn makai on Kalihiwai Rd. (first). It's before crossing over the highway bridge. Go 1 mi. down to beach.

BIKE: No mountain biking trails in **Kalihiwai Bay**, but if you're traveling the island on a bike, you can turn off the highway here, and, if the river is not at flood stage, cross a sand bridge at the river mouth and connect with **Anini Beach**, as described in TH13. This coastal option is not for those in a hurry or wishing the easiest passage.

PADDLE: The .75-mile slack waters of **Kalihiwai River**, with bananas and other fruits in the small river valley, might remind you of Southeast Asia. Commercial trips are not permitted here, but locals dip their paddles. The navigable part extends about one-quarter mile inland from the bridge, to below thundering Kalihiwai Falls. Access is in the ironwood grove at the far end of the bay.

SURF: **Kalihiwai Bay** is a consistent and popular surfing spot. To check out the surf, stop on the way down, .75-mile from the highway, at an unimproved two-car turnout along the guardrail. Usually a dozen or more boarders are gathered below to surf a four-tier right-break, extending from the mouth of the bay inland. Sets are usually narrow, breaking close to the cliff. Kalihiwai Bay usually has a low shore break, a spot for boogie boarding or swimming around with snorkel and fins.

15.   KALIHIWAI RIDGE   BIKE

WHAT'S BEST: Tropical trees and gardens galore adorn a paved ride through the Beverly Hills of Kaua'i. Private property borders Kalihiwai Ridge, but you can get a darned good look at it.
PARKING: Take Hwy. 56 past Kilauea and turn mauka on Kahiliholo Rd., .4-mi. after mm. 24/56. You'll see yellow sign noting a left-hand turn. Park at highway. This road also makes for an excellent scenic drive.

BIKE: Paved **Kahiliholo Road** is a 7- to 10-mile ride, roundtrip, to the top, depending on whether you take one of the side-road options. Your route is lined with ferns, palms and monkeypod trees, winding steadily upward, passing grand estates with gardens, and other, more modest homes. All are set on large gardenlike parcels, with the cloud-topped ridge looming surrealistically as a backdrop. At this part of the island, the dense tropical valleys typical of the north shore transition to the sloping moist-forest uplands of the northeast Kaua'i. Kahiliholo Road extends up privately held lands between the Moloa'a and Halelea forests, and is bordered by the Kalihiwai River on one side, and by a series of streams that feed Kilauea Bay on the other.

On the left side of the road, about 2.5-miles up, is Haulauani Road, a dead end which gives you the best tree-filtered view toward Mount Namahana in the foreground, and the Makaleha Mountains in the distance. Another side jaunt is to ride left on Kamo'okoa road toward Silver Falls Ranch, an abundantly scenic area with ridge views. They offer tours from horseback; see *Resource Links*. The top of Kahiliholo Road ends at a private drive. Turn around here and coast back down to Hwy. 56.

16.   SECRET BEACH   HIKE, SURF

WHAT'S BEST: A hike-to, beach-lover's beach, with a long sand-and-surf walk and dramatic view of Kilauea Lighthouse on the cliffs above. Hike down and find a spot to lose your sense of time.
PARKING: Take Hwy. 56 to .5-mi. past Kilauea. Turn makai on Kalihiwai Rd (first), before reaching mm. 24/56. Pass the driveway to the school bus yard, and then turn right, just .1-mile from the highway, on a dirt road cut through a 15-foot-high embankment. Continue .5-mi. to unimproved parking.

HIKE: Secret Beach (.5-mi. to 2.5 mi., depending on length of beach walk.)

Secret Beach, officially Kauapea Beach, might be renamed Not-So-Secret Beach, since this access is widely known. The beach is a long and deep deposit of fine sand, running from the lighthouse at Kilauea Point to Kapuka'amoi Point, which is the mouth of Kalihiwai Bay. Crowds are never a problem on the beach, but parking is limited.The trail starts out flat, along the fence of a two-horse paddock in the shade of broadleaf kamani trees. At the end of the fencing, the trail heads down on wood-and-dirt steps, roots, and rocks—all of which can be slippery after rains. You walk the last hundred yards or so through a flourishing pandanus grove—those tropical trees with pom-poms of drooping sharp leaves. Hats and mats are made from them.

Locals divide the beach into three, almost equal segments: "First" Secret Beach is the part you first access from this trail; "Second" Secret is the middle part that has black rocks poking up along it surf line; and "Third" Secret is the last beach which is nestled up to the cliffs that lead out to the lighthouse. Sand is a hundred yards deep in places, but winter surf moves tons of sand around to reveal black rocks and bedrock. *Be Aware:* Be alert for rogue waves. Also, keep your pants on: nudity is unlawful on all beaches.

SURF: **Secret Beach** commonly has an onshore break that is dangerous, especially during winter months. Another drawback is the long board carry down the trail. During calmer periods of onshore break, Secret is good for boogie boards, and during some winter storms the locals are known to ride the offshore swells. *Be aware:* Secret Beach is not one to try without observing the locals.

17.   KILAUEA LIGHTHOUSE   HIKE, BIKE, SURF

WHAT'S BEST: Take a gander at magnificent shorebirds and crashing surf at the lighthouse and wildlife refuge on Hawai'i's most northerly point. This place is powerfully beautiful.
PARKING: From Hwy. 56, turn makai toward Kilauea on Kolo Rd., near mm. 23/56. Jog over to Kilauea Rd. behind the gas station and continue makai for 2 mi. Pass a first lighthouse parking lot and go down a steep road to paved lot at

Kilauea Point National Wildlife Refuge. *Note:* Three other parking areas, all within a mile of each other, are described in the hiking instructions.

HIKE: **Kilauea Lighthouse (.5-mi.); Crater Hill (2 to 3 mi., depending on route selected); Kilauea Bay (5 mi. or less, depending on where you park.)**

Kilauea Lighthouse, although drawing many tourists, will still give you a faraway feel, standing on the most northerly part of the main Hawaiian Islands and looking down 200 hundred feet to seas crashing on tiny Mokuaeae Island. Tropicbirds, Laysan albatrosses, nene, great frigatebirds and other seabirds soar about—the lighthouse sits on Kilauea Point Wildlife Refuge. In the seas, whales and spinner dolphin vie to steal the show. Binoculars are provided for free. Although you cannot walk to the top of the historic lighthouse, you can peek in its doors. You'll also want to step inside the visitors center, both for brightly presented exhibits and nature-themed gifts. *Note:* A small donation is charged to visit the refuge.

Crater Hill, the grassy knob above the lighthouse, is part of the wildlife refuge and gives you a great view of the point as well as of the north coast and inland ridges. Two ways to enjoy Crater Hill: Volunteers at the U.S. Fish and Wildlife Service lead a 2 mile hike daily, beginning about 15 minutes after the refuge opens and lasting about two hours. A small fee is charged, which includes admission to the lighthouse, and reservations may be made by calling 808-828-0168. To check out Crater Hill on your own, park at Iwalani Road, the entrance to Seacliff Plantation, a gated residential development about .25-mile before the entrance to the lighthouse on Kilauea Road. Using the pedestrian access, walk up through the upscale neighborhood, bearing left on Makana'ano Place near the top. People are prohibited from entering protected areas—you can't get to the very top of Crater Hill— but you do arrive at a paved cul-de-sac. Go through an opening provided in the fence and walk a short distance out to a grassy patch to an ideal coastal viewing area.

Kilauea Lighthouse

The back way to **Kilauea Bay**—whose beach is called **Kahili Beach**—is again off Kilauea Road—on your right about .25-mile past Kong Lung store. Look for a paved road, marked by a green gate and upright poles near telephone pole #21X. Turn right and park at end of pavement. The road/trail is flat for the first .5-mile, along a pasture with inland views, and then drops more than 200 feet through a profuse banana patch. *Notes:* You can shorten the hike by driving in the first .5-mile. You can also drive directly to the bay via another route; see TH18. After passing the bananas, the trail to Kilauea Bay descends and soon opens to a pastoral, river valley view. You arrive at the bay across the river from the kayak spot for Kilauea Bay, TH18. Continuing on the road, in another .25-mile, you come to trail's end at an abandoned rock quarry.

BIKE: With the exception of the lighthouse itself, all of the areas in the hiking section make for good riding. The trail to **Kilauea Bay** is a particularly good ride, as is the paved pedal up to **Crater Hill**.

SURF: Surfers try their luck at **Third Secret Beach**, but the onshore break here is often hazardous and you have about a .5-mile board carry. The back way to the **Kilauea Bay**, as described in the hikes above, is also a surfing spot, at the offshore break near the quarry. This area, sometimes called **Rock Crusher** or **Quarry Beach**, is more readily accessed via Kilauea Bay, TH18.

18. KILAUEA BAY   HIKE, PADDLE, SURF

> **WHAT'S BEST:** Put this beach with a stream on the A-list with Kauaʻi's other out-of-the-way wonders. After wave play and beach time, seek a mini-adventure walk in the verdant stream delta or out to the rugged coastline.
> **PARKING:** Take Hwy. 56 toward Kilauea. Turn makai 6-mi. after mm. 21/56, on Wailapa Road. A yellow highway sign marks the intersection. Continue for .4-mi. and veer left down a steep but well-surfaced dirt road for .5-mi. to unimproved parking area at beach. Avoid this road during rains.

HIKE: Quarry Beach (.75-mi.); Keilua Point (up to 1 mi.)

For **Quarry Beach**—which is as close as you can get to Mokolea Point that juts out to form the riverside mouth of the bay—head down the beach to your left as you face the water. You need to cross the stream at a sand dam at the surf line, which is normally easy but, of course, not possible if the water is high. A path leads up to the trail that comes down from Kilauea the back way, as described in TH17. It's a short walk to your right on the road to the viewpoint at the old quarry, bordering the wildlife refuge. From rocky perches, you can watch the backside of waves rolling inland.

Walking the other way on the bay's soft sand—called **Kahili Beach**—you quickly leave the beach and walk up flat rock ledges, gaining 50 feet, to a grassy perch among ironwoods and just out of the salt spray. Continuing down from there is a small beach and cliffs of **Keilua Point**.

More Stuff: One of the more charming and ambitious botanical gardens you'll find anywhere lies at the end of Wailapa Road. The sprawling Na Aina Ka grounds are decorated with life-sized bronze statuary and a hedge maze, alongside a lagoon with fountains. This formality gives way to treed hillsides that extend to a wild beach. Call for reservations; see *Resource Links*.

PADDLE: Kilauea Stream curves inland for more than a mile, wide and deep through an open valley with upland views, before losing itself in dense foliage. Commercial kayakers are not permitted on this river. Access is good: Make a left at the main parking area, through two upright pipes on a narrow road section through ironwoods. This road leads to a sandy, open riverbank. The navigable portion of the stream ends below the cascade known as Slippery Slide of *South Pacific* fame.

SURF: Boogie boarding and board surfing is often good on the relatively gentle shore break of **Kahili Beach**. Locals also take advantage of an offshore break at the riverside mouth of the bay. This area is called **Quarry Beach** or **Rock Crusher**. Kilauea Bay, in spite of better than its decent waves, is not among the most popular surfing areas. You can drive down and check it out. *Be Aware:* Shore breaks can cause impact injuries and hazardous conditions during high surf periods.

Nene, Hawaiian state bird

Kong

"Kong" is the familiar name for the pointed peak on Kauaʻi's northeast shore, looking much like the head of the mythical ape, forever watchful seaward. The peak's real name is Kalalea, which in Hawaiian means "prominent." But Kong's 15-minutes of Hollywood prominence came not from *King Kong*, but as the opening shot for *Raiders of the Lost Ark*.

The gap-toothed ridge in which Kong is centered, commonly called the Anahola Mountains, is the subject of Kauaian mythology that has been altered by recent geology: The ancient "Hole in the Mountain," an opening through the ridge behind Kong, was said to have been made when a rival king from the Big Island threw his spear across the entire island, piercing the ridge and earning the kingship for his effort. In the mid-1990s, a landslide closed the hole to a tiny crescent.

Kong's ridge is a branch of the Makaleha Mountains, the east-side range that intersects the sloping forest reserve and agricultural lands that sweep around the coast from Kilauea on the north to the Royal Coconut Coast on the east. This area is known for numerous hike-to coves, beachcombing beaches and coastal bike trails. With several trails and four-wheel drive roads leading into forest reserves, the Kong region also offers an excellent inland access toward Mount Waialeale and adjoining ridges.

Heading away from Kilauea toward Kapa'a, begins a long coastline, perhaps the least-hiked of Kaua'i's accessible shore. Waiakalua beaches are among the best-kept secrets, featuring three cocopalm coves. Down the coast from Waiakalua is Larsens Beach, better known and much larger—more than two miles of coral beach and ragged reef, fringed by low bluffs. Tide pools, reef currents and wave action make Larsens' shore ever-changing, and winter trade winds bring eclectic flotsam ashore.

Continuing toward Kong from Larsens, the coast becomes a series of coves and inlets large enough to be called bays—Papa'a, Moloa'a, Aliomanu and Anahola. Moloa'a Bay, though the site of several homes, is a classic getaway cove for sunbathing, swimming, and short hikes along its bluffs. Off-highway paved roads around Moloa'a, including the one to Larsens, make this a place to tour on a bike. Anahola Bay, just below Kong, and Aliomanu Bay, which lies beside Anahola, offer three snorkeling and surfing beaches, a navigable stream and a variety of beach hiking. Bordering Hawaiian Homelands, Anahola is the most-Hawaiian community on this side of the island.

Around the point, on the Kapa'a side of Kong, are miles of coastline accessible by foot and mountain bike—some of it wild, and some of it through resort paths and beachside parks—extending all the way from Anahola along the Royal Coconut Coast to the Wailua River. Surfers and boogie boarders in this neck of the woods head for Donkey Beach, Kealia Beach or Wailua Bay, while snorkelers duck in at one of several lesser known spots behind funky Kapa'a Town and the hotels of the Coconut Coast. Although waters are shallow here, the swimming can be good.

Sacred Forest, Hindu Monastery

Donkey Beach, fresh coconuts

This coral-reef coast is not without its paddling waters, with two streams to inland areas that practically no one paddles. Unlike other streams on the island that fit this description, Kong's are close to kayak outfitters. Outrigger canoes and kayaks also stroke the waters off the coast, although Kauaʻi newcomers should check with locals before venturing beyond the breakers in a kayak.

Some of the best inland hiking is to be had on this east portion of the Kong trailheads. Above Kealia is the Spalding Monument, pointing the way toward the upper Makaleha Mountains and Waipaheʻe Falls. Above Kapaʻa on Olohena Road is more access toward these mountains, as well as three trailheads to Nounou Ridge, better known as the Sleeping Giant. The landmark Sleeping Giant is a forest reserve and excellent viewpoint to get a bearing on the east side.

Heading up the Wailua River—the place where the first aliʻi, or kings, chose to call home—leads to the Keahua Arboretum. From the arboretum, bikers and hikers can pick up the south end of the Powerline Trail that connects with Princeville on the north shore, or head up another ridge that twists through jungle to abut the Makaleha Mountains. Another trail from the arboretum leads to an up-close look at Mount Waialeale, below the rippling waters of its vertical face. Also from the arboretum are trails that poke out to views of Kilohana Crater above Lihue.

The rural roads around Kapa'a and the Coconut Coast are also a scenic tour for cyclists wishing to catch a glimpse of local-style living and maybe snag a papaya at an honor-system fruit stand. Behind the Sleeping Giant is a gardenlike expanse.

After a day spent recreating, Kapa'a Town is a good choice to grab a smoothie or a shave ice, and walk around the quaint streets and neighborhoods—a blend of the cultures that combine under the umbrella of aloha to make Kaua'i. Buddhist temples stand near Catholic churches, and brew pubs adjoin sushi bars and Hawaiian diners.

Anahola Stream, Coconut Coast in Kapa'a

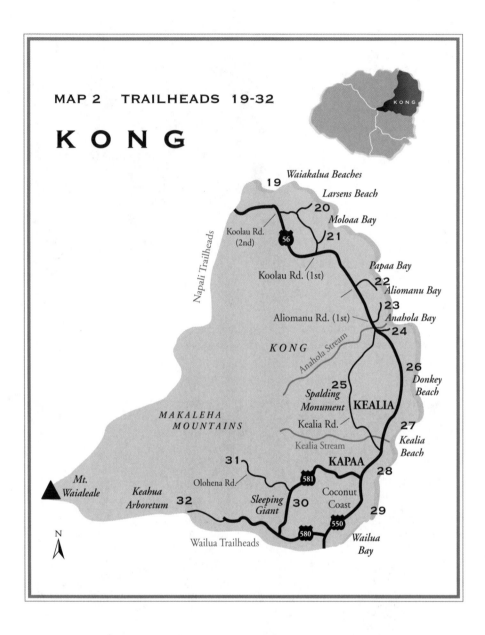

MAP 2   TRAILHEADS 19-32

KONG

KONG

Waiakalua Beaches

19

Larsens Beach

20

Moloaa Bay

Koolau Rd.
(2nd)

56

21

Papaa Bay

Koolau Rd. (1st)

22

Aliomanu Bay

23

Aliomanu Rd. (1st)

Anahola Bay

24

KONG

Anahola Stream

26

Donkey
Beach

25

Spalding
Monument

KEALIA

*MAKALEHA
MOUNTAINS*

Kealia Rd.

27

Kealia
Beach

Kealia Stream

31

KAPAA

Olohena Rd.

581

28

Mt.
Waialeale

Keahua
Arboretum

32

Sleeping
Giant

30

Coconut
Coast

29

Napali Trailheads

N

550

580

Wailua Trailheads

Wailua
Bay

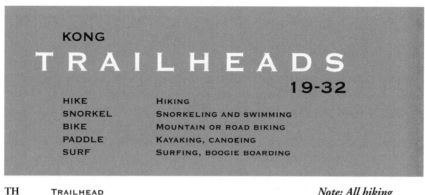

KONG

TRAILHEADS
19-32

HIKE	HIKING
SNORKEL	SNORKELING AND SWIMMING
BIKE	MOUNTAIN OR ROAD BIKING
PADDLE	KAYAKING, CANOEING
SURF	SURFING, BOOGIE BOARDING

TH	TRAILHEAD	
Makai	TOWARD OCEAN	
Mauka	TOWARD THE MOUNTAIN, INLAND	
mm.	MILE MARKER, CORRESPONDS TO HIGHWAY SIGNS	

Note: All hiking distances are roundtrip unless otherwise noted.

19. WAIAKALUA BEACHES   HIKE, SNORKEL, SURF

WHAT'S BEST: Adventurous hikes to idyllic, hidden tropical beaches. If you want to go native, try this place.

PARKING: Head beyond Anahola on Hwy. 56, past second Ko'olau Rd. Turn makai on N. Waiakalua Rd., about .8-mi. past mm. 20/56. Go .75-mi. on N. Waiakalua to end of road at cul-de-sac, and turn left on dirt road, which is lined with ironwood trees at telephone pole #17. Go .25-mi. to unimproved parking. Leave car free of valuables.

HIKE: Waiakalua and Pila'a Beaches (.25-mi to about 2 mi. depending on how many beaches you visit.)

Waiakalua Beaches are two little jewels tucked away on a remote section of coastline between Larsens Beach, TH20, and Kilauea Bay, TH18. To the most-readily accessible, start down the steep steps, improved by cut logs. Pause at a viewpoint not far from the trailhead and look to your right: You'll see the more secluded Pila'a Beaches—palm-fringed crescents of sand on a black rock coast, under cliffs rich with plant life. (See *More Stuff* for advice on getting to these babies.)

Proceed down over roots and a slippery section, in shade all the way. One short rock section requires attention to foot placement, just above the soft sand beach. Waiakalua is a fairly small beach, with a view of Crater Hill, looking up through palm fronds as you walk to your left. Keep going and you'll see a second second beach that lies beyond the first. At the far end of the beach from the trail, and about 100 feet up, is the site of Kapinao Heiau—remnants are hard to find and are more readily accessed from the top of the trail.

More Stuff: One access to the Pila'a Beaches is via a difficult passage along the black rock coast. Both beaches have dwellings; rustic plantation-style shacks, beautifully situated among palms and other beach trees. Above the beaches, land is privately held and a former access, near mile-marker 19/56, is no more. Instead, intrepid surfers use a route over private property located .25-mile from the highway on second Ko'olau Road, which follows uphill of a stream drainage. *Be Aware:* Slippery footing and large surf can make the coastal access hazardous, if not impossible. Land access may constitute tresspassing, so use your own judgment.

SNORKEL: **Waiakalua Beaches**, on pretty days, fill the bill for an ideal tropical beach, the perfect place to take a dip with the fishes. It's just the ticket to shed city skin. But it faces into the trade winds and features an exposed section of reef with confusing currents. Get a good read before venturing in.

SURF: Surfers take a gander at **Waiakalua** from the viewpoint mentioned in the hiking section, and die-hards carry their boards down. This is a place for locals and advanced surfers to look for something exciting. Because of the reef break and remoteness, Waiakalua is a risky surfing area. During periods of epic surf, big-daddy wave riders, partnered with buddies on jet skis, ride the rolling mountains: quite a show.

20.   LARSENS BEACH   HIKE, SNORKEL, BIKE

WHAT'S BEST: Larsens is definitely not on the tour-bus circuit. Roam an open beachscape for miles, looking for washed-up treasure and a well-chosen place to take a dip.
PARKING: Take Hwy. 56 past Anahola and turn makai at first Ko'olau Rd., which is about .75-mi. past mm. 16/56. Drive past Moloa'a Rd. and, at 2.5 mi. from hwy. turnoff, turn makai again, sharply right at white beach access pole. Go 1 mi. down to large parking area. Leave car free of valuables. *Note:* Ko'olau Rd. loops around to Hwy. 56, and the Larsens turnoff is about 1.2 mi. from the highway if you come in from that side.

HIKE: Kephui Point (3.5 mi.)

Larsens Beach is visible from a grassy perch a short distance down from the parking—the beach is about 200 feet below and little more than .25-mile away. **Kepuhi Point** is beyond two beach segments, lying to your left as you face the water. Take the trail down, not a very steep one, and head to your left at the beach. Along Larsens Beach, which extends from Moloa'a Bay to Kulikoa Point near Pila'a, you will discover drifts of yellow sand beside tilting sections of broken reef, foaming with aquamarine tidal action. *Be Aware:* You may also discover a few flop campers and nudie sunbathers, although neither of these activities are lawful in Hawaii. Larsens is an unusually complicated and interesting coast. The backshore slopes fairly gently, allowing for

Larsens coastline

several red-dirt routes through ironwoods and occasional broadleaf beach trees, like kamani and heliotrope, interspersed among flowering shrubs.

The first part of Larsens is also called Ka'aka'aniu Beach. After this first .5-mile beach, you leave the sand, taking a trail over a .25-mile stretch on a low point and dropping down to the next beach segment, a cutie called Waipake Beach. At the far end of Waipake, you'll see a ruddy, hog-back bluff. Make your way along the beach and then over this bluff—take a gradual route before coming to the end of the beach, and follow a sketchy trail through ironwoods. As you you come down the other side—crossing a lush gully—you'll see Kepuhi Point. The point is a volcanic formation set low to the surf, with a frothing tidal pool and a blunt tip that thwarts the sea to create a sometimes thunderous display of white water. The entire length of Larsens is a beachcomber's delight, with the possibility of glass balls, buoys, message bottles and shells. This beach is exposed to the trade winds coming over 2,500 miles of Pacific Ocean. *Be Aware:* Don't confuse this with a point of the same name near Haena. Also, inland is private property, so use coastal paths and heed signs.

SNORKEL: **Larsens Beach** is not known as a snorkeling spot. Before dropping down to the beach, study the reef from the viewpoint mentioned in the hiking section. You'll be able to spot the main blue channel, at the far left of the beach; current usually runs right-to-left and out this channel. Farther down the beach are other vantage spots to observe the current. Throw a stick in the water to see which way it floats, and once you enter the water, be mindful of the direction your body starts moving on its own. Still, on certain days in the right spot, Larsens is a beautiful place to get in the water with mask and fins. The second beach over, Waipake, has better spots, but they

Anahola Mountains

are more remote, and therefore more dangerous in the event of a mishap. *Be Aware:* Do not swim here without making sure it is safe. Conditions are often hazardous.

BIKE: **Ko'olau Road** and the road to Larsens invite a pavement pedal through pastoral countryside. One possible ride, which is an 11-mile loop, is to start at the first Ko'olau Road and ride down the lush valley to Moloa'a Bay on Moloa'a Road, then backtrack. Turn right on Ko'olau and continue to check out Larsens. You can even ride the .5-mile down to the beach with moderate effort. Come back out to Ko'olau and continue until you join Hwy. 56. Turn left and ride the highway back to your car.

21. MOLOA'A BAY   HIKE, SNORKEL, BIKE

> **WHAT'S BEST:** A lush tropical bay, made for an afternoon of swimming, short walks and relaxing. Though a cluster of homes crowd the parking area, privacy is a short hop away.
>
> **PARKING:** Take Hwy. 56 past Anahola and turn makai on first Ko'olau Rd., past mm. 16/56. Go 1.5 mi. and turn makai again on Moloa'a Rd. Continue down 1 mi., bearing left to beach access parking area amid private homes. Do not park unless you can fit into the designated area.

HIKE: Kalaeamana Point (1 mi.); Moloa'a Forest Reserve (.75-mi.; different parking area, see hiking description.)

From the parking to **Kalaeamana Point**, walk the short remainder of the road, through beach access area, and immediately cross Moloa'a Stream. Continue around the fine arc of this medium-sized bay, and cross under the spreading heliotrope at the far end. From this picnic ground-like area, hike up and around the point—a sketchy path leads safely between the rocks near the cliff and some well-marked private property.

You leave the bay behind and stop climbing about 50 feet above the water. Contour your way through a surprisingly dry area, with grasses and the occasional ironwood, with some flowering vines thrown in for good measure. On the upslopes before reaching the point, Layson albatrosses have been known to rest or make their awkward, "gooney bird" take-offs. If you see one of these remarkable birds, give it room. A sturdy fence and private-property signs prevent you from reaching the full distance of Kalaeamana, but you get close enough to sense it, and Larsens Beach, TH20, which lies around it to the north. It is possible to drop down at the fence line and hop the black rocks around toward Larsens, a route best attempted during dry weather and low surf. *More Stuff:* You can also walk a fair distance, perhaps .5-mile, the other way around Moloaʻa Bay, but it requires boulder hopping. Be mindful of slippery rocks and high surf.

The **Moloaʻa Forest Reserve** is not a spectacular hike, but it is the only place you can access the Anahola Mountains on this side; the trailhead is below a pointed peak named Amu. To get there, drive past the first Koʻolau Road for 1.2 miles. You'll be going up a grade, passing a series of guardrails; as the guardrails end—and about .1-mile after mm. 18/56—look mauka at a red-dirt bank to see a large brown mailbox. Park on grass shoulder on either side of road. *Be Aware:* The trailhead is hard to spot on this busy road. You might end up passing it and hanging a U-turn.

To begin the short hike, walk up the grassy approach and through a plywood gate in the fence, next to the mailbox, which reads, "B-14, Moloaʻa Hunter Checking Station." Then go through the closed, not locked, silver gate to your left and follow the wide path as is curves upward toward Anahola. After a little more than .25-mile, notice a grass-cut trail veering left—the hunter's road continues toward Anahola. The left-veer takes you a few hundred feet to a blue-water viewpoint of Moloaʻa Bay. Also of interest on this little-used trail: Halfway to the viewpoint spur described above, you'll see a red-dirt embankment, from which a poor trail leads. This trail gives you an option to look at Amu, a feature of the Anahola Mountains. Don't go too far in; this is really not much of a trail and walking off-trail is not safe. *Be Aware:* Hunter's area; weekdays are best for hiking.

SNORKEL: The perfect crescent of the **Moloaʻa Bay** is broken at various places by black-rock reef, making this an interesting place to snorkel around, with good visibility on calm days and enough fish to make it interesting. Moloaʻa is not known as a snorkeling destination, however. It is more a place to take a plunge and go back to the beach mat. *Be Aware:* Moloaʻa is fairly well protected, but avoid the rocky areas during periods of high surf. Choppy incoming surf can push you onto the reef inside the bay.

BIKE: Moloaʻa-Larsens area is suitable for a rideabout, mostly on pavement. See the mountain bike description for Larsens Beach, TH20.

WHAT'S BEST: Aliomanu contributes to Kaua'i's wealth of beachcomber's specials. This lesser-known getaway is easy to get to.

PARKING: Take Hwy. 56 past Anahola and Hokualele Rd. and turn makai on second Aliomanu Rd., past mm. 15/56. Then turn left on Kalalea View Dr., toward Aliomanu Estates. Go .5-mi. and then turn makai at beach access sign. Go .25-mi. on paved road and then veer right a short distance to developed parking below a bluff. *Note:* Papa'a Rd., the next road past second Aliomanu Rd., is also a way to get to this beach if you're coming from the north shore. Turn makai and follow beach access signage for about .6-mi.

HIKE: Anahola Bay (2 mi.); Papa'a Bay (1.5 mi.)

Aliomanu Bay is a shallow depression in the coast between Papa'a and Anahola bays— you probably wouldn't think of it as a bay. The bluff just above the parking is an airy spot that gives you a good look at the bay as well as the Anahola Mountains inland. Head down a red-dirt road, making easy curves to the beach, .25-mile away.

To **Anahola Bay**, head to your right as you face the water at Aliomanu Beach. You'll walk the coarse sand at first and then pick your way around Kuaehu Point, which is just below a lone house with a bright blue roof. A trail through sand and over black rocks soon leads to a view of Anahola Bay and Kong. Along the way you're bound to find nets, floats, and other colorful flotsam lost by fishing boats. High tide may make for a wet trip around the point, but this beach is made for wading. Once around Kuaehu Point, you can continue down Anahola Beach, as described in TH23.

To **Papa'a Bay**, walk to your left as you face the ocean at Aliomanu Beach. You'll soon run out of sand and find yourself rock-hopping around the shallow point—looking across Papa'a Bay's mouth to the far point that extends much farther seaward. Follow fishermen's mud tracks on the rocks, and watch out for high surf. Papa'a is a cozy bay, an ideal tropical setting, although a huge trophy home has recently been constructed there.

More Stuff: You can access Papa'a Bay more directly along the bluff: Where the road makes a right-angle above the Aliomanu parking, head seaward with a house to your left, and then hang a left on a trail that skirts along the bluff in front of newly built homes. At the far end of the bluff, a steep trail leads down you down to sea level. From there, pick your way inland to the sandy cove. *Be Aware:* The fun-loving owner of the trophy home has blocked access to Papa'a Bay via Old Government Road, which extends from Papa'a Road. Locals, having used this route for generations, staged a walk-in and were arrested for trespassing. The beach is public property.

SNORKEL: Aliomanu Beach has excellent scenic values, with kamani and ironwood trees interspersed along a grassy inland and a generous swath of yellow sand looking onto a two-mile long coral reef. Rocks and shallow waters make for interesting wave actions and tidal surges. All in all, this is a decent beach for snorkeling, with ample fish, although don't expect large, sparkling schools. *Be Aware:* Shallow waters, confused surf, and unpredictable northeast exposure make for strong currents. **Papa'a Bay** can be a good snorkeling spot on calmer days, as the cove offers protection from the surf. It's a real hassle to get to, but worth it.

Anahola Bay

SURF: It's a long paddle or steep board-carry to **Papa'a Bay**, but locals head here to take advantage of a quick-breaking, offshore swell. These fast-riding waves can be available at any time of the year.

23. ANAHOLA BAY   HIKE, SNORKEL, PADDLE, SURF

WHAT'S BEST: Snorkel, beachcomb or paddle. Though not normally on the list of starred attractions, charming Anahola may just become your first choice.
PARKING: Take Hwy. 56 past Kealia and turn makai on first Aliomanu Rd., which is past the Anahola Post Office and just past mm. 14/56. Go .5-mi. down the paved road to stream mouth at beach. Park there or at one of several turnouts proceeding to your left on Aliomanu along the beach, the last of which is about .5-mi. from the river. An excellent midway access is near 4746 Aliomanu.

HIKE: Anahola Beach (up to 3 mi.)

Anahola Beach, where the Anahola Stream flows down from nearby Kong and enters the bay, is a narrow, long strip of yellow sand along a coral reef. Ironwoods, cocopalms and several kinds of broadleaf trees shade widely spaced beach cottages. The stream bank near the surf line is one of those perfect spots. Start the beach walk with the stream at your back, heading for Kuaehu Point and Aliomanu Bay (connecting up with TH22). The last short section of this walk involves black-rock hopping, or jogging inland on an easement through private homes.

About halfway on the walk, a few beach cottages sit close to the water and you may have to walk the top of a short seawall for a bit during high tide. Just after the seawall, you come to a stream that gives you a romantic look at Kong, rising in the background, framed by cocopalms over still waters. Fishermen routinely walk the rocks around the Kuaehu Point; not a dangerous route. You may wish to walk the rural road on the home stretch.

SNORKEL: All in all, **Anahola Bay** is an above-average snorkeling beach, with clear pools large enough to do lap swimming, a moderate number of fish, and a long coral reef. You'll find sandy access in selected spots, although rough coral borders much of the shore. The better snorkeling is farther down from the stream. *Be Aware:* Rip currents head out channels, flushing the wave-surge from the coast, particularly strong during high-surf conditions. Observe and test the waters. Also avoid the river mouth area when the river is high and rip currents develop.

Anahola Beach Park

PADDLE: The **Anahola Stream** lazes inland almost a mile before petering out into flora near the highway overpass. The Anahola Valley is lush with tropical fruit trees. Birdsong dominates the airwaves. This is a non-commercial paddling area, but you'll usually see a canoe or kayak parked in the ironwoods at the stream bank, where Aliomanu Road comes down. Kayakers also head out into the bay, although these are not benign seas under most conditions, due to variable winds and currents. If you do venture into saltwater, make sure to spot the way back, as crossing the shallow water over reef can be hazardous. *Be Aware:* Flash floods occur after heavy rains.

SURF: Locals do surf this area, offshore of where the stream breaks through the reef. It's a long paddle out to a reef break, both right and left. For good surfers only. Not a good idea to venture out here without advice from local boarders.

24. ANAHOLA BEACH PARK   HIKE, SNORKEL, BIKE

> **WHAT'S BEST:** Stop in for a swim on the locals' side of the bay, taking in views of the Anahola Mountains in afternoon sun.
> **PARKING:** Take Hwy. 56 past Kealia. Turn makai on Anahola Rd., past mm. 13/56, and drive .75-mi. to white-rock sign noting the beach park. Veer left, drive short distance to end of road and beach parking.

HIKE: Anahola Beach Park (1.5 mi. to 5 mi.); Kahala Point (.5-mi.)

Anahola Beach Park, the getaway spot for the Hawaiian community of Anahola, is just across the stream from TH23. About .75-mile of sand stretches from the Anahola Stream to the black rocks that are the beginning of Kahala Point. From the beach are beautiful views of the Anahola Mountains, seen through a healthy grove of coco palms that border the sand. On the walk down the beach to the stream, you pass the beach park, a popular weekend picnic-and-party spot for locals. You can cross the stream under most conditions, connecting with the beach walk described in TH23.

The trail to **Kahala Point** is just beyond beach parking, where a road/trail leads up past picnic tables through ironwoods. This takes you on a gradual rise to Kahala, the point that forms the southern mouth of the bay. *Note:* This side of Anahola Bay, and the lands around the point are Hawaiian Homelands. Although the road continues around all the way to Kealia, it's best to respect the lands of the native Hawaiians and not venture farther than the point, especially on weekends.

SNORKEL: The waters off **Anahola Beach Park** are shallow and the water clarity is not the best. But you'll see a few fish in this relatively safe swimming area. The beach has sandy entry points and a good swimming lane that extends toward the river. Bordering trees allow for both sun or shade, and the view inland toward Kong is remarkable. All in all, Anahola Beach Park is a fairly good snorkeling spot. *Be Aware:* Under high surf conditions, currents can be a problem.

BIKE: **Anahola Beach Park** connects via coastal roads to Kealia Beach, TH27. Some unofficial restrictions apply to riding on Hawaiian Homelands, as noted in hiking description above. A better approach is from the Kealia trailhead.

Road to Spalding

25.   SPALDING MONUMENT

WHAT'S BEST: Hikes and bikes of varying distances along the pastured upslopes of Kealia, with blue-water views and in-your-face exposure to Kong and the Anahola Mountains.

PARKING: Take Hwy. 56 from Kapaʻa. Turn mauka at Kealia Rd., about .4-mi past mm. 10/56, across from main Kealia Beach parking area. Keep right past the tiny post office, and head uphill on paved road through bougainvillea, which becomes pothole paved. Pass pastures on the left and cane fields on right, and look for line of Norfolk pines up and to your left, which mark Spalding Monument. The decrepit monument is 2.25 mi. from Hwy. 56.

HIKE: Spalding stroll (up to 2 mi.); Waipaheʻe Falls (6 mi.)

The **Spalding stroll** is down the dirt drive fringed by tall Norfolk pines that lead away from the palm-encircled monument. Although the monument to honor a pineapple scion has been trashed, blue-water views from there remain pleasing. As you walk down the path, the embankment and flora sometimes obscure views, you do get looks of the Kapaʻa coast on your left and close-up views of a moist woodland valley on your right, as you make your way down the path. This hike will delight bird watchers. In about a mile, where a road veers to the right toward a private home in the distance, the path you're on starts to drop steeply. By this time the stately pines have given way to dwarfed ones, swallowed up by a profusion of other trees and shrubs. The road continues down to a valley inland from Kealia, but you'll probably want to turn around.

You should know from the get-go that **Waipahe'e Falls**—once a renowned tourist attraction—has been fenced off and closed for years due to flash flood and other hazards. Still, the walk to Kaneha Reservoir, near the falls, is beautiful, taking you through scenery evoking the green hills of Africa. Also be ready to see some roadside garbage at the outset, since illegal dumping sometimes takes place on this back road.

The trailhead for Waipahe'e Falls is down Kealia Road. As you face the gate at Spalding Monument, go .75-mile to your right and look on your left for a Kealia Hunter Checking Station, Unit C mailbox. (This marker may be missing.) Park there. At first, the red-dirt trail is cut through fallow cane, which allows only occasional glimpses of the Anahola Mountains on your right. At .3-mile, veer left when you have a choice, and at 1 mile also go left as you pass a paved airstrip on your right. Beyond the old airstrip, views open up, and in another .25-mile you reach the road that comes in from the locked gate at the monument—you'll see another gate on your left. Continue to your right on the road. At about 2 miles in, you'll start to get big views of the Makaleha Mountains to your left, and, in the mid-distance, of fleecy monkeypod trees scattered over lime-green slopes. At 2.75 miles, take a left fork in the road that leads to the reservoir and fenced-off spur trail to the falls.

BIKE: The trail to **Waipahe'e Falls**, as described above, is an excellent mountain bike route. You can either start at Hwy. 56 or start at the gate near Spalding Monument as per hiking description. The **Spalding stroll** road continues down to Kealia on a snotty, rutted road, connecting with Haua'ala Road, which is part of an inland ride described in TH27, Kealia Beach. To make this fairly difficult loop, you hang a left at the bottom of Spalding Road and ride out to the highway along the stream. From the highway, go left to Kealia Road, and pedal back up to Spalding. All of this is about 6.5 miles. Plan on hosing down the bike after it's over.

From Spalding Monument, you can also do a mostly paved **Anahola loop** by heading down to Anahola on Kealia Road—it cuts back to the right at the monument. You'll pass hunter's roads and a Japanese cemetery, coming close to Kong. At Anahola, turn right and ride Hwy. 56 back to Kealia Beach. Then take Kealia Road back up to Spalding Monument. The Anahola loop is about 7 miles.

26. DONKEY BEACH   HIKE, SNORKEL, SURF

WHAT'S BEST: A big beach offers to room to roam on a wild-and-scenic coastline. With a new development planned on the hillside, Donkey Beach may not be the hideaway it once was, but it still delivers the scenic goods.
PARKING: Take Hwy. 56 past Kealia Beach. Pass the signs for Kealia Kai development, and look for signed trailhead parking, makai at the top of the hill, near mm. 11/56.

HIKE: Donkey Beach (.75 mi.); House Beach (2 mi.)

Rental cars mingle with surfmobiles at the trailhead parking. A shrub-lined path leads down a hillside to **Donkey Beach**, which is also known by its real name, Kumukumu Beach. Donkey Beach is one of those well-known secret beaches, but its .5-mile wide crescent of sloping sand accommodates a number of people. Walks to either side of the bay afford good views back toward the beach as well as of the rugged coast—Paliku Point is to the right as you face the water, and Ahihi Point is left. *Be Aware:* Some doff their duds at Donkey Beach, but nude sunbathing is unlawful on all Kaua'i beaches.

To **House Beach**, also known as Anapalau Beach, head away from Donkey Beach, going to your left as you face the water. You can take coastal fishermen's paths or the road that runs along the coast. Pass a small cove before Ahihi Point and proceed to the next cove over. Look for a dirt road, used by locals for weekend picnics, that cuts down to House Beach alongside a fairly major drainage, Kamalomaloo Stream. The cove, which no longer has a house, is formed by Ahihi Point on one side and Anapalau Point on the other. You'll find ample sand between nests of black rock, and shade is supplied by mostly heliotrope ironwoods. You might hear-see an ATV rooting around, more probably on weekends.

SNORKEL: With a shore break, **Donkey Beach** is not the best snorkeling spot on the island. No reef protects the shoreline, but at the edges of the bay you can find entry points among rocks, and, on calm days, enjoy swimming around with a mask on. Water is deep and clear, with no freshwater incursion. *Be Aware:* Surf and rip currents can make this an unsafe snorkeling beach.

Snorkeling at **House Beach** is better—the best on the Coconut Coast during ideal conditions—but this is a more remote area with no help nearby if you get in trouble. Be wary of confused currents during high surf. On calm days, the fishermen's perches along the cove make for good entry points to swim ashore—through deep, clear water. When precautions are observed, House Beach is a very good snorkeling experience. Try walking out to the point to the left as you face the water, toward the lone ironwood, and swimming back in toward shore.

Above House Beach

SURF: **Donkey Beach** is on the circuit for east-side surfers. Most avoid the shore break and surf inside the point to the right as you face the water, where right-breakers peel off into the beach. You can tell if the surf is up by looking at the cars on the road: Look for surfmobiles and pickups parked amid the shiny rental cars. *Be Aware:* A powerful shore break means impact injuries. Donkey is not a beach for beginners.

27. KEALIA BEACH
HIKE, SNORKEL, BIKE, PADDLE, SURF

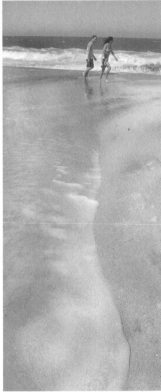

WHAT'S BEST: Coastal and inland bike or hike, beachcombing, whale-watching, and a boogie boarding extravaganza: spend the day at Kealia or drop in for a beach break on your way around the island.
PARKING: Take Hwy. 56 through Kapaʻa, about .5-mi. past mm. 10/56. Park at the large lot on the right before the hill.

Kealia Beach

HIKE: Kealia lookout (1.75 mi.); Donkey Beach (2.75 mi.)

To the **Kealia lookout**—where you may spot a whale during winter migrations, and are promised a fine seaward view on all clear days—walk to your right as you face the water. Near the far end of the beach, about .5-mile from the parking, you cross Kealia Stream. If the water is high, or as an alternative route, you can cut inland and use the bike-pedestrian bridge that spans the stream near the highway. Regardless, at the end of the beach, get on the non-motorized path and continue another .25-mile to a point visible from Kealia Beach. This is a spot below the scenic turnout on the highway between Kapaʻa and Kealia.

To **Donkey Beach**, go to your left as you face the water, walking on a former cane haul road that has been graded and is now commonly used by hikers, cyclists, and surfers. This coastline, with its grassy hills dotted with ironwoods, was once cane fields and is now being converted to large-parcel real estate. Its flora was also given a crew cut by Hurricane Iniki. About .5-mile along on the road from Kealia, you'll cross a gully where a bridge use to be—hug the coast here and don't take the sweeping turn inland. Across the gully is an abandoned pineapple pier, used when that fruit was prominent on Kaua'i. The pier is an exciting side-trip for those steady on their feet. On the way to Donkey Beach, you'll see a number of coastal vantage points, before dropping down to the large baylike beach.

SNORKEL: To your left as you face **Kealia Beach**, a black-rock breakwater creates a sandy area for snorkeling and wading. Swimming can be fairly good here, although fish are not abundant. Surfers usually don't frequent this part of the beach. If you've forgotton beach gear, or are in need of a snacking treat, try across the highway at quaint Kealia Kountry Store. They'll fix you up. *Be Aware:* Stay out of the water on big-surf days, and watch out for current sweeping the inside of the breakwater.

BIKE: From **Kealia** offers the island's best coastal riding, scenic and open. You have several options. Ride toward **Donkey Beach**, as per hiking description, and continue almost to Anahola, which is 6 or 7 miles, roundtrip. You can actually ride to Anahola Bay, although to do so infringes upon Hawaiian Homelands, and is not recommended. The ride has its ups and downs, but is essentially flat, curving with the coast, with options to duck in and out of coves and viewpoints. After Donkey Beach you'll find single-track riding areas inland as you approach Anahola.

You can also ride the other way from Kealia, toward the **Kealia lookout**, and continue on the coastal path for about two miles to Kapa'a. In Kapa'a Town, TH28, you hook up with a coastal route taking you almost to Lihue without having to venture on to the highway.

Another option from Kealia, is the **Haua'ala loop**, which takes you on a little-traveled, 5-mile swing through the Kealia Stream valley. Take off from the parking area toward Kapa'a on the riding path, crossing the Kealia Stream on the footbridge. Then cross the highway (heads up) and take a right, up Mailihuna Road. Pump uphill, past Kapa'a High School, joining Kawaihau Road, in the 'burbs. Then leave that behind by hanging an immediate right down Haua'ala Road, which takes you down quickly to the valley. In the valley you pedal with views of the stream, shaded by banana plants and broadleaf trees with massive limbs.

After about 2 miles, Haua'ala Road becomes dirt and crosses over Kealia Stream— water may be flowing over the road—surrounded by pools and under large monkey-pod trees. Shortly after this serene juncture, and an uphill stretch, the road hairpins

Kealia backroad

back toward the ocean, now on the other side of the stream. Just after the turn-back, you'll see the muddy swath that comes down from Spalding Monument, TH25.

Haua'ala Road continues its loop, down now, through puddles, surging roadside grasses and overhanging, vine-encrusted limbs. You pass small farms and agricultural home-steads, before coming to exotic views of Kealia Stream. You pop out of these tree tunnels into pasture and marshlands, about a mile inland from the Kealia post office, in view of beach parking across the highway.

PADDLE: Kayakers should park at the footbridge, very near mm. 10/56. **Kealia Stream** gathers the waters from several streams and has a wide passage of navigable water for about 1.5 miles inland. The Haua'ala bike loop, which can be driven on dry days, is a good way to check out the stream. You start out paddling in pasturelands—having to pick your way through grass patches at the beginning—and head increas-ingly into the subtropical flora as branches create sun-filtered shady pools. Birdsong is pronounced. The stream is navigable almost to the crossing described in the moun-tain bike loop. This is a stream not used by commercial outfitters, and may be the sleeper paddle on the island. *Note:* Kealia and Kapa'a streams join in this valley, and the stream that enters at the beach is shown as Kapa'a Stream on some maps.

SURF: The shore break at **Kealia Beach** invites board surfers and boogie boarders, often several dozen at a time. Boogie boarding is often good off the breakwater to the left. Near the stream mouth at the other end, swells also attract surfers, although be aware of submerged rocks. Although Kealia can be good at any time of year, normally the onshore trade winds fight the break; look for offshore wind, or none at all. Surfers crane their necks driving by Kealia to other surfing spots, looking for one of the beach's good days. *Be Aware:* Kealia is one of Kaua'i's most dangerous beaches, with rip currents, exposure to trade winds, and an onshore break. You're safer on a boogie or surfboard, but be mindful of currents and breaking surf.

28. KAPA'A TOWN   HIKE, SNORKEL, BIKE, PADDLE, SURF

WHAT'S BEST: Tool around a colorful Kauaian town, on foot or by bike, and enjoy one its several coral beaches. Try Kapa'a on a sunny weekend to see the mix of cultures that blend to create island-style living.

PARKING: The Kapa'a Town trailhead covers a 1.75-mi. portion of coast, beginning near mm. 7/56, just past the Kapa'a Shores condos, and extending to Kou Rd. on the other end of town, behind Otsuka's furniture store. For parking: Turn makai on Keaka Rd., at the Chevron, drive a short block and park at Niulani Rd. along the water. *Note:* Additional access points are imbedded in activity descriptions below.

HIKE: Kapa'a Town stroll (up to 4 mi.)

Begin the **Kapa'a Town** stroll at Keaka Road parking spot, and head toward the Waikaea Canal, about .75-mile to your left as you face the water. You start out walking in a quiet community, a two-block grid of beach cottages between the coast and the highway. A footbridge spans the canal and leads to the large sandy beach behind the Pono Kai condos. The Pono Kai beach extends to Kapa'a County Beach Park—with picnic pavilions and rest rooms—which is behind a soccer field that borders the highway. Most of the way on this hike, you can choose between walking the beach or a paved footpath. Palms and ironwoods shade the way, and beachside cottages are as colorful as the coral. Keiki birthday parties, neighborhood events, and fishermen enjoying a daytime brewskie add to the atmosphere.

Passing the beach park—having walked .75-mile from the Waikaea Canal—you reach another footbridge, at Kapa'a Library. Across this smaller canal is the Coral Reef Hotel, a modest place set among palms and a trimmed lawn. A small sand beach is to your right. The pleasant path continues for another .25-mile, passing a community center and swimming pool, and coming to an end behind Otsuka's at Kou Road. Here, a groomed stand of cocopalms faces the shore leading to Kealia.

On the way back, you may wish to take a look at Kapa'a Town. To do so, walk the beach path back to the soccer field, and continue right on Niu Road. Then go left on the main street, checking out the shops and sights of Kapa'a's triangular downtown.

Continue down the main street to Inia Road, at the Pono Kai, and cut through the grounds of these condos to the beach. To the right at the beach is the footbridge that crosses Waikaea Canal to the quiet residential roads that take you back to Keaka Road, and your car.

Pono Kai Beach

SNORKEL: **Baby Beach** is a sandy area for toddlers and moms. From Keaka Road, walk or drive two blocks to where Makaha Road comes in. The little beach section is between Makaha and Panihi roads. Note a long, shallow pool near the road.

Pono Kai Beach, the best swimming beach in Kapaʻa, extends to your right as you face the water at Kapaʻa County Beach Park—which is behind the large grass field at Niu Road. Pono Kai Beach has ample sand and trees providing a choice between sun and shade. Shore break is usually gentle due to an offshore reef. The sandy shore makes for easy entry, and you'll find interesting rocks and a reef not far out, although great schools of fish are uncommon. Current is generally onshore. Visibilty is often only fair. *Be Aware:* Don't drift too far out, especially if swells are large; current pulls into the channel under these conditions.

Coral Reef Beach—which you can access most easily by parking at the Kapaʻa Library and walking to your left across the footbridge—has shallow waters, but decent places of entry with the best fish along this part of the coast. Water clarity is good. For drying off, you can choose between a small strip of sand and a grassy area with shade among palm trees. *Be Aware:* Rip tides here can be dangerous, and sharp coral is also a factor. Not a good beach under turbulent conditions. Float and watch the bottom to make sure you're not drifting.

BIKE: The **Kapaʻa Town** coast is the most bike-friendly developed spot on the island. Read the hiking description for coastal walk, or just get on your bike and roll. Starting near the Kapaʻa Shores condos on Niulani Road, make your way along paths and footbridges, hugging the coast and heading toward Kealia. At the far end of town, near mm. 9/56 behind Otsuka's—across from Kawaihau Road—you pick up the coastal bike trail and jogging path that runs about a mile to Kealia Beach—and beyond. See Kealia, TH27.

Going the other way on a bike, toward **Wailua**, is not quite as simple, but not difficult, either. To connect with the Coconut Coast, TH29, stay on Niulani Road until you are forced to loop out around the Kapaʻa Shores condos. You can turn seaward toward the Kauaʻi Coconut Beach Resort or even earlier at a beach access sign for little-known Waipouli Beach County Park. See Coconut Coast mountain biking descriptions to take it from there.

PADDLE: Local kayak outfitters in Kapaʻa take the **Waikaea Canal** out into the ocean. Due to tricky currents and reefs, this is not one you want to do on your own. You can, however, paddle the canal inland for a little more than a mile. During the first part you'll be getting an unusual look at a commercial area. After that, you'll float into the natural flora that borders the open space behind Waipouli, next to Kapaʻa, with views of the Sleeping Giant. Commercial kayakers don't go here, and the scenery is not wild, but Waikaea Canal is a pleasant paddle, especially on a day when people are fighting for space on nearby Wailua River. Access is via a boat ramp. Turn makai on Kaloloku Road, behind the Hongwanji Mission.

SURF: **Kapaʻa Town** is not surf city. But local boarders sometimes try the reef break outside of Waikaea Canal. Head for the boat ramp on Kaloloku Road, and look seaward to the right. Due to shallow break and tricky currents, don't try this area unless the local boys are out there.

29. COCONUT COAST   HIKE, SNORKEL, BIKE

WHAT'S BEST: Strolling or pedaling Kauaʻi's lesser-known resort coast, with its classic coco palms and quiet coral beaches. Take a mellow walk to start or finish the day.
PARKING: Take Hwy. 56 from Lihue and cross over the Wailua River. Pass mm. 6/56 and park makai at Coconut Marketplace.

HIKE: Coconut Coast stroll (up to 3 mi.)

The **Coconut Coast** is a 1.5-mile long coral beach sometimes called Papaloa, running from Alakukui Point at Wailua Bay to Waipouli, the area before Kapaʻa. This is Kauaʻi's mostly serenely beautiful, easy-walking coastal resort stroll.

From the parking, walk through the mall-like Coconut Marketplace and continue, on a path or plots of grass, to the beach that is behind the Islander on the Beach Resort. As you face the water, go to your right, either on a paved path or the narrow strip of yellow sand. You'll pass mid-range resorts, set back from the water. Past the Kauaʻi

Kapaʻa

Sands, walk out a trail to a patch of greenery, which is Alakukui Point. From the point is a view of Wailua Bay and farther down the coast beyond Lydgate Park. You can continue from Alakukui Point, skirting two small coves behind tasteful condo complexes, and reach the beach of Wailua Bay.

Going the other way, to your left from the Islander, you have a choice between the paved path or the beach, which is a narrow strip of coarse sand and exposed reef running along a low bank fringed by palms and ironwoods. Coral bits and shells are scattered about. You'll pass a large grass field and then come to the Kaua'i Coconut Beach Resort, the fanciest place in this area. Crossing a small ditch on the other side of the Kaua'i Coconut, you are again in an open area, with ironwoods and a coral beach—the unimproved Waipouli Beach Park. This funky park is a close-in getaway.

SNORKEL: On **Papaloa Beach**, just behind the Islander on the Beach as described in the parking instructions, you'll find sandy entrances in an otherwise sharp-coral beach with the reef running close to the shore. A fair number of fish swim here, but the water is shallow and often made turbulent by northeasterly winds and wave action. If you're staying close by, dip your flippers, but this is not a destination spot.

Waipouli Beach Park, just to the left as you face the water at the Kaua'i Coconut Beach Resort, has the best sand in the area and several places that are shielded, relatively, from strong currents and wave action. One beach access to Waipouli Beach Park is via a road in front of the luau restaurant, which is in front of the Kaua'i Coconut Resort. A second access to Waipouli park is off Hwy. 56, just past mm. 7/56; look for a beach access pole between the large coconut grove and an outfitter's shack. A public lot behind Snorkel Bob's leads to a short pathway to the beach. *Be Aware:* Shallow waters, currents, and wave action combine to make this coast a place to take precautions.

BIKE: The **Coconut Coast** is ideal for exploring on a slow-moving mountain bike. Hug the water, being watchful for pedestrians and sections near hotels where walking the wheels is advised. Between the coastal paths and the highway, roads and parking lots provide safe passage for a bike. To connect with Kapa'a Town, TH28, you can ride the coast all the way, with the exception of a short carry across the narrow ditch at the Kaua'i Coconut Resort. A little farther down from the resort, you have to walk the ocean side in front of the Kapa'a Shores condos and Bull Shed restaurant. You can cross the canal on the other side of the Bull Shed where it's dry not far inland, except after heavy rains. If you want to cover more ground faster, however, you might want to pop out to the highway past the Kaua'i Coconut Resort, and cut back in again just past the Kapa'a Shores.

Going the other way, towards Lihue and Wailua Bay, you need to ride through the Coconut Marketplace parking lot and pick up Papaloa Road, which fronts the highway before joining it near the defunct Coco Palms Resort. You need to get on Highway 56 and cross the river via the marginal bike lane on the main bridge. After the river, cross the highway again and pedal toward Lydgate Park, TH34. A new concrete bike path makes for easy going from there.

30. SLEEPING GIANT   HIKE

> **WHAT'S BEST:** A tree-lover's hike to an east-side landmark, 1,200-feet high, with coastal and inland views. This forest reserve ranks high on the list of excellent half-day hikes.
>
> **PARKING:** Three different trailheads lead to the top of Sleeping Giant. Parking directions for each are imbedded in hike descriptions below, with the recommended route listed first.

HIKE: Sleeping Giant via west-side trail (3 mi.); Sleeping Giant via Kuamoʻo Rd. trail (5.5 mi.); Sleeping Giant via east-side trail (3.5 mi.)

All Sleeping Giant trails are part of Nounou Mountain Forest Reserve in the state's Na Ala Hele trail system. The Nounou Mountains, as you can observe from the coast, would be part of a ridge connecting with Kalepa Ridge, TH37, were it not long ago cleaved by the Wailua River. Inland of the Sleeping Giant, now Wailua Homesteads, was where the ancient Kauaian royalty, the aliʻi, chose to first settle the island.

For the **Sleeping Giant west-side trail**, which is the most direct way to the top, take Hwy. 580, Kuamoʻo Rd., mauka from Wailua Bay (at the Coco Palms). Continue on Hwy. 580, passing mm. 2/581, and turn right on Hwy. 581, Kamalu Rd. Continue about 2 miles on Hwy. 581, past Heamoi Place, and park at telephone pole number 11—public access is between two homes. Begin the hike passing private homes on a gentle upslope for about .5-mile, where you meet the trail from the Kuamoʻo trailhead, joining at an obscure junction on your right.

Sleeping Giant

Continue up the trail alongside tall Norfolk pines. The trail then switchbacks steeply—total elevation gain for this hike is about 700 feet—traversing a variety of trees planted in the 1930s by the Civilian Conservation Corps. You meet the east-side trail, coming in from your left. Veer right to a picnic shelter near the top for views of the Coconut Coast, Wailua River and the Makaleha Mountains. Keep going, to the right as you face seaward, as the trail snakes a ridgeline to the the top of the Giant, at his forhead. *Be Aware:* Thrill seekers will want to tiptoe to the left near the top to reach the chin of the Giant, but take your time since slips here lead to a free-fall.

For the **Sleeping Giant Kuamo'o trail**, take Hwy. 580 again, up for about 2 miles from Wailua Bay, passing Opaeka'a Falls. Look for a sign and trailhead parking on your right—across the highway from Melia Street. The Kuamo'o trailhead is best for car-shuttle hikers and those wishing less of a workout than the summit requires. The trail runs along the west side of Nounou Mountains, through richly varied forest with green views inland, meeting the west-side trail described above after about 1.8 miles. After .25-mile on the trail, you come to Opaeka'a Stream, at a point about .5-mile above the falls—which are not accessible from here. About .75-mile in you come to a picnic shelter, the Valley Vista Hale, about 200 feet in elevation from the trailhead, and affording a good view of Kalepa Ridge across the river. Valley Vista Hale is a good choice for a shorter walk into the Nounou reserve.

For the **Sleeping Giant east-side trail**, take Haleilio Road inland. Haleilio is about .25-mile toward Kapa'a from the junction of Highways 56 and 580 at the Wailua River. Drive about 1 mile up Haleilio and look for a trailhead as the road makes a big sweeparound to the left—near a water pump station. Topping the Sleeping Giant from this side requires about 1,000 feet of elevation gain. This trailhead has better footing and it gives you blue-water views on the way up. You'll see more flowering shrubs on this side, compared to the more forested west side of the ridge. The east and west trails join about .25-mile from the picnic area near the top.

31. OLOHENA HIGHLANDS   HIKE, BIKE

> **WHAT'S BEST:** Hiking or biking an open ridge into the island's tropical interior, or riding around the rural countryside above Kapa'a to get a take on local-style living.
> **PARKING:** Take Hwy. 56 to the center of Kapa'a Town and turn mauka on Hwy. 581. Hwy. 581 is Kukui Rd. Kukui becomes Olohena Rd. Take Olohena up for about 6 mi., making sure to bear right where Hwy. 581 turns left and becomes part of Kamalu Rd. Continue up Olohena on narrower paved section until it ends at a gate. *Note:* If the gate is open you can drive in about 1.25 mi. to a parking area and subtract 2.5 mi from hiking distances.

HIKE: Moalepe Trail (3 mi. to 6 mi., depending on hike selection.)

The **Moalepe Trail** is one of the lesser-used segments of the Na Ala Hele state hiking system. The trail begins on a gradual incline, a red-dirt road flanked by dwarf vegetation and pasturelands. White egrets will often be seen winging their way up a narrowing valley. To your back are blue-water vistas and a good look at Kong and the Anahola Mountains. After a mile the ridge narrows, with ferns, eucalyptus, and monkeypod trees at arm's length. At about 1.5 miles, the Kamali Ridge across the valley is dramatically close, on its way to abut the Makaleha Mountains, which in turn are heading toward Waialeale, as most all Kauaian ridges do.

After the 1.75-mile mark, the trail becomes decidedly steeper, gaining most of its 600-foot elevation on the way to join the Kuilau Ridge Trail, at 2.75 miles into the hike. Gravel is often added to this section, to aid equestrians, but count on big mudholes winning out in the long run. You'll get close-ups of the Makaleha Ridge all the way. The trail junction—actually the trails just blend together, getting renamed in the middle—is at a hairpin left turn.

The Kuilau Ridge Trail is described in TH32, Keahua Arboretum. The point at which the trails join is deep into the Halelea Forest Reserve, at a small grassy opening in the tropical flora, above Moalepe Stream. *More Stuff:* The Kuilau Ridge to Moalepe is 4.5-mile car-shuttle, which works out well if you have a non-hiking driver in the group. Instead of a car-shuttle, hikers may wish to continue .75-mile beyond the hairpin; at .5-mile you get to a footbridge, and .25-mile beyond that is a scenic view of Waialeale and the coastline around Hoary Head Ridge and Lihue.

BIKE: The **Moalepe Trail** is well-suited for all level riders for nearly 2 miles, but after that, count on standing in the pedals. This trail is popular among equestrians, and horses turn the route into pudding—although gravel patches remedy this for a while. Although this trail does connect with TH32, Keahua Arboretum, it is not well-suited to mountain bikes on that end—it's muddy and wheels damage portions of the trail. One option is to ride in on Moalepe for about 1.5 miles, and then try one or both of the countryside pedals described below.

For the **Hauiki-Waipouli loop**, a 5-mile, down-and-up ride, take Waipouli, the road that hairpins to your right where Olohena ends. Ride a narrow tree tunnel, bordered by country gardens—making sure not to go left on Kainahola Road—and then veer left on Hauiki Road. Hauiki is a gentle downslope, through open acreage and a few local-style houses, with plenty room for party in the carports and big views down toward Kong. At the bottom of Hauiki, turn right on a .25-mile paved section at a reservoir, which is closed to cars. You join Waipouli on the other side of the reservoir. Pump up Waipouli to the parking area, passing one or two honor-system fruit stands along the way. Those obscenely large power poles were necessary after Hurricane Iniki put Kaua'i into a blackout for a month or more in 1992.

Another paved option from the Olohena trailhead is the **Puʻuopae Loop**, which is also about 5 miles. Take Olohena down for 1.5 miles, and turn right on Puʻuopae Road. Puʻuopae dips and turns through countryside, replete with a wide range of tropical greenery, for more than a mile, and then stops at Opaekaʻa Road. Go left on Opaekaʻa Road for .5-mile, to where it adjoins Kamalu Road, or Hwy. 581. Here you hang a left, traveling through widely spaced homes and rural splendor behind Sleeping Giant. In about 1.5 miles you hit Olohena, at the section where it narrows. Turn left on Olohena and ride back up to the Moalepe parking area.

32. KEAHUA ARBORETUM   HIKE, BIKE

WHAT'S BEST: Hike or bike into the tropical highlands—to the basin of Mount Waialeale, along a jungle ridge, or head out across the island to Hanalei Valley. Several of Hawaii's prime forested hikes are right here.
PARKING: Take Hwy. 580, which is Kuamoʻo Rd., mauka at the Wailua River (at the Coco Palms). Arboretum parking is about 7 mi. from Hwy. 56. Park before spillway.

Note: The Keahua Arboretum area is best enjoyed under drier conditions. Four-wheel drive vehicles are recommended after the pavement ends. But when the water at the spillways is about six-inches deep or less, passenger cars can drive the Waikoko Forest Management Road across this first spillway, and even across a second, which is .5-mile farther in, and continue a mile or two beyond that. The roadway improves after the second spillway.

HIKE: Keahua Arboretum circle (1 mi.); Kuilau Ridge Trail (4.5 mi.); Powerline Trail hikes: Kualapa Ridge (9.5 mi.), trans-Kauaʻi car-shuttle (13 mi.); Waialeale stream convergence (6 mi.); Waialeale basin (10 mi.) *Note:* **Hiking distances are from first-spillway parking.**

For the tame stroll around the **Keahua Arboretum**, drive or wade across the spillway or cross the stream near the parking area. Walk up to your left, toward a picnic area. At the top of the rise is a grassy basin, planted with both native and introduced tree species by the University of Hawaii. This young arboretum is intended as an outdoor classroom for students and tourists alike. It's maturation was stalled by Hurricane Iniki, but it's beginning to grow into its own. Begin to your left as you face the arboretum. A trail encircles the grounds, but the grasses are rather thick on the homestretch and you may feel more comfortable going out partway and returning on the same path.

The **Kuilau Ridge Trail**, part of the state Na Ala Hele system, becomes the Moalepe Trail about 2.2 miles in; see TH31. This is a hike to remember. The trailhead is about

Kuilau Ridge Trail

.1-mile up from the parking area at the spillway—you should see it on your right driving down. The beautiful forest walk begins up a mud ramp, with tree-filtered views of Waialeale basin in the distance and two stream drainages in the foreground— bursting with shrubs, vines, and trees. You can also see the Powerline Trail making its way to the Kualapa Ridge that transects the middle of the island. At about 1.25 miles, the trail levels, reaching a large grassy area with picnic shelter. From the picnic shelter are views seaward of Sleeping Giant and Hoary Head and, straight ahead, of anvil-shaped Makaleha Ridge. You can see trail's end at the monkeypod trees in the middle-distance below Makaleha Ridge.

Second spillway, Keahua Arboretum

Press on. The trail jogs right from the picnic area, and, for the next .5-mile, you're on a narrow, twisting ridge, amid lush tropical greenery with a Japanese-garden feel. A variety of birds will be seen and heard. This squiggly ridge is one of the most striking and scenic walks on Kaua'i. *Be Aware:* The profuse greenery at the edge of the trail hides steep drop-offs on either side. Stay on the trail.

Crossing the ridge, the trail makes a switchback, climbing to your right and then descending over a stream on a footbridge. *Note:* A sign at the footbridge says this is the end of the Kuilau Trail; disregard the sign and continue. For the next .5-mile you ascend a straight, wide path, through a tree tunnel formed primarily by peeling paperbark trees—from which paper is not made. At the top of the tree tunnel is a small grassy opening, where the trail hairpins to your right. This is where Kuilau Ridge joins Moalepe, the end-point for this hike. *Note:* A spur trail that led straight toward Makaleha Ridge from the hairpin is now abandoned and overgrown. To get other views of the Makaleha Ridge, as well as the Kapa'a coastline, head down the Moalepe Trail for about .5-mile. Continuing all the way to the Moalepe trailhead, TH31, makes for a 4.5-mile car-shuttle hike.

The **Powerline Trail** begins about .1-mile from the arboretum parking, on your right after the first uphill across the spillway. You'll see a hunter's checking station for Unit C, and a muddy scar of a road going up. The **Kualapa Ridge** is nearly 5 miles in on the Powerline Trail, and about 1,500-feet up from the trailhead.

From the Kualapa Ridge you can see down the more-gradual north slopes of the trail to the Hanalei Valley, and, looking the other way, the upslopes of the Kilohana Crater area and the Sleeping Giant. These views are in addition to close-ups of the wrinkled ridges beside the Powerline Trail. The **trans-Kauai hike** is an all-day trek to be attempted by fit hikers on a sunny day. To acquaint yourself with Powerline Trail, you may wish to walk in from this trailhead as far as you want, and then pick another day to try the trail from the other side of the island, Powerline Trail North, TH12. *Be Aware:* Prepare for this hike with plenty of water, food, rain gear and a hiking pole.

From Powerline Trail

To the **Waialeale stream convergence**—where three streams join—and to **Waialeale basin**—a point 4,000 feet directly below the fabled peak—stay on the Waikoko Forest Management Road. You circle up and behind the forest gardens, drop down and cross a second spillway and walk up a grade, under a canopy of subtropical trees. After the second spillway, you come to where power towers cross the road. From the power towers, the road undulates heading fairly straight for a mile, and then it makes a right, beginning a west-heading approach to the Waialeale basin. Continue for .5-mile. Then, for the **Waialeale stream convergence**, take a right bearing fork. You'll see a sign announcing Hunting Unit C and telling people not to pick up lost dogs. This right fork follows a water ditch for a mile and ends under a tree canopy alongside the swift-flowing North Fork of the Wailua River, at a gauging station. If you carefully cross the river on rocks, you'll discover a point at which two major streams join the Wailua River, which is coming down from the Waialeale and headed for Wailua Bay. *Note:* Don't attempt to drive the road from the fork, even in four wheel drive.

For the **Waialeale basin**, take the left fork at the Unit C-dog sign. From this fork you are 2.5 miles from the basin. Continue up a grade through eucalyptus, avoiding spur roads and trails—this is a place where coonhounds get lost. After .5-mile

Waialeale Basin

Waialeale Convergence

from the fork, you pass a spur road on the left to a picnic area, and enter an open forest of monkeypods and African tulip trees. A mile beyond the picnic road you come to a gate, with tall concrete poles that frame a view of Waialeale. Beyond the gate, the relief becomes pronounced, and the scenery real darned pretty. Be careful of getting too close to trailside viewpoints that may be nothing more than snarls of plantlife. *Note:* Even four-wheel drive vehicles should park at the gate.

The trail ends at a gauging station, a rough-poured concrete dam, creating a face-on spot to sit and enjoy the fast-flowing North Fork of the Wailua River. Across from the dam is a profusion of jungle greenery, leaves as big as elephant ears lost within great vine tangles. Upward is the concave face of Waialeale, with a half-dozen gouges in its vertical face that become falls during rains. *More Stuff:* From the dam, a sketchy trail across the river leads through the jungle and along rocks to the Blue Hole at the bottom of Waialeale; this trail is difficult and should be attempted only by fit hikers traveling in pairs on nice days. *More Stuff:* For rest and contemplation, try two stops at the 51-acre grounds of Kaua'i's Hindu Monastery: The intimate Sacred Forest is on the main road, on your left as you head mauka near mm. 5, at 7345 Kuamo'o Road. This spot will calm everyone down, whether they like it or not. The monastery itself is down the road about .5-mile; turn on Kaholalele Road, near mm. 4.5. The church, garden, and visitors center is at 107 Kaholalele. The groomed banyan on the path to the church is a world unto itself. *Note:* Visitors are welcomed, but if you plan to go inside the monastery people ask that you use one on the sarongs supplied at the teahouse to cover up shorts.

BIKE: The **Powerline Trail** and **Kuilau Ridge Trail** are used by some advanced riders, but you will be much better off taking a bike in from the other access points for these trails: Powerline Trail North, TH12, near Princeville; and Moalepe Ridge Trail, TH32, above Kapa'a. The trails from this side are steep, muddy and rutted. The Kuilau Ridge Trail has portions that would be damaged by wheels. The better mountain biking option for this trailhead—one of the best anywhere— is the **Waialeale basin** trail, as described in the hiking section. Although mud may fly, the elevation is only 400 feet over the 5 miles, and the roads are very rideable, cobblestones notwithstanding. The toughest climbing for this ride is during the first mile as you negotiate steep hills on either side of the spillways. From the spillways, the ride is gradually up. On a bike, you can afford to explore the spur roads—although make sure to keep your bearings. *More Stuff:* Another adventurous option off this trail is to cut left where the power towers cross the road, as described in the beginning of the covergence and basin hikes. A network of roads lead to the Wailua River watershed, above the falls. Some of this area may be private property, however. You make the call.

Waterfalls on Mount Waialeale

Wailua

Wailua Falls

When the ancient Polynesians completed a 2,500-mile voyage from the South Pacific, thus making their mythical homelands a reality, their first steps were on the banks of the Wailua River. In the years to come, they built seven heiaus—temples—along the course of the river, the last near its source at Mount Waialeale. The heiaus line a sacred path from the bay to the birthplace of all waters.

To Hawaiians, Wailua was the Vatican, and for centuries the aliʻi, or kings, of all the Hawaiian Islands could trace their lineage to these hallowed grounds on Kauaʻi. Wailua in Hawaiian means, "waters of the spirits," a name reflecting the Hawaiians' reverence for their ancestors and kinship with nature.

Short walks from Wailua Bay and Lydgate Park lead to three heiaus, including one nearly intact. Intact heiaus are rare, since, as Christianity was embraced by the royals, the heiaus were sometimes used as livestock pens or their rocks removed and used for roadwork. Also at the mouth of the river are the remnants of a city of refuge, a place where vanquished warriors or criminals could escape to do penance.

Wailua Bay is the best surfing spot along the coast between the river and Nawiliwili. But most people get on the water here in canoes and kayaks, heading up the widest, deepest, longest river in Hawaii. A simulated Hawaiian village and the Fern Grotto, both tourist attractions, may be seen from the river. Naturalists can observe native subtropical vegetation, such as hala and hau trees, along with the rare pili grass, used to make grass houses, that still grows on the banks.

Beginning at Lydgate and extending toward Hanamaulu Bay are several miles of beach that are surprisingly secluded. This coast runs behind the Wailua Golf Course as well as behind a resort hotel. At Nukoliʻi Beach, strollers will find interesting bits of coral and shells, and usually will be able to see net fishermen casting from shore. Mountain bikers can find a trail most of the way—pushing the wheels as needed in one spot—completing a continuous run of coastal pedaling that goes from Hanamaulu Bay to Anahola Bay.

Hanamaulu is a locals' beach, where families gather on the weekends. Its sheltered cove makes for safe swimming as well as boogie boarding, and the bay's waters are safe for kayakers who can paddle out to Ahukini Landing at its mouth. An annual outrigger canoe race begins at Hanamaulu, heads into open water, and finishes by rounding Ninini Point and entering Nawiliwili Harbor.

Fern Grotto

Huleia Stream

The coast between Ahukini Landing and Ninini Point, despite being behind the airport, is a scenic ride or hike, and Ninini, with its lighthouse, is an eye-popping spot to watch cruise ships enter the harbor under Hoary Head Ridge.

Nawiliwili Harbor, Kaua'i's largest port, displays both the muscle and romance of a tropical island. Walking around Nawiliwili, or riding a bike, can easily take up a day. Included in that day might be swimming or surfing at Kalapaki Bay, the beach below the Kaua'i Marriott Resort that features Duke's Canoe Club. Walks along two breakwaters and a small harbor for cruising sailboats add charm to the lively harbor.

Almost unnoticed in the harbor, but one of its more remarkable features, is Huleia Stream. The stream's calm waters lead into the Huleia National Wildlife Refuge and past the Menehune Fish Pond. Some of the movie *Jurassic Park* was filmed here, and, although private property restrictions prohibit exploring the shore, much can be seen from the water.

The most-visited spot in the Wailua area, however, is not the coast, but Wailua Falls, a few miles inland. A very steep trail takes hikers to the base of the falls. In ancient times, warriors dove from these falls to prove their courage to prospective wives. Just inland of Wailua Falls, is a viewpoint of the north side of Kilohana Crater, Waialeale and Kawaikini, the tallest peak on Kaua'i.

The entire Wailua area can be viewed from Kalepa Ridge, which runs just inland, parallel to the coast between Wailua Bay and Hanamaulu Bay—a vantage point of historical significance. From the sandalwood trees that grew on this ridge, Kauaian warriors kept watch for a dozen years, beginning in 1795, for the invasion of Kamehameha the Great—an attack that never came. Once, a fierce storm on the

Kaua'i Channel thwarted Kamehameha's ships, and a second invasion fizzled when warriors were stricken by disease after they again had set sail for Kaua'i.

The sandalwood trees on Kalepa Ridge were clear-cut in the early 1880s and the fragrant wood became Hawai'i's first export. A hundred years later, from a bunker on the ridge, American soldiers kept watch during World War II for another invasion that never came. The ridge affords a mid-distance view of the coast and a panorama inland of the Kilohana Crater and Waialeale ridge.

Wailua River, County Courthouse, Sounding the Conch

MAP 3   TRAILHEADS 33-41

W A I L U A

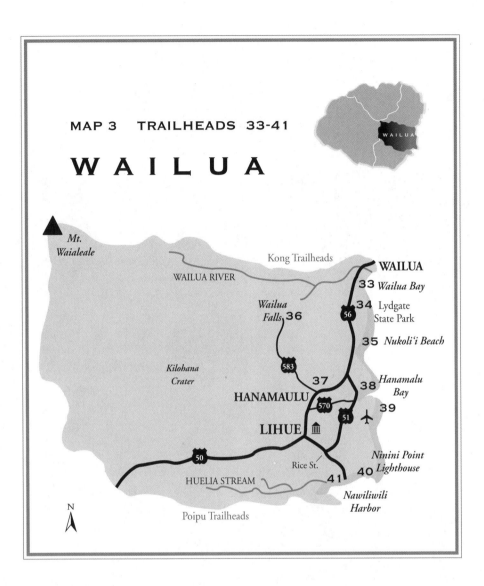

Mt. Waialeale

Kong Trailheads

WAILUA RIVER

WAILUA

33 *Wailua Bay*

Wailua Falls **36**

34 Lydgate
State Park

56

35 *Nukoli'i Beach*

Kilohana Crater

583

37

38 *Hanamalu Bay*

HANAMAULU

570

39

51

✈

LIHUE 🏛

Ninini Point Lighthouse

50

Rice St.

40

41

HUELIA STREAM

Nawiliwili Harbor

N

Poipu Trailheads

33. WAILUA BAY

HIKE, PADDLE, SURF

WHAT'S BEST: A variety pack: Walk the shore or paddle up the river of kings, the most sacred place in the Hawaiian Islands. Or take excellent family strolls to Kaua'i's largest heiau and its most underrated botanical garden.

PARKING: The jct. of Hwys. 56 and 580 chops this trailhead up into four parts, although everything is located close together. Read hiking descriptions for places to park.

HIKE: Wailua Beach (1.25 mi.); Malae Heiau (up to .5-mi.); Wailua Marina and Smiths Tropical Paradise (up to 1.5 mi.); Birthstone Heiau and Royal Cocopalm Grove (.5-mi.)

Access to **Wailua Beach** is easiest if you're heading from Lihue to Kapa'a; cross the river in the right-hand lane—on the one-lane bridge—and use the parking lot on your right immediately after crossing the river; or park at a second turnout on your right at the far end of the bay. In spite of its on-road location, Wailua Beach is a scenic stroll, especially when the river is running high after rains, colliding with choppy incoming surf. When the river is low, you can wade the sand bridge at the river mouth and connect with Lydgate Park, TH34. Or, heading left as you face the water, you can make your way around Alakukui Point and connect with the hike in TH29, Coconut Coast.

To walk the **Wailua Marina and Smiths Tropical Paradise**, turn mauka toward Smiths on the Lihue side of the bridge. This is a tourist-trot around the docks where boats depart for Fern Grotto. The grotto is a large dripping cavern creating acoustics for the old-timey serenade provided by your guides. The river boat tours, many family operated for generations, are a kitschy classic and well worth the price of tickets. The marina docks, surrounded by several grassy acres, yield a splendid view across the wide Wailua toward the Sleeping Giant; quietly one of the most scenic views on the island. The cultural and botanical gardens inside Smiths Tropical Paradise are also well worth the modest admission price. Footbridges span lagoons amid flowering tropicals and forests of native and fruit trees. Kaua'i's Japanese, Polynesian, and Filipino heritages are represented. Shrieking peacocks waft down from towering banyans. You'll likely give the place two thumbs, especially if kids are along.

The **Malae Heiau** is the most intact of seven heiaus the ancients constructed, beginning at Wailua Bay and extending to Waialeale. Today, it's right across the highway from the Aloha Beach Resort (unless that property has changed again). Access is easiest when heading toward Lihue. Cross the bridge, pass the entrance to Smith's, and look for a turnout and dirt track headed up a hillside. You can also access at a little farther on the highway, at a gate for a cane haul road. Head through that gate and look right for a 10-foot wide path that leads a short distance up to, and around, the 300- by 400-foot edifice. Its walls are about six feet high and more than twelve feet wide, vertical in the center and sloping down around the perimeter. *Notes:* The heiau was uncovered from underbrush, but the brush grows back quickly. Take care not to disturb the walls of this sacred place. A plaque commemorating the site as a State Historic Marker in 1928, located on the highway side, has been removed.

To the **Birthstone Heiau**, drive less than .5-mile up Hwy. 580 and park on the left at the Wailua River State Park Poliahu Area. A stairway with pipe railing leads up from behind this historic site to a small Japanese cemetery and a tree-filtered view of the Wailua River. Across the street from the Birthstone Heiau is small arboretum, a State Soil and Water Conservation Park. Between the park and the river is the **Royal Coconut Grove**. The royal grove lies behind the old Coco Palms Resort, closed due to Hurricane Iniki and subsequent insurance hassles. The lagoon inside predates the hotel, built for enjoyment by Queen Emma. Entrance to the grove is prohibited, but you can get a good look at it by walking along the road.

PADDLE: Kayakers may access the **Wailua River** by turning on Hwy. 580, Kuamo'o Road, and making an immediate left, just past Smith's ticket area, into a Wailua State Park boat launching area. The Wailua Marina also has a boat launch area. This is Kaua'i's most popular river, and kayak rentals and tours are limited to prevent overcrowding. Even so, it can get cozy. Wailua River Kayak, located near the Safeway and Movie Tours company, is an excellent choice for independent travelers who want the enrichment provided by competent guides. They are family owned, run small daily tours—mornings are best—and can customize a trip for you; see *Resource Links*.

The Wailua is very wide, with several miles of slack waters. Two miles upriver is a confluence: The left fork is the South Fork of the Wailua River, which comes from Wailua Falls, TH36; the right fork is the North Fork of the Wailua River, which

Coco Palms lagoon, Wailua River, Fern Grotto tourboat, Malae Heiau

Koholalele (Secret) Falls

comes from Waialeale basin, TH32. The Wailua was the landing spot for the ancient Polynesian mariners, where the first Hawaiian settlements were established. **Fern Grotto**, part of Wailua River State Park, is a little more than 2 miles upriver, just up the left fork. The right fork leads past the privately owned Kamokila, a recreated Hawiian village where much of the movie *Outbreak* was filmed. Many tours go past the village and take out a little farther up, where the river narrows at rapids and shallow water. A trail leads from the left side of the river for about a mile to **Koholalele (Secret) Falls**, a popular destination.

SURF: With its eastern exposure and river-mouth location, the surf at **Wailua Bay** varies more than most places. Surfers take advantage of an offshore break, from about the middle of the bay extending over to Alakukui Point. Boogie boarders try the shore break, though shallow water makes this hazardous to your health. *Be Aware:* Swimming and snorkeling can be dangerous due to rip currents near the river and near the rocks at the other end of the bay.

34. LYDGATE PARK
HIKE, SNORKEL, BIKE, SURF

WHAT'S BEST: A short walk of historical significance or a longer beach walk. Families flock to fantastical play area and the island's safest snorkeling.

PARKING: Take Hwy. 56 from Lihue and turn makai at mm. 5/56, on Leho Dr. Follow Leho around to large improved parking lot. *Note:* Coming from Kapaʻa, turn makai after crossing the river, at left-turn lane for the Aloha Resort; this is also Leho Dr. as it loops back out to Hwy. 56.

Lydgate Park

HIKE: Hikinaʻakala Heiau (.25-mi.); Lydgate Beach (up to 3 mi.)

At the **Hikinaʻakala Heiau**—located at the river mouth just above the beach and below the hotel—is an interpretive center, describing heiaus in general, and this heiau in particular. Not much remains, but this was the first of seven heiaus leading inland from the bay toward Waileale. Adjacent to the heiau are the remains of the **Hauola City of Refuge**, a place for Kauaian miscreants to go during periods of banishment from proper society.

Lydgate Beach, a state park with showers and rest rooms, is part of a beach that starts at the mouth of the Wailua River and extends about four miles, almost to Hanamaulu Bay. Large Kamalani Playground and picnic area is just inland of the park's man-made snorkeling pools. Heading away from the river on the beach, you leave the developed area of the park in about .5-mile. Ironwoods encroach on a fairly narrow strip of yellow sand. A wide concrete bike path runs inland from the beach, through a primitive camp area and the park's surprise: a several-story, mazelike Play Bridge that could accomodate several classrooms of scurrying younsters. You then come to the ocean side of the Wailua Golf Course, beyond which you connect with Nukoliʻi Beach, TH35. Along this entire coast are long views up and down the coast, particularly scenic at sunrise.

SNORKEL: **Lydgate Park** features an oval, man-made swimming area, which breaks the surf near the river mouth. This large pool provides snorkeling free of concerns about riptides. Fish at times may be outnumbered by snorkelers in the shallow water, which can sometimes be turbid due to wave action outside the enclosure. Lydgate is ideal for children. It's a sure thing for a swim.

BIKE: Although **Lydgate Park** may not be a mountain biker's destination, it is a pleasant segment of a long bikeable shoreline, connecting on one side with TH35, Nukoliʻi Beach, and on the other with TH29, Coconut Coast. Heading toward Kapaʻa and the Coconut Coast, you may be able to carry your bike across a sand bridge at the river mouth and up to the highway along the bay. If the river is high, you have to ride up to the highway and take the main bridge across the river on the marginal bike lane.

Biking the other direction, toward Lihue, you can roll along the concret path until it ends past the play bridge. (The bike path will be extended in both directions.) From here you need to trailblaze: paths lead through the ironwoods—along which you will notice big black boulders that were taken from the heiau for road improvements. Eventually you spill out onto the sandy road along the beach. To avoid the beach trails, you can also push and ride along the out-of-bounds perimeter of the golf course, which is marked by upright pipes.

SURF: **Black Rock**, at the mouth of the Wailua River off the point of Lydgate Park, offers a fairly deep reef break. It's a long paddle out, to a right-break. Recommended for intermediate-level surfers.

35. NUKOLI'I BEACH HIKE, BIKE

WHAT'S BEST: Comb the east side's longest beach, looking for coral and shells, and watching Hawaiian net fishermen. You get far away in an instant.

PARKING: *First (easiest) Nukoli'i access:* From Lihue or the airport, head toward Kapa'a on Hwy. 56—from the jct. of Hwys. 56 and 51. Turn makai on Kauai Beach Dr., .25-mi. past mm. 3/56, toward the Hilton Kaua'i Beach Resort. Turn right just before resort lot, and follow the road around to developed lot, which is Nukoli'i Beach Park. *Second (prettiest) Nukoli'i access:* Continue .6-mi past Kauai Beach Dr., nearly to mm. 4/56, and turn makai on a dirt road running along the edge of the golf course. Follow the road, which may have major potholes, around to parking area among ironwoods at beach.

HIKE: Nukoli'i Beach (4.5 mi.)

Starting at the beach park, at the **first Nukoli'i access**, take off down the beach to your left as you face the water. Nukoli'i is also called Kaua'i Beach and Kawailoa. Aside from a camper or two, this beach sees few visitors, especially beyond the immediate grounds of the resort. At any time of the day you are likely to see net fishermen, plying their ancient trade. The onshore reef deposits bits of coral, polished glass and shells along water's edge. About .5-mile from the beach park, you pass the hotel, where you cross a ditch and come to the best swimming area along a beach that is not recommended for swimming. A sandy road parallels the beach. Nukoli'i extends more than two miles, joining the beach behind the golf course—where the second access area described above brings you in—and continues seamlessly to Lydgate Park, TH34.

BIKE: Beginning at the **Nukoli'i Beach Park** and heading toward Kapa'a, is a bike route that allows you to ride to Anahola with little or no on-highway pedaling. At the park, take the sandy road that fronts the beach to the hotel, which you can pass either on the beach or parking lot side. It's smooth going from there, bordering the Wailua Golf Course for awhile, until the road dumps out onto the beach. Here, with the large

Nukoli'i Beach

black screen at the Wailua Golf Course as a landmark. You may need to push your bike along a short beach segment, befor you reach Lydgatge's concret bike path that connects with Nehe Road.

Going the other way, toward Lihue, you need to cross the sweeping highway bridge, Hwy. 51, that spans the Hanamaulu Bay drainage. Once across, you can head makai on Ahukini Road toward the airport, or take coastal roads to Nawiliwili—see mountain bike descriptions for Ninini Point, TH40, and Nawiliwili Harbor, TH41.

36. WAILUA FALLS   HIKE

> **WHAT'S BEST:** Viewing the falls, from above or below, or popping inland for vistas of Waialeale and Kawaikini, the island's tallest peaks.
> **PARKING:** Turn mauka on Hwy 583 which is off Hwy. 56, between Hanamaulu and Lihue. Take Hwy. 583, also called Ma'alo Rd., 4 mi. to end at falls parking area.

HIKE: Wailua Falls (1.5 mi.); Waialeale view (.5-mi. or more)

Wailua Falls trailhead is a dirt turnout past a railroad trestle and .25-mile before the falls parking at the end of the road. A sign warns of hazardous conditions. You should drive to the end and take a peek at the falls beforehand. *Be Aware:* If the river level is high, flowing over the entire top of the falls (normally it is comprised of twin cascades), or if it is raining, do not attempt this hike. Also do not take a trailhead that is near the guardrail at the falls overlook.

The Wailua Falls trail is very steep and often greasy, but roots and branches make for steps and handholds. It's doable. After reaching the bottom, head upriver through ferns and a shade canopy, courtesy of huge mango trees. The trail becomes sketchy, and you need to cross to the far side of the river where it narrows to a ledge. After crossing, a hard-to-follow trail leads to the vast pool beneath the falls. Follow your ears and watch your footing. *Be Aware:* Falling-rock danger under the falls.

To the **Waialeale view**, look for an unmarked opening in the seed cane, opposite the falls overlook about midway in the cul-de-sac parking lot. Trailblaze through this opening, not more than 20 feet, and you come upon a red-dirt road that curls around about .25-mile before joining a wider cane road. By walking a short distance on the road you can look inland, over the upper Kilohana Crater, to Waialeale and Kawaikini, the island's tallest peak at 5,243 feet. Kawaikini lies just to the left of Waialeale, both in the same jagged ridge. This trail from the parking lot is also a way to access the river above the falls, by bearing right and finding one of several accesses. *Be Aware:* Needless to say, avoid the lip of the falls. These routes are not signed; use at your own risk.

37.   KALEPA RIDGE   HIKE

> **WHAT'S BEST:** Walk the path of Kauaian warriors, a sweeping mid-elevation vista of the Wailua coast, Kilohana Crater and interior mountains.
> **PARKING:** Take Hwy. 56 toward Lihue from its jct. with Hwy. 51. At .4-mi. past the jct., turn mauka on red-dirt Hulei Rd. Go .25-mi. on Hulei Rd. and park at gate, where concrete ramp goes up straight in front of you, and cemetery is visible around to the right. *Note:* A permit is no longer required for this hike; property owners are not liable. Use at your own risk.

HIKE: Kalepa Ridge (4 mi. to 8 mi.)

Kalepa Ridge is where Kauaian sentinels kept a watchful eye seaward for Kamehameha's invading ships from Oahu. Start up the concrete ramp, gaining 400 feet in elevation and passing a water tank. The ramp may turn to crumbling asphalt and back to concrete again. Continue to where the concrete ramp turns sharply left—the concrete continues to a telecommunications installation. Take either of two trails to right at this point—they both go to the same place. The right-most trail crests the first Kalepa knob, a good choice for those wishing to bag the view and turn around. The left-side trail avoids the elevation gain and continues along the ridge.

The Kalepa Trail, like life, has its ups and downs. Avoid side trails. After the viewpoint at the beginning, the next major knob on this ridge is Kokomo, nearly 1,000 feet up from the trailhead, and about 1.25-miles from where the dirt part of the trail begins.

Those game for more may continue, dropping off Kokomo, and navigating a rough, eroded red-dirt zone, to Nailiakauea, another bump in the ridge. At this point, you are near, but high above, the Wailua River. Beyond Nailiakauea is another protuberance, called Mauna Kapu. Just below these features, as you face inland, is the fork of the Wailua River featuring Fern Grotto, and you may hear faint hula music from a tour boat. Mauna Kapu is about 2 miles of rough walking from Kokomo. The ridge, comprising the Kalepa State Forest Reserve, is an ideal place to gain a perspective on the entire east side of Kauai.

Hanamaulu

Note: Kilohana Crater, inland from the ridge; the expansive dome of green is not easily recognized as a former volcanic eruption—one that came millions of years after the first episodes formed the island.

38. HANAMAULU BAY   HIKE, SNORKEL, PADDLE, SURF

> **WHAT'S BEST:** Picnic, swim at a locals' beach with a Hollywood setting.
> **PARKING:** Turn makai off Hwy. 56 on Hanamaulu Rd., at traffic light. Hanamaulu is .5-mi. toward Lihnue from the jct. of Hwys. 56 and 51. From Hanamaulu Rd., veer right on Hehi Rd., continuing down to the beach park, which is about 1 mi. from Hwy. 56 turnoff.

HIKE: Hanamaulu Beach Park (up to 1 mi.)

No hiking trails lead from **Hanamaulu Beach Park**, but short walks inland through boggy banana fields and around the park and beach of this cozy bay, will give you a look a the east-side's most Kauaian beach and community. This ain't no tourist place. On the weekends, expect a family party in one of the picnic pavilions.

Hanamaulu Bay is the only indent in a seven-mile coast running from Wailua Bay to Nawiliwili Harbor. Looking out to sea, on the right, is Ahukini Landing, TH39. Hanamaulu Bay was the scene for several of the earlier movies shot in Kauai, including *Pagan Love Song*, in 1950, and John Wayne's 1963 classic, *Donovan's Reef*.

SNORKEL: Water near shore at **Hanamaulu Bay** is often not the clearest, due to the stream, but this is normally a safe spot to swim around with mask and fins. Farther out, water visibility improves, and better swimmers can venture out into the bay. *Be Aware:* Rip currents can accompany high surf.

PADDLE: **Hanamaulu Bay** is the launching spot for canoe races that go around Ninini Point and into Nawiliwili Harbor. Although novice kayakers might want to avoid that voyage, except on the calmest of days, Hanamaulu is perhaps the best place to safely venture into the saltwater, with intimate views of the bay, shrouded with cocopalms and ironwoods. You can even get a few strokes inland on the stream, .25-mile or more, amid bananas and lush fields.

SURF: A gentle onshore break invites safe boogie boarding and body surfing, though the local boys don't often clamor to catch these combers.

39. AHUKINI LANDING   HIKE, SNORKEL, BIKE

> **WHAT'S BEST:** Say a scenic aloha before leaving Kauai, or on any day, with a walk around a historic pineapple pier.
> **PARKING:** Take Hwy. 570, which is Ahukini Rd., toward Lihue Airport and veer left, staying on Ahukini. Go 1.5 mi. to road's end.

HIKE: Ahukini stroll (.5-mi.)

That a place like **Ahukini Landing** can be so close to the airport is testament to Kaua'i's scenic beauty. Once a major port, and principal shipping dock for the flourishing pineapple trade, Ahukini today is a decrepit pier where locals fish on weekends. The pier area makes for an interesting stroll, with a view of Hanamaulu Bay. Ahukini's black rock breakwater is another option to explore but the most common actvity here is the park 'n' stare, a tradition among Hawaiian drivers taking a break from the workaday world. Ahukini is a state recreation area. *Be Aware:* Observe the surf before venturing onto the breakwater.

SNORKEL: With no beach and all the fishermen, you may not want to swim at **Ahukini Landing**. Not many people do. But the water is deep and clear, sheltered by the breakwater, and fish are plentiful. This is a place for those seeking an unusual snorkel to take the plunge. Entry is easy, but over rocks. *Be Aware:* You may find current and tidal action near the mouth of the bay; stay behind breakwater.

BIKE: A fine dirt road fronts the shoreline from Ahukini Landing all the way to Ninini Point, TH40. The shoreline road is marked by a pipe gate, just before Ahukini Road makes its 90-degree turn on the way to the landing. Going the other way on a mountain bike, toward Kapaʻa, you need to follow Hwy. 51 around Hanamaulu Bay and duck in at Nukoliʻi Beach, TH35.

40. NININI POINT   HIKE, SNORKEL, BIKE

What's Best: From the lighthouse is an exotic look at ships entering Nawiliwili Harbor. Check out a secluded beach or a long, level pedal along the coast and a resort lagoon.

Parking: Take Hwy. 51 toward the Lihue Airport. At .6-mi. past Hwy. 570, turn makai at beach access sign, which is Ninini Rd. You'll see an entrance station for the Kauaʻi Marriott—not the main entry for the resort. Follow running path signs around on Ninini Rd., curving left and then right, around golf course. At 2 mi. from highway, look for a golf hole number 12 sign, shaped like an alligator; go left on dirt road for .4-mi. and park at fenced radio antenna installation.

HIKE: Ninini Point (less than .5-mi.); Ahukini coast (up to 4 mi.); Running Waters Beach (1 mi.)

Ninini Point is just down the dirt road from parking area. You'll see Ninini Light-house, which sits close to the sea at the mouth of Kalapaki Bay, also the entrance to Nawiliwili Harbor. Across the bay is Hoary Head Ridge, a backdrop for the white cruise ships that slide past Ninini Point. To walk the dirt track along the **Ahukini coast**, go back to the parking, and take a grassy, two-track road to your left as you face the water, going behind the fenced installation. You walk along ironwoods and a low-set bank on a rugged coastline, with an open view inland (near the boundary for the airport). In about .5-mile you reach Kamilo Point, just beyond a freshwater pond that flanks the shoreline. About 1 mile from Ninini is a rocky cove with a beach, a good destination for this hike. The road continues, veering inland slightly—past a "white balloon" looking communications tower—before dipping back out to the coast at other rocky beaches at 2 miles. Finally, at 2.5 miles, the road joins with Ahukini Road.

To get to **Running Waters Beach**, get in the car and go back to the alligator sign at the golf course, and veer right instead. Continue a short distance and park in lot behind the old shopping mall. Head toward the brew pub that sits above the bay and golf course, walking to your right either in front of or on the water side of the restaurant. You'll see beach access signs. An improved path winds down along the golf course at the parking lot for the brew pub. The path gives way to a short, red-dirt trail and a view of Running Waters Beach, which will be on your right as you face the water. Running Waters is a sloping curve of sand, pocked with black rocks. It lies outside the breakwaters of Kalapaki Bay. *Note:* See TH41 for easier access.

Snorkel: **Running Waters** is better for sight-seeing and relaxing than anything else. Large waves from varying directions wash the rocky shore, making this a turbulent area for swimming on most days. But, during calm periods, Running Waters is known as a good area for experienced snorkelers.

Bike: The **Ahukini coast**, as described in the hiking section, is ideal for mountain biking. Another option for cyclists, which could also include the coast, is to park at the entrance station described parking instructions, and tour the area in a loop. Start by riding out to Ninini Point and then go down the coast to Ahukini Landing and back. Then pedal over to Running Waters—at the brew pub—and coast down to the Kaua'i Marriott. From there you can loop back up to the entrance station on the path that encirlces the resorts's huge man-made lagoon, crossing over artful bridges and skirting the golf course. This loop ride is about 10-miles.

41. NAWILIWILI HARBOR   Hike, Snorkel, Bike, Paddle, Surf

What's Best: Get a look at the guts and the glitz of tropical Pacific seafaring life and enjoy the beach that lured Kaua'i's first major resort. Or paddle up a river into a wildlife refuge or on the tranquil waters of a resort lagoon. It's all happening at Nawiliwili.

Parking: Take Hwy. 50 to Lihue, turn makai on Rice St. and continue about 2 mi. down. Or take Hwy. 51 toward the harbor from airport, turn makai or on Rice St. Once down to the harbor, park at beach access on left just before crossing small concrete bridge; or at Anchor Cove shopping area just after bridge. *Note:* Additonal access points described in the activities sections.

Hike: Nawiliwili Jetty and Kalapaki Beach walk (1.5 mi.); Kuki'i Point (.5-mi); Running Waters Beach (.5 mi.); Nawiliwili Small Boat Harbor (1 mi.)

Nawiliwili Beach Park, a canoeists' enclave, is behind the Anchor Cove shopping center. **Nawiliwili Jetty** extends seaward from the beach park, about .5-mile into the harbor. You can drive out the entire distance, but a path closer to the water gives you a close-up look of surfers and boaters, as well as a perspective of beautiful Kalapaki Bay with the Kauai Marriott Resort Hotel perched above it. Across from the bay is Hoary Head Ridge. From the end of the jetty, looking out the bay, is the Nawiliwili jetty light, on a breakwater that is not accessible by foot. To your right from the end of the jetty is the Huleia Stream and the small boat harbor.

Going the other way from the parking, toward **Kalapaki Beach**, you cross a footbridge on a path passing Duke's Canoe Club, leading to the beach—or you can cross the stream at the surf line. Kalapaki Beach is more than .25-mile long, a curve of sand ending at cliffs, upon which homes overlook the bay. The resort's gardens and paths blend into the beach. *More Stuff:* You can also access Kalapaki Beach by driving toward the main entrance to the Marriott. Pass the resort and turn right, following Shoreline Access signs down to a large parking lot.

Kuki'i Point is the mini-lighthouse across from Nawiliwili jetty light that heralds the entrance to the harbor. You could walk up through the Marriott, and follow the road that runs behind the houses above Kalapaki Bay. It's shorter, however, to get back in the car, head up Hwy. 51 for a short distance, and turn right toward Marriott. Pass the resort entrance. Veer right toward shoreline access and Chapel by the Sea. Kuki'i Point is not far from the chapel parking. From the paved lot next to the golf course, walk up to a path, and turn right, back toward the bay. The path curves down, around a green, and then out a rocky trail to Kuki'i Point. The point is a wave-lover's hangout, with its own perspective on the harbor. Try it at sunset with your favorite libation. You'll likely be joined by fishermen.

To **Running Waters Beach** drive past the Marriott and continue through the golf course to the road's end. Park in a large lot, closest to the restaurant and shopping center. The path to the rugged beach skirts the golf course and curls down to your right, as described in TH39. To **Nawiliwili Small Boat Harbor**, you need to make a .75-mile drive from the beach park. Follow Wa'apa Road around the harbor, away from Kalapaki,

Ninini Lighthouse, Kuki'i Point

Marriott Hotel

turning left on Wilcox Road and passing Matson shipping and the anchorage for the massive cruise ships. Continue and then turn makai on Halemalu Road toward the boat harbor. Several kayak outfitters, as well as sailing and fishing guides, are based in this low-key area. Boats in the harbor will strike a romantic chord for anyone who has fantasized sailing the South Seas. For the full effect, try walking the jetty that shields the vessels from both the harbor and the fresh waters of Huleia Stream.

SNORKEL: **Kalapaki Bay** is known for surfing rather than fish-peeping, but relatively sheltered waters do provide a scenic and reliable place to don the mask and fins and take a good swim. People do lap swimming just offshore of the beach. Safer waters are near the east end of the beach, closer to the cliffs, where you will also spot more fish. Kalapaki is a roomy bay, but if you drift too far off shore you might run into trouble with surfers and boating lanes.

BIKE: As might be guessed from the varied parking descriptions, **Nawiliwili** is a trailhead well-suited for tooling around on a mountain bike. You can range from Kukiʻi Point to the small boat harbor, taking in the jetty and nooks and crannies around the shops and restaurants. Bicyclists might also drop in on the island's biggest Banyan tree by pedaling into the Banyan Harbor Condominiums—an asphalt-happy development—bearing left through its parking area. The spreading Banyan there has been pruned so it can be ridden through, and is about 100-feet across.

Cyclists can also connect up with the Marriott lagoons and **Ninini Point**, TH40; read mountain bike section for that trailhead. Going the other way, toward Poipu, a coastal route is not possible. But you can ride inland through the rural **Kipu** area. Take Waʻapa Road and Wilcox Road along the coast from Nawiliwili, past the small boat harbor and ride up Hulemalu Road. You have an uphill pump for a while, past the Menehune Fish Pond, and then hit countryside along the Huleia Wildlife Refuge in full view of Hoary Head Ridge. Some 5 or 6 miles from Nawiliwili, Hulemalu Road comes out on Hwy. 50. *Note:* The bike lane on Hwy. 50 ends not long after Kipu; proceed with caution.

PADDLE: Kayakers will enjoy stroking into well-protected **Kalapaki Bay**, although keep an eye out for surfers and boat traffic. For access to the **Huleia Stream**, go to the Nawiliwili Small Boat Harbor. Outfitters there rent kayaks and offer guided tours up the wide stream, which goes into the Huleia Wildlife Refuge. Or, better yet, stop in at True Blue-Kauaʻi Beach Boys, located next to Duke's at the Marriott. True Blue has

river and waterfall tours, and also will rent kayaks to independent paddlers. They also can put you in the tranquil, beautiful waters of the 40-acre lagoon above the Marriott— a mellow experience that families and birdwatchers will particularly appreciate.

The Huleia Stream was a setting for the movies *Jurassic Park* and *Raiders of the Lost Ark*. It is not readily accessible on foot, due to private property restrictions and wild- life refuge regulations. As wide as any river except for the Wailua, the stream curves inland for about 2 miles. About 1 mile in, you pass the Menehune Fish Pond, a streamside reservoir constructed by Kaua'i's legendary settlers around 200 to 400 AD. A mile past the fish pond, waters ripple over a cascade, the end of navigable waters. No hiking is permitted inland, except with the li- censed outfitter. *Be aware:* Brace yourself for a headwind on the homeward paddle.

SURF: Kalapaki Beach is site of Duke's Canoe Club, named for surfing legend Duke Kahanamoku. Hardwood longboards are displayed inside. Duke's beach has several good surfing spots, although often too tame for the local boys. The onshore break is suitable for boogie boards and body surfers. Farther out, near Kuki'i Point, is an area called **Lighthouse**, a left-slide next to a rock wall suitable for good surf- ers only. Near the breakwater across from lighthouse is an area sometimes called **Hang Ten**, near the right side of the bay; Hang Ten also has rock hazards. Both these Kalapaki spots often suffer from low surf. On the other hand, good breaks for beginning and in- termediate surfers may be found on any given day.

Kalapaki Bay, Duke Kahanamoku

Mahaulepu

The last volcanic eruptions on Kaua'i took place 40,000 years ago from craters that are now obscured by cacti and brush, a long tee shot from the golf links and resort hotels of Poipu Beach. Kaua'i's first eruptions were 10 million years ago, under the sea.

More recently, but long ago in the 1300s, the Poipu shores at Mahaulepu were the scene of a great battle, when a powerful king from the Big Island, having conquered all the other islands, landed here with a flotilla of war canoes. The Kauaian king, Kukona, outfoxed the powerful enemy, coaxing the invading forces inland, where they were defeated. Rather than kill the captured king, Kukona is said to have taken him on a tour of the island. The next unified invasion of Kaua'i was not attempted for almost 500 years, by Kamehameha the Great, and his forces did not succeed either.

From Mahaulepu, which lies along the ocean side of Hoary Head Ridge, to Lawai Bay, at the other end of the south coast, is a varied coastline—reef-protected coves, wave-bashed bluffs and sandy beaches. These features make Poipu ideal for hiking, cycling, and all water sports. Horseback riding is also popular here.

On the bluffs between Shipwreck Beach and Mahaulepu is a sandy path with open views amid dwarf flora, one of the most spectacular coastal walks on the island. The Hyatt Regency at Shipwreck is rated among the world's top tropical resorts.

The whole coast from Spouting Horn to Mahaulepu is well-suited for exploring on a mountain bike—some of it by zigzagging through resort areas and other parts by riding on four-wheel tracts and disused cane roads. One dirt road, just up from the Poipu-Spouting Horn junction, leads inland to parts of the island not reachable by any other means.

Windsurfers are drawn to the waters with the surfers off Shipwreck Beach. Ocean kayaking and canoeing are popular within the protected waters of Poipu Beach, but paddlers should get the advice of a local before stroking out to sea.

Poipu Beach is flanked by resorts and condominiums, basking in the south shore's more arid climate. In the winter, Poipu will have sun when the rest of the island may not. The beach is a two-mile run of small sandy coves separated by short peninsulas, creating pools suited for snorkeling and swimming. Surfers come here year around to Brennecke's Beach, but the real surfing action along this coast is during the summer when Kona winds bring larger swells.

Koloa Landing, at Whalers Cove, today is often bypassed by tourists heading for Spouting Horn or Poipu. But in the 1800s Koloa Landing was the third busiest anchorage in Hawaii among whaling and trading ships, surpassed only by Honolulu and Lahaina on Maui. Although the shore is rocky, snorkeling is good at Whalers Cove, but not quite as good as a little farther up the coast at Prince Kuhio Park. Named in honor of Prince Jonah Kuhio Kalanianaole, delegate to the U.S. Congress in the early 1900s, today the place is just "PK's." An audience gathers at PK's to watch the surfers during the summer, and in the winter the little beach is packed with snorkelers.

The road ends at Lawai Bay, not far from Prince Kuhio Park. Two of Kaua'i's three National Tropical Botanical Gardens are located up the Lawai Valley—Allerton and McBryde gardens. The gardens, part of a botanical research center working to preserve and study tropical plants, were once the retreat of a Hawaiian queen. Many movie companies, including those shooting *Honeymoon in Vegas*, *Jurassic Park*, and *Donovan's Reef*, have selected the gardens for locations. Visitors wishing to see the gardens must take a tour, starting from the visitor's center across from Spouting Horn.

Spouting Horn is where pressurized sea water erupts like a geyser through a lava tube, created from sea swells trapped below. Reputedly, a second, larger geyser was located nearby, but it was dynamited in 1910 by plantation owners who wanted to keep salt spray from killing cane crops just inland.

Agricultural lands and rural neighborhoods comprise the lands sloping up from Poipu toward Kahili Peak. The hikes to Kahili Ridge provide exhilarating views of the

Poipu Beach

south shore, as well as a close-up of the ridge's complex flora and topography. Kahili rises above Koloa Gap—the passageway between Lihue and Poipu. The view from this jungled spine was once utilized by outlaws who could swoop down on horseback and surprise their victims.

An easier walk, and perhaps the best place on Kaua'i to view the south and west shores, is Kukuiolono Park on a hillock above Kalaheo. The park will interest history buffs and botanists, as well as provide a 260-degree blue-water vista.

Mahaulepu, Chelane Kauilehua Weaver, Spouting Horn

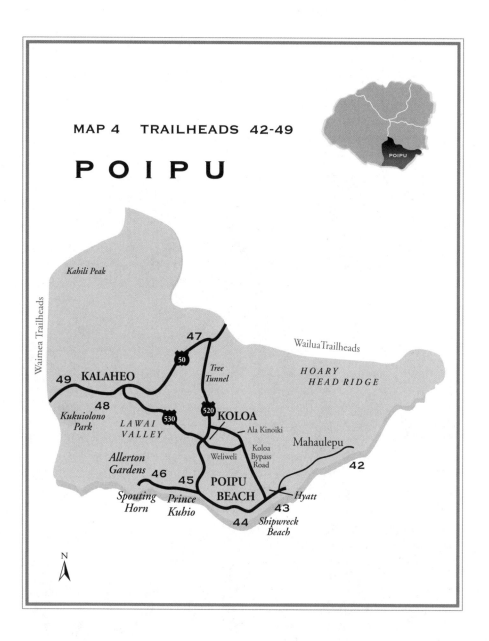

MAP 4   TRAILHEADS 42-49

POIPU

POIPU

Kahili Peak

Waimea Trailheads

WailuaTrailheads

47

50

Tree
Tunnel

HOARY
HEAD RIDGE

49 **KALAHEO**

48

Kukuiolono
Park

LAWAI
VALLEY

530

520 **KOLOA**

Ala Kinoiki

Mahaulepu

Weliweli

Koloa
Bypass
Road

Allerton
Gardens   **46**

45

42

Spouting
Horn

Prince
Kuhio

**POIPU
BEACH**

Hyatt

43

44 Shipwreck
Beach

N

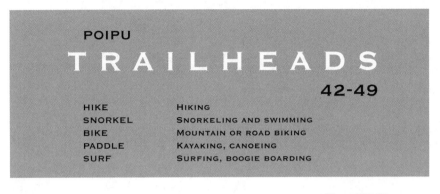

POIPU

T R A I L H E A D S

42-49

HIKE	HIKING
SNORKEL	SNORKELING AND SWIMMING
BIKE	MOUNTAIN OR ROAD BIKING
PADDLE	KAYAKING, CANOEING
SURF	SURFING, BOOGIE BOARDING

TH	TRAILHEAD
Makai	TOWARD OCEAN
Mauka	TOWARD THE MOUNTAIN, INLAND
mm.	MILE MARKER, CORRESPONDS TO HIGHWAY SIGNS

Note: All hiking distances are roundtrip unless otherwise noted.

42. MAHAULEPU   HIKE, SNORKEL, BIKE, PADDLE

WHAT'S BEST: You'd never guess this natural place is so close to the resorts of Poipu Beach. Take a swim or nap where the monk seals sun themselves, or walk along the south shore's wild coast.

PARKING: Take Hwy. 50 from Lihue and turn makai on Hwy. 520, which is Manuhia Rd., the Poipu tree tunnel. Go 3 mi.and turn left, before Koloa, on Ala Kinoiki. Continue to stop sign at Poipu Rd. Turn left. Pass Hyatt Regency, pass road to stable, and turn right, about 1.5 mi. from Hyatt. Enter gate for Kawailoa Bay—open from 7:30 a.m. to 6 p.m. Continue .5-mi to first beach parking, turn left, continue .5-mi and park in unimproved area at Kawailoa Bay. *Note:* Beyond the Hyatt, the road is unpaved and seriously potholed. The bumpy drive dissuades some tourists.

HIKE: Haula Beach (1.5 mi.); Mahaulepu Beach (1 mi.)

The bright seascape from Kawailoa Bay to **Haula Beach** may inspire you to take up watercolors. Start to your left as you face the bay—a road goes in that direction but most hikers will prefer to take coastline trails, curling through the ironwoods along low bluffs. Waves often pound the point at Kawailoa Bay, and when conditions are right you may hear a resultant whoosh of air coming up just inland through old lava tubes. Open sand dunes and sculpted cliffs highlight the middle of the walk. Then you drop into a cove, rugged, but with a good beach. Continue along the coast.

After the first cove, you'll encounter a fence. You may pass unobstructed at the shoreline—a dicey little move around a post over a 20-foot drop. Stroll up a sparsley treed slope and curve around to the left. You'll have to pick your way down to the beach.

Haula Beach is a weekend favorite among locals, and the only access to Haupu State Forest Reserve, which rises above it. It is a generous curve of sand, in the shadow of steep-rising Kawelikoa Point. *More Stuff:* Lands around this point are private, including mysterious, photogenic Kipu Kai Beach. A hunter's trail leads from the upslope of the beach and switchbacks up the ridgeline to an awesome view spot. *Be Aware:* Inland areas are private property.

Haula Bay, Kawailoa Bay

Going the other way from Kawailoa Bay, toward **Mahaulepu Beach**, walkers will find easy going along a strip of sand bordered by the ubiquitous ironwoods. Monk seals commonly beach themselves in this area—stay away from this endangered species. The monk seal, one of three mammals—along with bats and humans—to make shore in Hawai'i, can trace their genealogical heritage back to primordial times. Near the far end of Mahaulepu Beach is a house, the only one on this coast. Beyond that, at the far end of the beach, is a trail leading to a cave, beginning just beyond a stream. The Waiopili Heiau lies inland, up and left after crossing the stream; but better access to the heiau is from a dirt road that goes off to your right where the pavement ends when you enter the Kawailoa Bay gate.

SNORKEL: Small **Kawailoa Bay** is enticing for snorkelers and swimming can be good. But much of the time, you'll find choppy surf, making swimming less desirable. Watch for sleeper waves along the shoreline. You may have better luck at **Mahaulepu Beach**, accessed best from the first beach parking area. Look for cars; a short trail to the beach is hidden in a hedge of ironwoods. The best swimming is to your left, a couple hundred yards down the beach. A rock barrier, about 30 yards out and running along the shore, creates a huge oval pool for beginners and younger children. Safer spots are nearest the sandy point. A deeper water entry is next to the beach's headland. *Be Aware:* Surf at Mahaulepu indicates dangerous current conditions. Don't drift.

BIKE: Sandy beach roads, horse trails, and cane roads in disuse all make **Mahaulepu** mountain biker friendly. Some of the best riding is inland. You can take Mahaulepu Road (go left where the beach road turns right before the gate) back toward Koloa, and get a look at the Koloa Sugar Mill, which was the first on Kauai. Closed in the late 1990s, the behemoth, red-stained structure is being swallowed by tropical foliage.

Cyclists also can make a 10-mile **Koloa loop**. Start by parking in Koloa. Take Weliweli Road from Koloa, but turn left on the cane toward Mahaulepu, rather than the paved Koloa-Poipu Bypass Road. Once at Mahaulepu, skirt the coast along Shipwreck Beach, TH43, and **Poipu Beach**, TH44. At the far end of Poipu, just past the Sheraton, head to the right, and come back up the pavement on Poipu Road to Koloa. *Be Aware:* Heed private property signs on cane roads, and watch out for cars on Poipu Road.

PADDLE: Experienced paddlers can put in at Kawailoa Bay and head to the left around the point to **Kipu Kai Beach**, which is not accessible by land to the public. This is a spectacular place. Check weather reports and seek advice from local outfitters before embarking on this challenging trip.

43. SHIPWRECK BEACH   HIKE, BIKE, SURF

WHAT'S BEST: The grand Hyatt Resort is a fitting start for a majestic walk along bluffs above the deep blue Pacific. Wide-open views inland preview a short, quirky walk to the site of the Kaua'i's last eruption.

PARKING: Take Hwy. 50 from Lihue and turn makai on Hwy. 520, the tree tunnel road. Before Koloa, turn left on Ala Kinoiki, a bypass road. Continue several miles. At stop sign, turn left on Poipu Rd., and, just past Hyatt Regency Resort, turn makai on Ainako St., a beach access road running between the Hyatt and Poipu golf course.

HIKE: Punahoa Point (4 mi.); Makahuena Point (1.5 mi.); Pu'u Wanawana Crater (.5-mi.)

To **Punahoa Point**, start toward your left as you face Shipwreck Beach in front of the Hyatt and walk down the beach toward Makawehi Bluff. The landmark bluff greets the pounding surf at that end of Keoneloa Bay—which is the proper name for the Shipwreck. Several footpaths lead to the top, where intrepid divers sometime wow beachgoers. Make your way down the coast, at first through a network of sandy paths woven amid dwarf ironwoods. You soon top a rise, from where reddish Punahoa Point is in view, more than a mile around the coast. Hoary Head Ridge looms inland. Make your way along the coast. Farther down the coast is Mahaulepu, TH42.

To **Makahuena Point**, head to your right as you face the water at Shipwreck. The beach walk is longer in this direction, but in short order you will be on a coastal path on the outer rim of condos and homes that carpet this bluff between the Hyatt and Poipu Beach. Development notwithstanding, this is a scenic jaunt, ending at Makahuena Point Light. *More Stuff:* A paved path extends from the Hyatt through the greenbelt of Poipu Kai condos, reaching Poipu Beach at Pane Road, which is off Ho'one.

Pu'u Wanawana Crater is a short drive from Shipwreck, hiding in plain sight. The crater is the site of Kaua'i's most-recent eruption—recent in geologic terms. Head mauka on Ala Kinoiki Road, up just .1-mile from the stop sign at Poipu Road. Park across from a fruit stand. Walk around a yellow gate and then go left on a two-track road that rises up to a road that goes around the crater. Don't take the trail in front of you as you get to the crater road. Instead, go to your right about 75 feet and look for a trail leading into some intimidating brush—a thicket of upright shrubs with cacti tentacles carpeting the ground. This stuff would stop a rhino. But the path leads through the foliage, twisting a hundred yards or more, and reaches a vantage point at the Stonehenge-like volcanic teeth the mark the perimeter of the crater. *Be Aware:* Use your own judgment when using this route. Access may be through private propery.

BIKE: Mountain bikers can head toward Mahaulepu, TH42, on a road that heads from the public access lot at Shipwreck Beach. This is a trailblazer's route, and you need to pick your way along the coast after this road ends. A better route is to pop out to Weliweli Road and ride it past the golf course, exploring roads after that. *Be Aware:* This is equestrian country, so be sure to yield to horses or dismount in tight situations.

Cyclists can get to Poipu Beach by taking Weliweli Road in that direction. Turn makai at stop sign, up Pe'e Road. This takes you up, winding in a circle through the condos and homes on Makahuena Point. Pe'e Road then drops down to Brennecke's Beach, which is just down the road from Poipu Beach.

SURF: **Shipwreck Beach**—the ribs of the wrecked ship were removed by Hurricane Iniki—is a popular spot for bodysurfing and boogie boards, as well as the stand-up boarders. Its popularity and location in front of a major resort hide the dangers of the waters here. Shipwreck is known for a shore break with rock hazards, swells in the winter and high surf in the summer. Make observations before entering the water, and avoid on rougher days. The coast off Shipwreck Beach is also popular among windsurfers, but only experts should venture into these seas.

44. POIPU BEACH   HIKE, SNORKEL, BIKE, PADDLE, SURF

WHAT'S BEST: Surfers, strollers, snorkelers, and people-watchers all can end their quest somewhere along sunny Poipu Beach. The arid surround and condos are a disappointment to some, but not to those seeking blue sky when it's raining elsewhere on the island.

PARKING: Take Hwy. from Lihue and turn makai on Hwy. 520, which is Manuhia Rd., the tree tunnel road. At Koloa, turn right at stop sign and then turn left immediately past the gas station on Poipu Rd. Veer left on Poipu Rd. at coast.

First (Sheraton) parking: Turn makai on Kapili Rd toward the Sheraton, about .5-mi. after veering left. Kapili Rd. ends at Ho'onani Rd., where you turn left and park immediately on right at public access lot.

Second (midway) parking: Continue on Ho'onani Rd. for about .25-mi. and park near the Kiahuna Plantation Resort. Puts you in the middle of the Poipu Beaches.

Third (Poipu Beach Park) parking: Continue on Poipu Rd. past Kapili Rd., about .75-mi. and turn makai on Ho'owili Rd. to Poipu County Beach Park.

HIKE: Poipu Beach stroll (2.5 mi.); Moir Gardens (.25-mi.)

Poipu Beach is more than a mile long, consisting of four small sandy coves separated by natural black-rock breakwaters extending not far seaward. This is not a nature walk, as beach chairs, boogie boarders, and sunbathers abound. Starting at the first parking, take a groomed path through a pleasant palm grove, around the back of the Sheraton, coming upon its sloping sandy beach. Continue, either along the beach or a path that runs parallel to it. You leave the resort, with its double-scoop beach, and walk a path past a time-share resort, in front of which stood the remains of Kihahouna Heiau until Hurricane Iniki finished if off in 1992.

After passing the rocky area at the former heiau, you come to Waiohai Beach, which soon blends into Poipu Beach Park. The park has a sandy peninsula, with a rocky tip, that creates a beach area to either side of the spit. The park extends inland from the beach to Poipu Road, cut across the middle by a quiet street, Ho'one Road. Continuing along the park, the next, rougher beach you come to is Brennecke's, across from the restaurant of the same name. Beyond Brennecke's, Makahuena Point intrudes into the water, separating this beach from Shipwreck Beach, TH43. (A path leads from Pane Street at the end of the park through resort homes to the Hyatt.)

To **Moir Gardens**, a.k.a Pau a Laka, go to the Outrigger Kiahuna Plantation, which is across Ho'onani Road from the second beach access parking. The gardens, begun in the 1930s, include native plants, succulents, and a display of cacti rated among the ten-best in the world. The gardens surround a lagoon and the plantation restaurant.

SNORKEL: Poipu Beach commonly offers some of the best, safest, and sunniest snorkeling on Kaua'i, especially during the winter. At **Sheraton Beach** and **Waiohai Beach**, a reef offshore breaks up the swell and waves, creating a large and fairly deep swimming area. Getting in and out is easy along the sandy shore, although the little shore-breakers might test your balance. Hotel concessions rent snorkeling equipment.

Directly in front of the **Poipu Beach Park** pavilion is a swimming pool-like area that is popular. The area close to shore, to the left of the sand spit, is sometimes called **Baby Beach**. The snorkeling is also good on the other side of the short peninsula. The only beach in this area snorkelers should avoid is Brenneckes, with a shore break and rougher conditions. At Poipu, you might want to park in the middle access point, and dip in and out of a number of good snorkeling spots. *Be Aware:* Don't be lulled too far out into Poipu's waters, where surfers, sailors, and reef action pose hazards.

Another snorkeling spot, often overlooked because it's in the seam between the roads that fork to Poipu and to Spouting Horn, is **Whalers Cove**. Take Ho'onani Road away from the Sheraton about .5-mile. Look for a turnout on the left. Whalers Cove has good snorkeling with clear water and plenty of fish, but getting past boulders at water's edge requires some balance, and the water can be choppy.

BIKE: **Poipu Beach** is more of a place to explore on a bike rather than take a bike ride. Follow the parking descriptions above, and you will find a wealth of places cars can't go within the resort community and beach front. To connect with **Shipwreck**, TH43, stay close to the coast from the Sheraton on Ho'onani Road, making your way on footpaths where Ho'onani ends. You come out at Ho'one Road, which takes you past the beach park and Brenneckes, and then comes to Pe'e Road, which climbs around to the Hyatt. Going the other way on a mountain bike, toward **Spouting Horn**, you need to take Poipu Road and turn left on Lawai Beach Road. Another option toward Spouting Horn direction is Ho'onai Road past Whalers Cove, if the bridge is intact.

PADDLE: **Whalers Cove**, going away from the Sheraton on Ho'onani Road, has a canoe landing. Go past the turnout described in the snorkeling section and look for a sharp left as the road heads away from the cove up Waikomo Stream. This is access for ocean exploration of the Poipu and Prince Kuhio areas. Recommended for calm days.

SURF: With occasional trade swells in the winter and Kona wind in the summer, Poipu is year-around surf city. During the summer, beginners surf **Poipu Beach Park**, off the spit in front of the pavilion. The beach features both right and left breaks. In the cove next door, rougher **Brennecke's** also breaks both ways. During the summer, board-

Poipu Beach, Moir Gardens, Sheraton Beach

ers try the reef off **Waiohai Beach**, to the right of the sand peninsula. This is for average surfers, but a shallow reef covered with sea urchins creates a hazard. Consult with local surfers or instructors. **Horseshoe** is in front of the Sheraton. Again, this is mostly a summer surfing beach, with a fast break and a long paddle from shore. Horseshoe (a.k.a. Cow's Head and First Break) is recommended for top surfers.

45.   PRINCE KUHIO PARK   HIKE, SNORKEL, BIKE, PADDLE, SURF

WHAT'S BEST: The coast may lack curbside appeal, but it has some of the island's best snorkeling and summer surfing. You'll also find beaches tucked away. **PARKING:** Take Hwy. 50 from Lihue and turn makai on Hwy. 520 toward Poipu. At Koloa, turn right at stop sign, then left immediately on Poipu Rd. At bottom of grade, veer right toward Spouting Horn, on Lawai Rd. Go 1 mi. on Lawai Rd. and park off road at Prince Kuhio Park—near Beach House Restaurant.

HIKE: Kukuiula Bay (2 mi.); Koloa Landing (1 mi.)

The coast along **Prince Kuhio Park** is generally rocky, developed, near a road carrying tourists to Spouting Horn, and close to well-known Poipu Beach. For these reasons, this good snorkeling and surfing area is often unnoticed. A good way to check out this coast is on foot. To **Kukuiula Bay**, a small boat harbor, head to your right as you face the water at Kuhio Shores. A paved path leads the way across from the beach, starting at the Lawai Beach Resort. From the resort, a grassy ditch makes for a footpath just far enough from the road to appreciate the agricultural inland, which includes papaya orchards (unless a planned development changes the landscape). When the grassy ditch ends, cross the highway onto a small road—Amio Road—that takes you to the sportfishing harbor. Kukuiula Bay's breakwater can be walked for a whale's eye view of the bay and a gander up the coast at Spouting Horn's eruptions. *Be Aware:* Monk seals also like this beach—give them at least 100 feet of space.

Heading the other way, to **Koloa Landing**, from the parking—to your left as you face the water—walk through small Prince Kuhio Park. This historic park features a monument to Kauaʻi's longtime congressional representative, grassy terraces, picnic areas, and a pond—a good place to have lunch away from the small beach. From Kuhio Park, cross Lawai Road and veer off to the water side on Hoʻona Road. Once on Hoʻona, look for a beach access pole near 5142 Hoʻona Road. Head out onto the beach—known as **Waterhouse Beach**—and make your way along the sand and then around black-rock tide pools, accented by dry areas filled with bits of white coral.

Around the point from Waterhouse Beach is Whalers Cove, in front of the resort of the same name. Keep going around the resort, heading toward the Waikomo Stream inlet. You will see a wooden stairway, which is the public access to Koloa Landing from the resort. Go up the stairs, through the resort parking lot, and back out to Hoʻona Road. From Hoʻona, walk back among beach cottages, passing the access pole at Waterhouse Beach, and continuing to Kuhio Park.

SNORKEL: **Longhouse Beach** is on the other side of the Beach House Restaurant from Prince Kuhio Park. Despite its unappealing roadside setting, Longhouse—also called Beach House, Keiki Cove, or PK's—offers excellent snorkeling, with enough sand, easy entrance and a nice population of fish swimming close to shore in deep, clear water. You might see a turtle swimming through coral heads. The beach is small, not the best for spending the day. For a picnic after a swim, consider nearby Prince Kuhio Park. *Be Aware:* During high surf, strong current runs from left to right.

Waterhouse Beach, described in hiking section, has an excellent baby beach, a protected, shallow spot for dunking and wading. Snorkelers will have better luck at **Whalers Cove** at Koloa landing, which is also noted in the snorkeling section of TH44, Poipu Beach. It looks a lot better from the water than the shore.

BIKE: The best bet for mountain bikes is to go back up Poipu Road, .5-mile up from the Spouting Horn-Poipu intersection. On your left, past the little shopping center and across from a fruit stand, you'll see **Cane Coast Road**. This road parallels the coast, a mile or so from the water, and continues above Allerton Gardens all the way to Numila—a distance of about 12 miles, one-way. *Be Aware:* The Cane Coast Road is on private property and access may not be permitted in all areas. Use at your own risk.

SURF: The offshore break at **Longhouse Beach** draws average-to-advanced surfers, mostly during the summer. Longhouse breaks in four places, which locals call—starting from left to right as you face the water— **PK's** (for Prince Kuhio), **Centers**, **Acid Drop**, and **Heroins**. Sometimes PK's is just called Longhouse. Just don't call it late for surfin'. Boardriders also try the right-break off the jetty at **Kukuiula Bay**.

Kukuiula Bay

From April through October, people line the shore at the Beach House Restaurant—which was formerly the Tahitian Longhouse—to watch the show. PK's and Centers draw good surfers—none of these beaches are for beginners. The kahunas test their skills at Acid Drop and Heroins. All Longhouse breaks are well offshore, two-way breaks—and vary greatly due to wind conditions.

PADDLE: Outrigger races from Nawiliwili Harbor end at **Kukuiula Bay**. Another popular paddle from here is toward Spouting Horn and Lawai Bay, which is not accessible to the public via land, except for garden tours. The bay is sheltered, although you need to be mindful of boat traffic.

46. ALLERTON GARDEN   HIKE, SURF

> **WHAT'S BEST:** Two of the nation's five National Tropical Botanical Gardens are right here. Across the street is Kaua'i's sea geyser.
> **PARKING:** Take Hwy. 50 from Lihue and turn makai on Hwy. 520 toward Poipu. Turn right at stop sign in Koloa, and then left on Poipu Rd. At bottom of grade, veer right toward Spouting Horn on Lawai Rd. Go about 2 mi. on Lawai Rd., turn makai and park at Allerton Garden visitors lot.

HIKE: Garden Visitors Center and Spouting Horn (1 mi.); Allerton Garden (1 mi.); McBryde Garden (1.5 mi.)

A path leads from the **Bill and Jean Lane Visitor Center** to **Spouting Horn**, which is directly across Lawai Road. Spouting Horn is Kaua'i's saltwater version of Old Faithful. Here, flumes of sea-foam erupt through an opening in a reef, powered by pressure of waves trapped below. You watch from a safe distance behind a fence, just off a parking lot with plenty of space for tour buses and booths for crafts people selling their wares. Safe viewing spots are also on the rocks, via an opening and short path to the left of the fenced area. Many a camera lense and shutter finger have poised at this sight.

The garden's visitor center, built using a grant from Bill and Jean Lane, former publishers of Sunset Magazine, is a restored 1920s sugar plantation home, set here on the coast after Hurricane Iniki destroyed the other center farther inland. A path leads through the grounds, featuring a number of native plants, tropical fruits and interpretive areas—a beautiful and informative introduction to the island's greenery. This garden is growing into its own. The center's artful offerings will end your quest for a gift.

Both garden walks are ticketed tours, leaving from buses at the center. The tours are popular and advance reservations are recommended for Allerton; an admission is charged. The National Tropical Botanical Garden is a nonprofit, privately funded organization, under Congressional charter to do scientific research and plant conservation. Three of the five NTBG sites are on Kaua'i. The **Allerton Garden** was once a retreat for Queen

Emma and is known for its landscape design and flowering tropical plants. With a private beach and lush valley, Allerton has been the set for a number of movies, including *Honeymoon in Vegas, Thorn Birds, Jussasic Park,* and TV's *Fantasy Island.* The guided tour includes the history estate— a lifelong labor of love.

You're left to wander and gander at your own pace at **McBryde Garden**, which is aimed more at scientific research. A dreamland of native plants and trees, as well as extotics, are spread along a falling stream, crossed by a bamboo bridge and punctuated by cascades and pools. Sit a spell here and there. Independent travelers and plant peepers will appreciate the McBryde. *Be Aware:* Many of the plants are rare and endangered; don't touch and stay on the path.

Allerton Garden, Monk Seal and friends at Longhouse Beach, McBryde Garden

More Stuff: To Kaiwa Point, which is as close as you can get on public land to Lawai Bay, take Lawai Road to its end. Park off-road safely, and away from the Allerton locked gate. A chain-link fence, which runs along the ocean side of the road, ends about 100 feet before the gate. Near the gate you will see a rough, unmarked trailhead that takes you down to the rocky coastline. To call this a trail is generous. Watch your step. Once at the water, walk to your right, making your way through grass patches and boulders to Kaiwa Point, which forms the south mouth of Lawai Bay. By inching your way around some bigger rocks, you can look into the beach and bay.

SURF: It's a long paddle, or a scramble using the trail described above, but board fiends manage to get to the left-right break offshore of **Allerton Beach**.

47.   KAHILI RIDGE   HIKE

WHAT'S BEST: A thrilling walk up a tropical ridge with blue-water views.
PARKING: Take Hwy. 50 from Lihue. Turn mauka .5-mi past Hwy. 520, which is the turnoff to Poipu. Look for Kahili Mountain Park sign, just past mm. 7/50. Go 1 mi. up road, turn left toward Kahili Mountain Park, circle around to left, between office and Adventist School, with cabins to your right across a grass field. Continue past cabin number 30, and park off road when you see a water tank on your right.

Note: Kahili Mountain Park and Adventist School are private property. They have been generous is granting permission to use these trails, but keep in mind that landowners are not liable for any injuries that may occur to hikers. The cabins (Kaua'i's best rustic) can be rented by visitors with some restrictions; go to www.kahilipark.org.

HIKE: Kahili Pine Grove (.75-mi.); Kahili Ridge (2.75 mi.)

For the **Kahili Pine Grove**, walk down the road from parking, making sure to look inland to view your destination, a stand of several hundred Norfolk and Cook pines. Once you get there, you can't see the forest for the trees. As the road dips down, look for a white rock and a short, three-foot high concrete wall on your right. The trail starts here; and there are two routes on this short walk. For the best trail, turn right about 50 feet in, just after the trail makes its first small step up. The straight-ahead trail leads to the grove, too, but it's a little tighter passage. The better trail loops around to the right, through fern hedges six-feet high, and then through a stand of ironwoods before leading into the grove. These are mostly Norfolk pines; their cousin, the Cook pine, has bushy branches, whereas the Norfolk is distinguished by its long, frondlike limbs. Outside the grove in all directions is an impenetrable growth.

The **Kahili Ridge Trail** is a climb of about 1,700 feet up a spiny feeder ridge that abuts Kahili Ridge. Begin at a road behind the water tower. After only .1-mile, you veer left off the road, following a homemade sign into a tunnel of a trail through pink-flowering shrubbery. Branches from this bush will provide helping hands as you navigate up and down this often muddy trail. Less than .5-mile in, and 200 feet up, you pop out to views of the 197-acre park, with Hoary Head Ridge and the Poipu shores as a backdrop. Kong and Sleeping Giant even appear in the distance.

The ridge trail gets steeper, never making switchbacks, before reaching another plateau, about 1 mile from the trailhead. You get a seaward view here, but now the mauka view draws attention, with four or five waterfalls often streaking down Kahili Ridge. By this juncture the trail has narrowed to a foot or two wide, falling very steeply on both sides. But any acrophobia is assuaged by the thick foliage, through which you couldn't roll a bowling ball. Still, exercise caution, for what appears as an embankment to the trail may be just tufts of flora.

The trail continues flat along this ridge for just a short distance, before launching skyward again, through trees whose roots provide steps to go with branch handholds. This rise gives way to another plateau, now that much closer to the face of Kahili. You make another significant upping, your final, before reaching the windswept heights. The trail ends at a radio antenna, down the ridge from Kahili Peak, which is not readily accessed *Be Aware:* This trail can be a mudder. Bring water and a hiking pole.

48. KUKUIOLONO PARK   HIKE, BIKE

> **WHAT'S BEST:** A short walk with long views, a scent of flowers and a sense of history. This park is a peaceful retreat for road-weary visitors.
> **PARKING:** Take Hwy. 50 to Kalaheo, which is about 5 mi. past Hwy. 520, the turnoff to Poipu. In Kalaheo, turn makai at the traffic signal, on Papalina Rd. Continue, passing first Pu'u Rd., for 1 mi. Turn right on Pu'u Rd., and right again immediately, at the stone archway that is entrance to the park.

HIKE: Kukuiolono Park Pavilion (.75-mi)

Kukuiolono Park is a golf course with grounds featuring an exotic Japanese garden and a Hawaiiana exhibit that includes rocks of archeological significance. From these attractions—which are located in trees just up the hill from the parking area—a path leads seaward to a picnic pavilion, resting high above the gentle slopes of the Lawai Valley. Cocopalms, ironwoods, plumeria, and Norfolk pines line the path to the pavilion, where you'll find a 270-degree view of the coast from Barking Sands and Ni'ihau on around to Poipu. You can extend the walk by continuing outside the golf course out-of-bounds markers to another hillock that is to your right, as you face the sea.

Walter McBryde, 19th century sugar magnate, is buried in the park. Also, if you look on the inside of the stone arch and gate that is the park's entrance, you will find a bronze plaque on which McBryde dedicates the park to his mother.

BIKE: **Pu'u Road** is a one-lane country road that encircles the park. It has enough curves and dips to provide exercise, but overall is fairly level pedaling. Bananas and shade trees line the road, along with tall grasses. Pastoral and blue-water views open up here and there. For this 5-mile ride, park outside the entrance to Kukuiolono Park. With the park gate at your back, head to your right. You'll be on

Kukuiolono Park

Pu'u Road most of the way, until reaching a neighborhood area closer to Kalaheo, where you turn right on Papalina Street and follow it back down to the park.

For another paved, rural-residential ride, go down **Papalina Road**, just outside the park gate. After coasting down a mile through a modest neighborhood rich with trees, you come to the administrative offices of the National Tropical Botanical Gardens. These offices were the site for Allerton Garden tours before the visitors' center was moved down to Spouting Horn. You can view the upper reaches of McBryde garden from the serene and shaded back patio of the offices.

49. ALEXANDER RESERVOIR   HIKE, BIKE

WHAT'S BEST: A little-known back way to jagged Kahili Ridge, for cyclists and hikers, affords long views from the island's high country.
PARKING: Take Hwy. 50 past Poipu turnoff, through Kalaheo, and past the jct. of Hwys. 50 and 540. Turn mauka on unmarked red-dirt road, .2-mi. beyond of Hwy. 540 turnoff. Proceed .5-mi. up road, with trees on right and cane on left. Park off road where red-dirt road reduces to narrower road, in view of a

large stone home. *Note:* If the gate is closed at the highway, walk in and add 1 mi. to roundtrip distance.

HIKE: **Alexander Reservoir (5 mi.); Kahili Ridge (9 mi.)**

The **Alexander Reservoir** trail—a four-wheel track—begins on a gradual, pastoral incline, up the Wahiawa Valley, situated between Kahili Ridge and the Hanapepe River Valley. On the jaunt to the reservoir, you climb about 800 feet on a red-dirt ramp. Over the first mile you have views of unusual rock escarpments and of Hanapepe Bay. You then enter a tree canopy, walking under the boughs of huge monkeypods, eucalyptus, and a number of flowering trees. Alexander Reservoir feeds two falls, Kaukiuki and Waiolue, which you may be able to hear on windless days, to your left beginning .75-mile from the reservoir—but which you cannot access by trail.

Nearing the reservoir the road wyes—either fork gets you there, but the left one should be less muddy. Both options take you to the right along the south shoreline of Alexander Reservoir, which looks like a fairly large woodland lake. Due to seepage, the road below the reservoir often turns to a mud swath that would bog a Humvee. Birds like this zone, with egrets most noticeable among a number of species.

From Alexander Reservoir, the route to **Kahili Ridge** becomes less of a road and more of a wide trail—steeper, curving and rutted, but very walkable. You'll be climbing another 800 feet before reaching road's end near the ridge below a radio antenna. Above the reservoir, you'll pass a large stand of Norfolk pines and pop out of the tree canopy with views of the upper Lawai Valley. You continue ramping up on the lip of this drainage, as foliage becomes dwarf and fern hedges dominate. The sky opens up and the route levels as you reach another fork; go right at telephone pole 2901.

After the fork, for the last mile, the trail is on top of the world, with saw-toothed Kahili Ridge beckoning straight ahead. Up the valley to your the left looms Kawaikini, the tallest peak on Kaua'i at 5,243 feet. Also on the left are the ridges of upper Hanapepe Valley. The open flat below on the left with dwarf trees is Kanaele Swamp. To your right—as the trail wiggles and climbs—is the vertical relief of two rippling green ridges coming together. The route ends tantalizingly close to the ridge, at a knob; but only a goat, and not a smart one at that, would continue on the overgrown and sketchy trail from here. *Be Aware:* The margins of the trail are only mats of ferns in places; don't venture off trail.

BIKE: **Alexander Reservoir** is well-suited for a hike 'n' bike. Park at the trailhead and pedal up to the reservoir, and hike the rest of the way to the ridge. You will have a pleasant coast down from the reservoir. Fit and experienced cyclists can make the entire ride. The tough parts—aside from the savage mud bogs—are steep ruts just beyond the reservoir, and some rutted hard-pack on the final approach to the ridge.

Waimea

Kilohana Overlook

In 1778, Hawai'i became the last major landmass to take its place on the modern globe. In that year British Captain James Cook and his ships, the *Discovery* and the *Resolution* dropped anchor in Waimea Bay, thus ending the Hawaiians' fifteen centuries without contact from the rest of the world's cultures.

Cook and his men, having sailed the South Pacific for a dozen years, recognized at once that these new people were of Polynesian descent, but prior to making landfall not even this great navigator knew that Hawai'i existed. Four hundred years had elapsed since the last Tahitian migrations, and islanders in those southern waters, like Cook, had known nothing of their descendants far to the north.

Cook's Kauaian visit lasted only three weeks, long enough to trade coveted iron nails with locals for equally coveted fruits and livestock, and for Cook and his officers to share a few peppery awa cocktails with the Kauaian ali'i. Cook's most-significant legacy, however, was not a welcome gift: Although he had prohibited fraternization with the local women, his men managed to infect them with venereal disease.

Upon surveying Kaua'i, these first Europeans chose the gently sloping coast of the drier west side for safe anchorage. But they barely caught a glimpse of what awaits today's visitors. Not many hikers in the tropics expect to find cacti growing on cliffs of red-walled river canyons. Waimea Canyon is appropriately dubbed the "Grand Canyon of the Pacific."

About ten miles long and almost 4,000 feet deep, Waimea Canyon takes its place alongside canyons in America's Southwest as a scenic wonder. Trails lead into the canyon, as well as along its cliffs and throughout the diverse forests that border its upper rim at Koke'e State Park—a wonderland for birds and countless varieties of trees. Forests include both native varieties and others planted by the Conservation Corps in the 1930s. Within Koke'e are a museum and interpretive nature path, as well as miles of trails through forests chock-full with a fantastical array of flora. Some trails—including the Cliff and Waipo Falls trails—pop out to big views of Waimea Canyon.

The west side of Koke'e State Park forests gives way to Napali—The Cliffs. All along the northwest quadrant of the island, ridges and valleys fan out like spokes on a wheel, starting at road's end on the north shore and continuing around to road's end on the west shore at Polihale State Park and Barking Sands Beach. Each ridge ends at a cliff along a coast with no roads. This is a wild forest reserve area that hikers and cyclists can spend weeks exploring.

At least eight of the Napali ridges can be hiked or ridden by mountain bike. The hikes begin through tropical greenery and end at bluffs, some 1,500 feet above the surf, with canyon walls of neighboring ridges to the left and right. Viewpoints at trail's end look down at remote valleys, once inhabited, and all steeped in Hawaiian mythology.

Heading up from Koke'e park headquarters, the road ends at a lookout of the Kalalau Valley. Road's end is the beginning of the Pihea Trail. From Pu'uokila Lookout, the Pihea Trail starts along the precipitous rim of the Kalalau Valley and then turns inland, going across the Alakai Swamp on a boardwalk. Alakai Swamp is a 60-square mile bog of dwarf vegetation that was once the caldera of Hawai'i's first volcano. The boardwalk ends abruptly at a platform looking 4,000-feet down into the rippling green Wainiha River Valley and, beyond the valley, to Hanalei Bay on the north shore. Even the most-avid among red-dirt adventurers may take several trips to Kaua'i before comprehending its geographic jigsaw puzzle.

Down from Waimea Canyon is a shoreline than includes the longest strip of sand in Hawai'i—some 17 miles—beginning where the road ends at Barking Sands Beach in Polihale State Park. Beach hiking and surfing are superlative at Barking Sands, as well as at Majors Bay and Kekaha, two other beaches that continue around the west side from Polihale.

Pihea Trail, Kekaha

This trailhead section also includes two of Kaua'i's quaintest places to walk around, each distinctly Hawaiian—Waimea and Hanapepe. Waimea Town, once the island's capital, is where the Royal Hawaiians make their monthly trips by ferry from Ni'ihau. Waimea, meaning "red waters," has a river for kayakers and a bay for surfers. An ancient trail also leads up Waimea Canyon from Waimea Town, along the ancient remnants of Menehune Ditch.

Between Waimea Town and Hanapepe is Pakala Beach, one of the best surfing beaches anywhere. Pakala is also dubbed Infinities, because the rides can go on forever. Right near Hanapepe is Salt Pond Beach Park, the best snorkeling spot on the west side, as well as the site of the ancient—and still functioning—salt ponds. In the 1800s, sailing vessels coveted the salt, not only for its taste, but also as a vital preservative for meats and fish.

Hanapepe is another uniquely Hawaiian town, funky around the edges with Kauaiana shops along its small main street. Browsers will enjoy the town's suspension footbridge over a river, and trails into a canyon that would be a main event were it not for nearby Waimea Canyon. Private property limits access as far as Hanapepe Falls— of *Jurassic Park* fame—but three rural roads and trails give hikers and cyclists a taste of the canyon floor. Paddlers can get the farthest into the variegated green-and-red gorge.

Port Allen, Kaua'i's working harbor, with a power plant and commercial dock, is a taking-off point for snorkelig adventures and the "Forbidden Island" of Ni'ihau. Kayakers can try the bay before heading up Hanapepe River. From Port Allen, hikers can also walk a coast trail to Wahiawa Bay, a destination for snorkeling tours not easily reached directly, since the bay borders a coffee plantation.

The Waimea area doesn't have hotels—with one notable exception in Waimea Town, and other ventures on the drawing board—so many visitors zip through on the way to Waimea Canyon or Barking Sands. But the west side could be an island unto itself and still be a world-class destination for muscle-powered sports nuts.

Waimea's historic 1843 Gulick-Rowell House, Hanapepe Falls, Kalalau Overlook

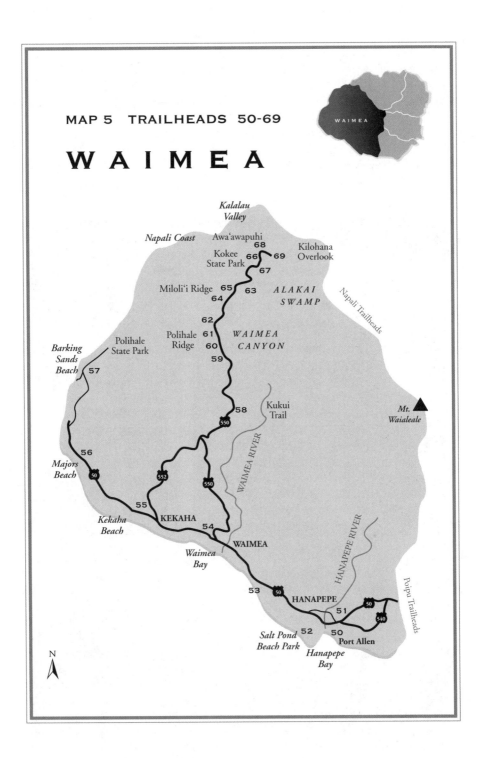

MAP 5   TRAILHEADS 50-69

W A I M E A

WAIMEA

Kalalau
Valley

Napali Coast   Awa'awapuhi
                        68
           Kokee 66   69   Kilohana
           State Park   Overlook
                        67

Miloli'i Ridge 65 63   ALAKAI
              64   SWAMP

              62
Polihale   61   WAIMEA
Polihale Ridge 60   CANYON
State Park
              59

Barking
Sands   57
Beach   58   Kukui
                   550   Trail   Mt.
                                              Waialeale

       56
Majors   552   WAIMEA RIVER
Beach   50   550

       55
Kekaha   KEKAHA
Beach   54
                     WAIMEA
       Waimea
       Bay

                              53   50   HANAPEPE
                                              51   50
                        52   50   540
              Salt Pond   Port Allen
              Beach Park Hanapepe
                          Bay

N

TRAILHEADS

50-69

HIKE	HIKING
SNORKEL	SNORKELING AND SWIMMING
BIKE	MOUNTAIN OR ROAD BIKING
PADDLE	KAYAKING, CANOEING
SURF	SURFING, BOOGIE BOARDING

TH	TRAILHEAD	*Note: All hiking*
Makai	TOWARD OCEAN	*distances are roundtrip*
Mauka	TOWARD THE MOUNTAIN, INLAND	*unless otherwise noted.*
mm.	MILE MARKER, CORRESPONDS TO HIGHWAY SIGNS	

50. PORT ALLEN-NI'IHAU   HIKE, SNORKEL, SURF

WHAT'S BEST: Take a look at Kaua'i's sightseeing and whale-watching port, or hike to out-of-the-way snorkeling bay. Or, spend the day cruising to the island of Ni'ihau, where you can't set foot, but you can place your face is some excellent snorkeling waters.

PARKING: Take Hwy. 50 past Kalaheo, and turn makai on Waialo Rd., at mm. 16/50. Go .75-mi. on Waialo and park at large lot near dock. Additional parking areas described below.

HIKE: Port Allen dock and breakwater (1 mi.); Glass Beach (less than .25 mi.); Wahiawa Bay (2.5 mi.)

Port Allen is not a place most people would want to spend their entire Polynesian vacation; fuel tanks, utility pipes and power poles are not subjects for postcards. Yet a tour around the port gives you a look at what makes Kaua'i tick and offers some colorful glimpses of dockside commerce. The main dock at Port Allen is popular for sportfishing and whale-watching boats, as well as commercial vessels. To walk out on the **breakwater**—and get a view back in toward Hanapepe Bay—you need to back-track up Waialo Road a bit, and turn right on a road running between metal ware-houses and fuel storage tanks. Park and walk along a series of pipes running on the ocean side of the warehouse toward the breakwater. The tip of the breakwater is a likely spot to see whales during winter migrations. *Be Aware:* Observe the waves for several minutes, and know that surf conditions can change suddenly.

To **Wahiawa Bay** and **Glass Beach**, continue driving beyond the parking for the breakwater. The road becomes dirt and bumpy just beyond the tanks. The beach is

where the road drops to the water. Zillions of colorful smooth glass pieces almost outnumber the sand particles at this tiny cove. The road continues a short distance and ends at a Japanese and Hawaiian cemetery. A fishermen's path leads down the coast from here to the bay, winding its way alongside tide pools on a sketchy trail. The mouth of Wahiawa Bay is about a mile from the cemetery. Once there, follow its low cliff inland, sloping down to a small sandy beach. Wahiawa Bay is a deep, narrow inlet, bordered inland by the Kauai Coffee Company plantation. *Note:* Local fishermen come use a road through plantation houses that is .3-mile up from the visitors' center. Permits for this access are available: Call Alexander & Baldwin Corporation at 808-742-2773. The office for permits is at Kukuiula Bay near Prince Kuhio.

SNORKEL: The ultimate Kaua'i snorkeling trip awaitng 20 miles offshore in the waters of the 'Forbidden Island' of **Ni'ihau** and the tiny island of **Lehua** that lies next door—a bird sanctuary. Several tours depart Port Allen, but the most experienced and popular is HoloHolo Charters. They'll zip you there in a diesel catamaran, and throw in lunch, gear, and a swing by the Napali coast on the way. Ni'ihau is privately owned, off-limits to all but native Hawaiians. Lehua is a cinder cone off its eastern shore.

Offshore Ni'ihau and Lehua

Snorkeling locations will depend on weather and sea conditions, but count on crystal clear water. *Be Aware:* Check the sea reports before booking your trip, as the ride can be bumpy. The cruise, including Napali, is an all-day affair.

Wahiawa Bay boasts a comfy sandy beach, ideal for sun bathers, but with shade as well. The base of its cliffs is lined with submerged rocks, and the bay is well-protected, especially during the winter when the trades blow from the northeast. All this makes for a snorkeling adventure for those wishing to try something different. Tour companies used to sail here. *Be Aware:* Few people snorkel here, meaning no help is nearby in case of a mishap. In summer, the Kona winds can bring high surf and poor visibility. Another swimming area is a small beach near the **Hanapepe River** mouth—between the small boat harbor at Port Allen and the river. The beach has poor sand, but a gradual entry makes for safe swimming. Keep an eye out for boats.

SURF: **Hanapepe River** mouth is a spot for beginners and boogie boarders. Small waves and rock-free waters make for safe conditions. Waves break either direction. Often, surf is too small, but this might be a choice during the summer, when surf elsewhere on the west and south coasts might be too large.

51. HANAPEPE   HIKE, BIKE, PADDLE

WHAT'S BEST: Exploring old-style Hanapepe Town and its river canyon—on foot, by bike, or paddling a kayak. Nose around and you'll be rewarded.
PARKING: Take Hwy. through Kalaheo. Veer mauka toward Hanapepe on Hanapepe Rd., which is about .5-mi. past mm. 16/50. Continue short distance beyond left turn and park near Pa Lane at parking for Swinging Bridge.

HIKE: **Bougainvillea view (.25-mi.); Hanapepe River (up to 3.5 mi.)**

In **Hanapepe**, dilapidation and gentrification have fought to a standstill, resulting in a quiet, old-style hamlet sprinkled with interesting shops. To see the place come alive, catch an art night, held monthly. For the **bougainvillea view**, walk back the way you drove in, past Ko Road, and look for a paved path with a pipe railing leading up to the

Hanapepe Town

left. Tour buses sometimes stop here to let passengers take a gander at the multicolored flowering plants that blanket the cliff on the way into Hanapepe. This short walk gives you a perspective on the town, bay and river.

For the **Hanapepe River**, walk across the swinging bridge that spans the wide river— the bridge is a destination itself. A levee trail on the other side goes both to the left and right. To the left, or downriver, you walk about .5-mile, to a one-lane car bridge on Hanapepe Road, about .5-mile up from where the river enters Hanapepe Bay. The downriver option might be a choice for someone wishing to take a stroll and then get picked up down the road by someone else who preferred to gallery tour in town.

Going to the right across the swinging bridge, or upriver, takes you, after about 1.25 miles, to a broad, agricultural area, with a variety of fruit trees, including bananas, as well as fields of seed corn. On the first part of the walk, you'll have river views, looking through large broadleaf trees at the red walls of the gorge, while, on your left, as a contrast, you'll pass a tropical junkyard, replete with rusting vehicles and chicken coops. Roosters and barking poi dogs are a likely audio. The path loops away from the river, ending at a farmhouse—this is where Awawa Road comes in, as per mountain bike description. Near the end of the levee road is a scenic vista of the river valley across agricultural fields. Farm roads lead across the fields, giving you an option on cutting over to take another look at the river.

BIKE: Three good rides await mountain bikers in Hanapepe, all up the valley on different routes. **Ko Road**, which is your first right on the way into town via the parking directions, snakes in 1.5 miles before coming to a locked gate. Beyond the gate is a hunter's road. Ko Road is bordered in places by the 200-foot high walls of the river valley, with views of the river and a patchwork of agricultural lands. Mountain bikers can ride the other side of the river by pedaling down Hanapepe Road from the suspension bridge parking area, crossing the river on the one-lane car bridge, and turning right on **Awawa Road**. Awawa Road takes you through a tree tunnel and past country homesteads. After 1.5 miles the road, now unpaved and ends at a cornfield.

The **Hanapepe River** trail, as described in the hiking section, is also an option for bikers. To ride this trail, pedal across the river as if going to Awawa Road, but instead jog behind a building to your right just as you cross the bridge. The levee trail comes in here, and you can ride about 2 miles upriver, although tall grass will sometimes hamper the going on this route. The levee road comes out on Awawa, giving you an option of looping back out via that road.

PADDLE: The **Hanapepe River** makes lazy, very scenic curves inland from the bay for 1.5 miles. The farmlands are lush and the canyon walls, reddish and spotted with greenery, are peculiar to this arid and yet tropical gardenscape. You see cacti in these hills as well as bananas. One access for kayakers is behind the structure across the bridge at Awawa Road, as described in the mountain biking section. Kayakers can also

put in at the river mouth, on Puolo Road. To get to this put-in, backtrack out to the highway and turn right toward Waimea. Cross the river and turn makai immediately on Puolo Road. Continue on Puolo, passing a ball field on the right, and park after .25-mile, where the road makes a sharp right. Make sure not to block the gate. This puts you at the mouth of the Hanapepe River across from the swimming beach at Port Allen. The river mouth put-in involves a short carry, but it extends the navigable river by .5-mile, and also more readily gives you the option of stroking around Hanapepe Bay. You need to be mindful of boat traffic in the bay.

Hanapepe Swinging Bridge and River

Drying fishing nets, Salt Pond

52. SALT POND BEACH PARK

HIKE, SNORKEL, BIKE, SURF

WHAT'S BEST: Salt Pond is best place to take a snorkeling break from touring the west side. Follow the swim with a picnic or seacoast hike.

PARKING: Take Hwy. 50 to .75-mi past Hanapepe River and turn makai on Hwy. 543, toward Salt Pond Beach Park. Hwy. 543 is Lolokai Rd. Bear right at Lele Rd. and continue on Lolokai Rd. to beach park, which is 1 mile from Hwy. 50.

HIKE: Pa'akahi Point (3 mi.)

Salt Pond Beach Park is an unflattering name for this more than pleasant park. From the parking, walk across the lawn of the picnic and camping area and then arc left around the beach. Almost unnoticed inland as you first leave the beach is the pond from which the ancients—and present-day Hawaiians—have extracted salt from seawater. Continue around, hugging the coast on a red-dirt road. The hike takes you around the chunky peninsula that forms the west side of Hanapepe Bay, across from Port Allen. As you walk you encircle Port Allen Airport, an asphalt strip that is the occasional launching pad for ultra-lights and tour helicopters—but these craft are enough removed and too infrequent to detract from the overall aesthetic. On the contrary, it's a fanciful sight to see the ultra-lights winging in from the sea.

The sharp point closest to Salt Pond Park is Ku'unakaiole, an ironwood-shaded contemplation spot. In the middle of the peninsula, Puolo Point is the location of Hanapepe Light which identifies the bay for sailors. From Puolo to Pa'akahi Point, the last .5-mile of the outward segment, black rocks supply the resistance for some explosive wave action. Near Puolo Point, dolphins and whales are sometimes spotted close to shore.

SNORKEL: Nature has made a saltwater swimming hole at **Salt Pond Beach Park**, complete with a crescent of sand and swaying palms. Local families picnic here. A reef protects the shoreline, and swimming is safe on most days within the lagoon the reef

creates. Don't drift beyond the reef, as currents get tricky not far out. Due to silt and wave action, visibility is most often just fair, and fishes are not profuse. To the right of the big beach is a keiki pond, made for splashing.

BIKE: The **Paʻakahi Point** hike, described above, is well-suited for pedal pushers wishing to take a 3-mile, half-paved loop. Ride the coast to Paʻakahi Point, pushing the wheels for a brief spot when starting out. You continue around the bumpy peninsula and then inland along the bay coast, meeting up with Lele Road. Ride on Lele past the veteran's cemetery, about .5-mile, and meet up with Lolokai Road, a.k.a., Salt Pond Road. Hang a left on Lolokai and ride back to the beach park. Don't be confused by another road, Kuiloko Road, that runs along the airstrip; this road takes you back to the park also, except on the sea-side of the salt pond.

SURF: Windsurfers and boarders alike take advantage of an off-shore break outside the reef at **Salt Pond Park**. It's a long paddle out, and known only as a summer spot

Salt Pond Beach Park, Pakala Beach

Beach at Makaweli

for surfers. Some locals also try the harbor break, at the mouth of the harbor just off the airport runway— **Pa'akahi Point**. Access is difficult, down a rocky embankment, and the right-breaking swells are recommended for good surfers only. Locals tend to gravitate to Pakala, TH53, just up the highway.

53. PAKALA BEACHES   HIKE, SNORKEL, SURF

WHAT'S BEST: Surfers rave about Pakala's long-breaking waves, but hikers will find a long, palmy beach walk, or a shorter one to view a quiet sugar-shack community right out of the 19ᵗʰ century.

PARKING: Take Hwy. from Hanapepe. Pass the makai turnoff to Makaweli and cross a highway bridge, at mm. 21/50, near an emergency phone. Park on highway shoulder, just on other side of bridge.

HIKE: Pakala Beaches (up to 2 mi.); Makaweli (1.5 mi.)

Access to **Pakala Beaches** starts just below the highway bridge. A path runs beside A'akukui Stream for about .25-mile under the boughs of large monkeypod trees to the beach. Turning right at Pakala Beach—which is also called A'akukui Beach or Infinities, because that's how long the waves roll—leads you about 1 mile to rocky Po'o Point. The point forms the mouth of Hoahuana Bay, along which the beach lies. *Be Aware:* On certain days, the stream can be filthy with agricultural runoff, making the beach a turn-off.

Going to your left at the beach, you cross the stream (if it's not too high or turbid) and follow the cocopalm-lined shores that border **Makaweli.** Makaweli is collection of several dozen weather-worn, red-stained sugar shacks, festooned with nets, glass balls, and hanging laundry, choked by tropical greenery and set in a grid of narrow, potholed dirt streets that make perfectly good sleeping spots for the occasional poi dog. This is not a tourist town. *Be Aware:* Although the people here are uncommonly friendly, visitors might want tread lightly at this quiet community.

SNORKEL: The water is shallow and the stream mouth used to have a reputation of being unhealthy due to upstream agricultural use. Although you would not come to **Pakala Beach** just to snorkel, you can find places to wade or take a float. Water quality is generally better toward Makaweli. *Be Aware:* Surf can make shores turbulent all year around, with rip currents in shallow waters.

SURF: Pakala Beaches, or **Infinities**, draw surfers all year, but during the summer the swells are particularly inspiring. If the surf is good, cars will be parked at the highway. To the east side of the beach, or left as you face the water, is Pakala Point, where left-hand slides take boards up the coast to infinity. To access this break, you need to walk to your right up the beach about .25-mile and paddle out through deeper

Makaweli

water for about 100 yards. Curls often begin at several sections, accommodating a fair number of surfers. Locals ride these fast tubes for two or three hundred yards. *Be Aware:* Infinities has a dangerous, shallow reef. Even the big boys and girls prefer high tide.

54. WAIMEA TOWN   HIKE, SNORKEL, BIKE, PADDLE, SURF

WHAT'S BEST: This most-Hawaiian of towns offes a mix: a long walk on a swimming beach, a navigable river, and exotic hiking into the "heart of darkness." Waimea is the West, cowboys and all.

PARKING: Take Hwy. 50 past mm. 22/50. Cross bridge over the Waimea River and turn makai at first opportunity, on Alawai Rd. Go short distance and park at river mouth at Lucy Wright Beach Park. *Note:* Additional parking in activity descriptions.

HIKE: Waimea Beach and Town walk (3 mi.); Menehune Ditch (1 mi. to 16 mi.)

You won't find many tiki torches in **Waimea Town**, but you will find some of old-Hawai'i. Outrigger canoes rest along the beach, fishermen hang out on the pier, families picnic and talk story about the town's fabled rodeos. Quiet streets with weathered bungalows and sugar shacks blend with tropical gardenscapes and plots of vegetables. Waimea has the most native Hawaiians among its population, and is the docking place for the Royal Hawaiians who make the ferry ride from Ni'ihau.

For the **beach and town walk**, start at Lucy Wright Beach Park, which was the landing for the first Europeans to set foot on Hawaii, in 1778, arriving in vessels led by Captain James Cook. Less than .5-mile down the beach is Waimea State Recreational Pier, where you can walk over the water and also pick up a few pointers from bamboo-pole anglers. Plantation-style homes are set back all along the beach, and fishing boats and canoes are parked next to cocopalms at their back doors. Waimea Plantation Cottages, a low-key, upscale vacation spot, marks the end of town; its spacious lawns with massive banyans invite a stroll. Kikiaola State Boat Harbor, almost a mile from the pier, marks the end of Waimea Beach. Walking back, you may wish to jog inland through sleepy Waimea Town. Quiet roads parallel the beach along the highway. Or, across the highway, other roads zigzag through Waimea's mom-and-pop commercial district.

For the **Menehune Ditch** hike up the Waimea River—one for trailblazers only—you need to get in the car. From Lucy Wright Beach, go out to the highway and turn left, and then turn right immediately on Menehune Road. About 1.25 mile up Menehune Road, you'll see a suspension footbridge and plaque commemorating the archeological site of the Menehunes' water-conveyance ditch, or what's left of it. Exotic birds and cacti growing in the rocks clue you that this isn't your normal tropical hike. About 2 miles in from the highway, still driving, look off to the right: Where a four-wheel drive

Around Waimea Town

road crosses the river is the trailhead. If the river is not easy to cross here, forget about going more than a mile or two on this hike, as the path crisscrosses the river.

An alternative and more scenic trailhead for the Waimea River trail is .5-mile beyond the river-crossing trailhead. The road ends in a jungle setting at a small farm for bananas and other tropical fruits, with a home and outbuildings. Locals access the river trail, part of Pu'u Ka Pele State Forest Reserve, through here. Park off-road just before this property. Get an okay on your parking spot if you see anyone around.

Proceed straight on the dirt road, past the bananas and papayas, continuing left of a gate and along a fence. Then go through a gate. The trail goes up to the left, through switchbacks, climbing about 150 feet, until you hit a ditch. You follow the ditch up the canyon, with birdsong and the rushing river for a soundtrack. You may need to push plants away in a spot or two, and step over a few rocks. In about .5-mile, you'll see an Indiana Jones-type suspension bridge crossing 20 feet above the river. You cross this plank-and-cable bridge—the safety of which cannot be assured—and meet up with the four-wheel drive trail coming upriver from the first trailhead.

About 2 miles in from the trailhead, the trail climbs again, perhaps 500 feet, and follows a ditch above the river for about 1.75 miles before dropping down again to the river. By this time you may feel like you've stepped into a Joseph Conrad novel. Signs of civilization are to be found in the form of a water conveyance system, built in the early 1900s, centuries after the Menehunes' 25-mile effort; plantation owners constructed an elaborate ditch system to feed the thirsty cane fields of the west slope. From where the trail drops to the river to where it meets the Kukui Canyon trail, TH58, is another 3.5 miles. To see this area, you're better off taking the Kukui Trail down from the canyon. *Be Aware:* Don't attempt this hike when river is high or when thick clouds indicate mountain rains inland. Hiking pole recommended. If you're going more than a mile in, prepare for a full-fledged trek. Although Kauaian hunters are a friendly lot, this trail is best for weekdays when hunters are not out.

SNORKEL: The water clarity is often poot, but swimming is safe under most conditions near the breakwater at **Lucy Wright Beach Park**. After storms, river silt will make water too clouded for swimming. People also swim farther down the beach toward the pier, but avoid fishermen's lines. *Be Aware:* No beach is safe every day; if you see several tiers of beach-pounders, most often during the summer, it's not a safe day.

BIKE: **Waimea Town** and **Menehune Road** to beyond the first suspension bridge invite cyclists to take a rideabout. From Lucy Wright Beach Park, hug the coast on quiet residential roads as far as you can, and then zigzag back toward town. You might want to head up Alawai Road instead of Menehune; this road follows the river levee and meets up with Menehune Road after a mile. A Waimea rideabout is some 8 miles.

PADDLE: **Waimea River** is navigable for maybe 2 miles inland, although after about a mile in you want to watch for rocks and debris. Not many people paddle upriver here. Waimea also invites a bay-and-river combination, as waters along the beach are normally fairly calm. You're more apt to be joined by an outrigger canoe than a kayak.

SURF: The river mouth at **Lucy Wright Beach** is usually a place for novice surfers and boogie boarders. But Wright's is not always okay for keikis: Summer swells break far offshore, and build in four tiers to a shore break that can be dangerous. Currents can be strong under these conditions.

55. KEKAHA   HIKE, BIKE, SURF

WHAT'S BEST: Pull off the road and catch a sunset view of Ni'ihau along miles of sand beach. When rains darken the rest of the island, sun seekers head for Kekaha.
PARKING: Take Hwy. 50 past Waimea. Pass Kikiaola Small Boat Harbor and park on makai shoulder anytime after mm. 25/50, which is the beginning of Kekaha Beach Park. Additional parking available along next 2 mi.

HIKE: Kekaha Beach (up to 4 mi.)

Kekaha, is an eclectic community known as a gateway to Waimea Canyon and for its long, long beach. You'll find locals along the shore—fishing, horseback riding, and surfing its year-around wall of waves. And when clouds hang over other parts of Kaua'i, sun often shines on Kekaha, making it the best choice for beach-goers. From the parking at curved O'omano Point, start walking to your right as you face the water—look for where a rock bulkhead ends at the side of the road. In about .25-mile you'll come to the only reef section on Kekaha Beach. During high tide you may have to rock hop.

Kekaha comber

Kekaha Neighborhood Center is about a mile up the beach, across the highway, a place for a restroom-and-water break. A mile after that, the highway veers away from the beach. Look for a lifeguard station at mm. 27. The open sand and surf continues for miles, part of the longest sand beach in Kaua'i, and blends into Majors Bay at the Pacific Missile Range Facility. *Be Aware:* Due to heightened military security, the beach may be closed about .75-mile north of the lifeguard station. One wonders if it will ever be opened again.

BIKE: A frontage road and wide shoulders allow passage for cyclists for most of the way along **Kekaha Beach**, but you'll want to keep one eye peeled for high-speed traffic. A better cycling option here is to take a pedal inland through the community. The gargantuan sugar mill, derelict since 2000, lies in the middle of Kekaha, on Kekaha Road, which is the farthest road away from the highway. Head for the towering chimney. The inland ride gives you a look at a middle-class neighborhood not usually trumpeted in travel brochures. Up from Kekaha are the sugar cane fields, sloping toward the canyon, and the beginnings of the ridges-and-valleys that become the Napali.

SURF: **Kekaha** gets pounded with south swells in the summer, and has predicable winter surf. But this beach is too far away from Kaua'i's numerous other surfing beaches to be well-known or become crowded. Good-to-average surfers try their luck at a half-dozen different spots. Among the most popular spots are the reef near **O'omano Point**, sometimes called **Davidsons**. The reef, which provides the break, also presents a hazard, and Davidsons is not for novices. There are four other breaks along **Kekaha Beach**, from the community park to the lifegurard station. *Be Aware:* Rip currents and high surf make this a beach to observe before paddling out. People swim here, but it is a dangerous beach—drownings and impact injuries do happen.

56. MAJORS   HIKE, SNORKEL, SURF

WHAT'S BEST: A beach-lover's beach, with sand two-hundred yards deep and many miles long, made for surfing and bagging some R&R. The catch these days is you need to apply for permit to enter the base.
PARKING: Access using day permit at Pacific Missile Range Facility, which is past Kekaha on Hwy. 50. Turn OS at main PMRF gate, which is .5-mi. CW of mm. 32/50. Stop at gate. *Note:* Due to heightened military security, the base may only be open on weekends, and only to persons who have obtained a permit. Call a week ahead of time for current procedures: 808-335-4221. It's worth the trouble.

HIKE: Majors Bay (3 or 4 mi.)

Majors Bay, another name for Waiokapua Bay, is the middle segment of the long beach—the longest in Hawai'i—that runs from the foot of the Napali coast at Polihale State Park around to Kekaha. Majors is next to what's left of Mana, the settlement of old-Kaua'i. Your permit allows access to several recreational areas, depending on what operations may be taking place on the base. One area is in the middle of the bay, and another is toward the north end, where monk seals have been known to loll about. The vegetation at Majors was given a buzz-cut by Hurricane Iniki, but century plants and low-growing trees are making a comeback. If you need shade with your beach, however, bring it with you, since Majors is nothing but sand, air and water.

Starting at either area on Majors Bay, walk toward your left as you face the water. You'll be heading toward Kokole Point, visible from Kekaha. Majors Bay is the kind of place to get lost right out in the open, a deep expanse of soft sand that gives way to a mesmerizing view of Ni'ihau. The Kawaiele Bird Sanctuary, located just inland between the two entrance gates, invites feathered friends to fly into the view. Albatrosses, also known as gooney birds, are often soaring in numbers.

Going to your right from the parking areas at Majors you can get to the coral reef that signals the beginning of Mana Point. At certain times, you can access **Barking Sands Beach** from the base, by taking a road to the right as you enter the main gate. Ask when you get your permit if this access area is open, called Recreation Area One. The road leads to the reef at the far end of Barking Sands, and then becomes a four-wheel drive sand road. The sand road continues for about .75-mile, ending near Queens Pond at Barking Sands, as described in TH57.

SNORKEL: On occasion, swimming is possible at **Majors Bay**, but more often, all year, the surf is unsafe for snorkeling. A rip current from right to left, or north to south, is also a hazard. The best snorkeling area—the reef near the airstrip—is sometimes off-limits. Receding tide sometimes creates keiki ponds.

SURF: **Majors** draws surfers, featuring some of the west side's biggest breakers during the winter. During the summer, swells can be outrageous. This is not a beginner's beach at any time of the year—some locals have proposed surfing championships be held here. Some surfers head toward the north end of the base, toward Barking Sands, but this access through the base is often limited.

57. POLIHALE STATE PARK   HIKE, SNORKEL, BIKE, SURF

WHAT'S BEST: Walking from the Napali coast over the sands of time on the longest beach in the Hawaiian Islands. Big mana.
PARKING: Take Hwy. 50 through Kekaha to end of highway at mm. 32/50. From the poorly paved road, turn left where a sign says "Polihale." Continue

for 3 mi. on an unpaved road notorious for its ruts and mud-holes (most recent repairs were scheduled for 2006 after storms forced closure). Turn right at a large monkeypod tree, with a sign that notes "camping by permit only." Continue for 1.75 miles, crossing a spillway, and park near a pavilion.

Notes: Near the end of the road, sand may be a hazard for passenger vehicles. Before the end, you'll see spur roads that lead to camping sites along the road that runs parallel to the main road on top of the dune. You can take any of these, park, and walk out to the beach. Also, see *Snorkel* paragraph for directions to the Queens Pond.

HIKE: Polihale and Barking Sands beaches (up to 4.5 mi.); Kapaula Heiau (.75-mi.)

Polihale State Park, which includes portions of Barking Sands Beach, is at road's end on this side of island. Here, a massive sand dune butts into Napali—The Cliffs. Inland from the tree-and-shrub-covered dune, is a wedge of agricultural

Polihale State Park

lands, Mana. The entire beach runs for about 17 miles, but you can't walk the whole way due to restrictions at the military facility. Polihale park has rest rooms, showers, picnic shelters and car-camping sites scattered atop the dune, providing the most remote camping on the island—although it sees a fair number of campers. *Be Aware:* For all hikes bring water, sun protection, and footwear to guard against hot sand.

From wherever you park, make your way through ironwoods and palms and out onto the sloping, fine sands. Going to your right, the beach gives way to black rocks in less than .5-mile, at the base of the Polihale Ridge. This may be the prize spot in the park. You can walk the rocks another .25-mile to Polihale Springs, or Sacred Springs, which flows from Polihale Heiau, where the spirits of the dead are said to have departed the island. This walk requires extensive rock-hopping.

The hike to your left along the coast will walk the legs out from under even the most ambitious beach walkers. About a mile from the last picnic grounds at Polihale Beach, as you begin to see coral reef offshore, the beach inland is Barking Sands. The beach gets its name from a "woofing" sound these 60-foot high dunes make when settling, or when someone walks down them. Kauaian mythology says the "woofing" is the other-worldly echo of an ancient fisherman's dogs—the first man to love dogs as companions rather than as a culinary delicacy. As you proceed, the reef and shoals become more pronounced—a vast, eternal seascape. *Note:* Due to military security, the beach may be closed to walkers, about 1.75-mile south the beach pavilion parking, which is about .75-mile beyond Queens Pond. You definitely don't want to put on a ski mask and skulk inland. *Be Aware:* Don't turn your back when walking the surf line and watch out for rogue waves.

The **Kapaula Heiau** is up a drainage from the camping area. Look for a short, steep inland valley from the dune at the campsite—the only place you would even consider walking inland. You can get a short distance on a road that leads to a water tank, which is right next to the heiau. The heiau site is not far inland, but enough to give a different perspective on the area. The site is overgrown and hard to locate.

SNORKEL: Queens Pond is often a safe swimming area on an otherwise dangerous swimming beach. To get there, take the left at the tee, where the sign is on the monkey-pod tree as you first get to Polihale. Continue for .25-mile to where the road makes a short uphill turn seaward and ends at the sand dune. You may wish to park at the bottom of this right-hand turn. Head through the dunes to the beach. Queens Pond is a few hundred feet to the right as you face the water. It is formed by a crescent-shaped reef that touches the shore at either end, making a large oval swimming area. When conditions are right, surf is spilling over the outside of the reef. Under extended calm conditions, Queens Pond can dry out and be a sand box. *Be Aware:* During storm surf it may be too turbulent for swimming. Rip current can be extreme.

BIKE: From the end of the highway past the Pacific Missile Range Facility to the first coastal road at Polihale is a little more than 3 miles of dirt road—safe and scenic for mountain bikers, but the number of rental cars makes this a lower priority ride. Also, as Hwy. 50 ends, you can ride right on Kiko Road which takes you inland on the wedge of agricultural land between the cliffs and the coastal dune. The road forks, with both forks ending after about .75-mile at locked military gates. Another choice for cyclists is to drive the bumpy three miles to the monkeypod tree, where the road tees on the way into Polihale, and ride the dune roads along Polihale State Park. If you go left at the tree, the road quickly makes an uphill turn toward the dune—the approach to Queens Pond described above, where you'll see a blocked-off sand road going toward Majors Bay. Going to the right at the tree, the road ends after about 1.25 miles at the last campsite and picnic pavilion. Between the "main road" and the beach are spur and dune roads, which you can ride in places where vehicles cannot.

SURF: **Polihale State Park** is known for a multi-tiered shore break with lots of wave action and fairly short rides. The waves normally pound all year, with winter surf and currents posing a significant hazard. You want to consult the locals before trying Polihale; this is a big beach, and its quirks are not commonly known.

Another spot, but one for experienced surfers only, is **Queens Pond**. Follow directions in the snorkeling description above. The break here, especially in the summer, may not be pondlike. Get advice from locals; if it's a good day to surf, they will be here. *Be Aware:* Barking Sands and Polihale State Beach are among the island's most dangerous. Swimmers should stay clear of the water in all but calm conditions.

58. KUKUI TRAILS   HIKE

> **WHAT'S BEST:** A hike to the bottom of a rainbow-hued canyon that rivals any in Arizona or Utah. This trail stands shoulder-to-shoulder alongside Kaua'i's scenic superstars.
> **PARKING:** Take Hwy. 50 to Waimea and turn mauka on Hwy. 550, which is Waimea Canyon Dr. Continue past jct. with Kokee Rd., Hwy. 552, to about .75-mi. past mm. 8/550. Look for trailhead signs on right and park off road.

HIKE: Kukui Trails: Iliau Nature Loop (.25-mi.); Wiliwili Camp, to bottom of canyon (5 mi.)

The **Kukui Trails** take you into the Pu'u Ka Pele Forest Reserve and are part of the Na Ale Hele trail access system. The **Iliau Loop** is a promenade around a flat below the parking area, on which the native scrub vegetation of the canyon rim is identified. The loop takes in a railed viewing area and its inspiring vistas of the variegated red-and-green canyon walls, often streaked with a waterfall or two. You can see up Waimea Canyon and also Waialae Canyon, which wyes off to the right.

Wiliwili Camp is 2,000 feet below, at the bottom of the canyon and alongside the Waimea River. Kukui Trail is the only way for bi-peds to walk the bottom of the canyon from the Koke'e area. Once down, you can go upriver another 3.5 miles to Lonomea Camp, or downriver, connecting up with the Waimea River trail, TH54; but most day hikers will have done enough after making it back up. The Wiliwili Camp trail begins to the right off of the nature loop trail. You start out switchbacking, and then walk out onto an eroded promontory that makes a destination for those not wishing to go all the way down. From the promontory, having descended the majority of the way, you hike left, traversing an eroded hillside, and then right, switchbacking down to the bottom through forest. The canyon floor, still about 600 feet above sea level, will give you a faraway feel (Burma?), with towering century plants and cacti. Go left on the trail and you get to it's first hairy portion, where it is cut into a cliffside, a high-dive above the river as courses through contorted geology.

Be Aware: This is a pig hunter's zone, best hiked weekdays. Also, be mindful of flash floods, as sunnier weather here might belie wet weather in the mountains; check it out from the viewpoint before descending. River crossings (required farther uspsteam) can be treacherous. Prepare for a full-on day hike, including food and water.

Wiliwili Camp, canyon bottom

Waipo'o Falls, Waimea Canyon

59. PU'U KA PELE   HIKE, BIKE

WHAT'S BEST: A short hike with a big payoff: an astounding viewpoint of mythological significance. Mountain bikers can take a different flight.
PARKING: Take Hwy. 50 through Waimea. Turn mauka on Hwy. 550, continue past Waimea Canyon Lookout. Just past mm. 11/550, park on left, off road on shoulder near access sign for Papa'alai Rd.

HIKE: Pu'u Ka Pele (.75-mi); Lapa Picnic Area (4.5 mi.)

Pu'u Ka Pele, or Pele's Hill, is an extinct sulfur vent located to the right of the highway, on the edge of Waimea Canyon across the highway from Papa'alai Road. The hill is said to be where Pele, the volcano goddess, left Kaua'i to create more fiery mischief farther south in the archipelago. At a pit at the top is Pele's footprint, made when she leapt from the island. From the road, take a concrete driveway to a phone company building, visible from the highway. Concrete stairs lead to a series of log-and-dirt steps with a cable handrail that go straight up to Pu'u Ka Pele. A fenced phone installation at the top takes up space but doesn't detract from the view. *Be Aware:* Don't press your luck by venturing out onto unsafe rocks. Also, although this is a historic trail within a state park and used frequently by hunters and hikers, it is along an improved easement utilized by the phone company. Use your own judgement, enter at your own risk, and stay away from the phone company's buildings and lines.

Lapa Picnic Area is partway along Contour Road, which runs along the forested contour on the left side of the highway as you drive up. Fanning seaward off the road are a number of out-and-back trails onto the ridges of the northwest Napali, all leading to blue-water and cliff views. This hike, though generally a contour, takes you through a few hundred feet of undulation. Start down Papa'alai Road. After about .5-mile the trail makes an "S" turn and crosses Koke'e Ditch. You then head seaward for another .5-mile, passing a road on your left that is the continuation of Papa'alai Road toward two ridge roads—see mountain biking description. Passing this road, you bear right, now on Contour Road. You loop inland through subtropical forest, cross a small stream, and then turn back toward the ocean. You walk seaward again for .5-mile or less, and finally hairpin back to your right, reaching Lapa Picnic Area in another .5-mile. *Be Aware:* Spur trails before the picnic area may be confusing; when in doubt, keep right.

Instead of backtracking from Lapa Picnic Area, you could continue on Contour Road, coming to the Haele'ele Ridge Road in about .5-mile. At this juncture, leave Contour Road and make a sharp right, taking Haele'ele Ridge Road. After a little more than a mile, you come to Highway 550 at TH60, Haele'ele Ridge. You'll pass Lua Reservoir on the way. This route is about the same distance as returning from the picnic area via Papa'alai Road—not counting the mile on the highway.

BIKE: A good way to get to know these Napali ridge roads is to tour **Contour Road**. Six different four-wheel drive roads head seaward from Contour Road, all going out its own ridge, each with valleys steeply falling to either side. These ridge roads are covered under separate trailheads—this one, plus TH60-TH62, TH64 and TH65. To ride Contour Road, follow the hiking description for the picnic area, but continue past the Haele'ele Ridge Road. After another twisting-and-turning mile you reach Polihale Ridge Road, which you could take out to the highway. Continuing on Contour Road, another 1.5-miles beyond Polihale Ridge Road, you come to Ka'aweiki Ridge Road—hang a right here and pedal about one curving mile back up to the highway. You'll reach Hwy. 550 at the TH62, Pu'u Hinahina, about 3 miles up from Papa'alai Road. *Be Aware: On* Contour Road, expect mud, puddles and a slippery surface littered with branches and cones. It's best to use these roads on weekdays, when hunters are not present (and when the gate is usually locked).

Papa'alai Road is also access for a ride off of Contour Road onto two ridges. After a mile from the trailhead on Papa'alai Road, take a left fork. This fork splits again after a short distance: Going left at this second fork takes you toward **Kahelu Ridge**, ending five miles and 2,000 feet down; the right fork leads out **Mana Ridge**, ending in about 6 miles and dropping 2,200 feet. *Be Aware:* Kahelu Ridge and Mana Ridge are not maintained; debris, ruts and mud are to be expected. Only fit riders should venture off Contour Road on these ridges. Hunters use this area on weekends.

60. HAELE'ELE RIDGE

HIKE, BIKE

> **WHAT'S BEST:** A tree-lover's ridge hike or bike for a bird's eye view of Barking Sands and a blue-water look at Ni'ihau.
> **PARKING:** Take Hwy. 50 through Waimea and turn mauka on Hwy. 550 toward Waimea Canyon. At mm. 12/550, park on left, off-highway on the shoulder near sign for Haele'ele Ridge.

HIKE: Haele'ele Ridge (13 mi.); Kepapa Spring (12.5 mi.)

Haele'ele Ridge drops 1,900 feet in its 6.5-mile run to a cliff that is due east, as the albatross flies, and 1,400 feet above road's end at Polihale State Park. The red-dirt surface gets snotty with rain, so watch your footing. Haele'ele trail is a broad swath through a forest of eucalyptus, Norfolk Pines, and other trees. Beginning in Waimea Canyon State Park, the trail takes you into the Pu'u Ka Pele Forest Reserve on part of the state's Na Ala Hele access system.

From the trailhead you hook left around the Lua Reservoir, and then cross Contour Road, about 1.5 miles in. From here you gradually come out of forest along a 3-mile descent. After about 2 miles on this descent—and that distance from Contour Road—is a side road to **Kepapa Springs**, which feeds Sacred Spring at Polihale Beach. Kepapa Springs road drops another 700 feet to the south, or left, becoming a trail after .75-mile. It's a down-and-up hike without question. The spring, while affording a canyon view, will probably be obscured by foliage.

Continuing on Haele'ele Ridge road, you drop down the remaining 500 feet over the last 2 miles to trail's end. During the last .5-mile, through a rocky section, the trail stops being a sort-of road and becomes a true trail. *Be Aware:* Hunter's use this area, so the usual precautions against weekend use apply. On the other hand, this is not a jungle area, so hikers are highly visible, and having vehicles on the road means someone is there to drive you out in the event of an accident.

BIKE: **Haele'ele Ridge** is ideal for fit, experienced cyclists. If caution is used—that is, staying aware of slick surfaces, ruts, branches and roots—the route is not difficult to navigate. The difficulty comes in having the wind and strength to ride back up. Coasting down on a bike, after leaving the junction with Contour Road, saves a lot of steps.

61. POLIHALE RIDGE

WHAT'S BEST: Exploring where the Napali begins on this side of Kaua'i, and where the spirits of the dead left the island from a sacred heiau below.

PARKING: Take Hwy. 50 through Waimea and turn mauka toward Waimea Canyon on Hwy. 550. Pass mm. 12/50, almost to mm. 13/550. Park at picnic area. Look for trailhead sign for Polihale Ridge Road. *Note:* From the guardrail at the highway is a knock-out view across the canyon to Waipo'o Falls.

HIKE: Polihale Ridge (10.5 mi.)

Polihale Ridge descends steadily 2,000 feet, through a forest of pine, eucalyptus and other trees, as well as flowering shrubbery. Conditioned hikers can step out on this four-wheel drive surface. From the A-plus picnic grounds, head down and take the first left, paralleling the road for a short distance, and passing a house with a large garden. Head through the yellow gate just beyond the house. From here to the end, the route is due west. For the first mile or more, you drop through moist forest, reaching Contour Road. The trail from Contour Road falls steadily, through large koa trees, mixed with ironwoods and Norfolk pines. About a mile from Contour Road, and 1,000 feet farther down from the trailhead, Polihale Ridge narrows, not to a spine, but you'll see pronounced relief of the valleys on either side. *Be Aware:* Hunters drive this road on weekends and holidays, when the gate is open. Hikers may prefer weekdays.

The road forks near the end, just past a small water tank, each fork a short spur leading to an exciting view from a 1,400-foot escarpment. The left fork ends at a turnaround among ironwood trees. Walk through the trees to an eroded, red-dirt area for a big view above Polihale Heiau, just past road's end at Polihale State Park. On calm days, you will be able to hear surf pounding and, using a hang glider, you could be there in a matter of minutes.

To the left is canyonlike Haele'ele Valley, and three ridges are visible: Haele'ele, Kolo, and Mana. The right fork ends after .25-mile at an eroded area, looking down 1,000-feet into the Hikimoe Valley. The next ridge over, Ka'aweiki Ridge, is close enough for those with keen eyes to spot a wild goat or two. You can see surf at a wild cove. Polihale Ridge, according to Hawaiian religion, was where the spirits of the deceased left the island for the other world. Aloha.

BIKE: Polihale Ridge is made for mountain bikes. It's a tough down-and-up pedal, but the down part isn't so tough. Ruts, cones, and roots, along with a slick surface, present the usual hazards, but this ride takes more endurance that skill.

62. PU'U HINAHINA   HIKE, BIKE

WHAT'S BEST: Combine a short walk to a dramatic canyon lookout with a long hike or bike down your choice of two west Napali ridges.
PARKING: Take Hwy. 50 through Waimea and turn mauka on Hwy. 550 toward Waimea Canyon. Pass mm. 13/550 and look for Pu'u Hinahina scenic turnout on right. Park in improved lot. *Note:* Different parking for ridge hikes; see hiking descriptions.

HIKE: Pu'u Hinahina (up to .5-mi.); Ka'aweiki Ridge (10.5 mi.); Kauhao Ridge (8.5 mi.)

Pu'u Hinahina Lookout is often overlooked, since other viewpoints precede it, but it affords a spectacular view down Waimea Canyon. Glancing left from the lookout, you can review the terrain of the Halemanu Valley Hikes, TH63. Along the road on either side of Pu'u Hinahina are unofficial lookouts with slightly different perspectives on Waimea Canyon, and to your back are the moist forests of Kokee State Park which blend into the very moist bog of Alakai Swamp.

The trailhead for **Ka'aweiki** and **Kauhao ridges** is on the other side of the road, and about .5-mile down the mountain, at mm. 13/550. Drive in, avoiding spur roads to the left and right, and continue straight for almost .4-mi. Park where the road forks. The right fork is Kauhao Ridge; the left fork is Ka'aweiki Ridge. *Note:* Under most conditions, you can drive another .5-mile either way at this fork, and park where each ridge road intersects Contour Road. Access is made somewhat confusing by a series of community and church camps situated between the highway and Contour Road.

From Contour Road, the **Kauhao Ridge** trail extends almost 4 miles and drops 2,000 feet. For the first 1.5 mile after Contour Road, the trail twists and drops through rumpled topography, before coming upon the wide ridge. Open eucalyptus and koa forest allow occasional blue-water vistas, with glimpses of Ni'ihau and its lesser known satellite island, Lehua. The proximity of church camps and mountain cabins bring more four-wheel vehicles to this road, but not so many as to distract from the hiking aesthetic. A short trail leads from road's end on Kauhao Ridge to a lookout of the Napali. At this lookout you are about two miles up the coast from Polihale State Park.

The left-forking **Ka'aweiki Ridge** trail extends more than 4 miles from Contour Road, descending about 2,000 feet. This ridge lies between Kauhao Ridge and Polihale Ridge, TH61. Ka'aweiki is narrower than its neighbors, with deeply cut Hikimoe Valley on its south side and Ka'aweiki Valley to the north. As is the case with Kauhao Ridge, the nearby community camps and private cabins draw a few more vehicles here than the ridges to the south. *Be Aware:* Hunters may be out on weekends, so pick a weekday.

BIKE: Just as with their sister ridges in Pu'u Ka Pele Forest Reserve, **Ka'aweiki** and **Kauhao ridges** are a mountain biker's wonderland. If these and nearby roads were on the mainland, Kaua'i would rival Moab as mountain bike city. *Be Aware:* Slick, packed dirt, road debris and ruts make these ridge roads a place where accidents do happen. Also make sure as you're breezing down that you have enough oomph to get back up.

63. HALEMANU VALLEY TRAILS   HIKE, BIKE

WHAT'S BEST: A tree-lover's hike with waterfall and canyon vistas, perfect for a day when fog is higher up the mountain.
PARKING: Heading up Waimea Canyon on Hwy. 550, continue to mm. 14/ 550 and park off road at marked trailhead, at sign near Kokee State Park Boundary—as you leave Waimea Canyon State Park.

Halemanu Trail toward Waipo'o Falls

Waipo'o cascade

HIKE: Halemanu Trails: Cliff Lookout (2 mi.); Canyon Trail to Waipo'o Falls (4 mi.); Kumuwela Lookout (7.25 mi.); Black Pipe Trail (3.5 mi.) *Note:* Distances are for on-highway parking. A steep road from the highway leads .75-mi. to trailhead; if you choose to drive this road, subtract 1.5 mi. from hiking distances.If you plan to do a lot of hiking in the woodlands of Koke'e, stop by the park museum and purchase an inexpensive map. Within the park area is a fishnet of trails and access roads which can be interconnected in a great number of routes.

The **Halemanu Valley** trails skirt the edge of the forested birdlands where Koke'e Park gives way to the eroded red escarpments of Waimea and Po'omau canyons. **For all trails**, go down the steep, wide Halemanu Road from the highway, which takes a big bend at the bottom and comes to another trailhead sign after .75-mile. Go right a short distance to where the road ends, usually in a big mud-hole, and the trails begin.

After a short distance the trail forks: The **Canyon Trail** goes left and the **Cliff Lookout Trail**, right. The Cliff Lookout is a scamper up to an overlook with a pipe railing and picnic table. You'll get a big sense of place. From Cliff Lookout, you can see down the canyon to your left and see the eroded promontory that is part of the Canyon Trail. Watch for wild goats, known to hang around on these cliffs.

Continuing left on the Canyon Trail to the falls and other destinations takes you down another 600 feet. You drop through dense forest and cross over part of the extensive irrigation ditch system, a subtle hazard, as this swift moving water comes from a tunnel and passes into another on its mysterious way. After the ditch, the Canyon Trail then climbs a bit, to where you get a view down the canyon, and where the **Black Pipe Trail** joins from the left. The Black Pipe Trail—perhaps best done to make a semi-loop on the way back from the falls—loops through a plethora of trees back to the road you walked down. After about .5-mile on the Black Pipe Trail, make sure to switchbak left up a hillside of koa trees, rather than continuing to down to the stream. About.25-mile after this little climb, you go left again when you come to a road. Just remember to keep circling to your left on the Black Pipe Trail. You'll come to the trailhead sign that is just down the road from the highway.

For **Waipo'o Falls** and **Kumuwela Lookout**, you continue on Canyon Trail past the Black Pipe junction, dropping a few hundred feet onto a dramatic barren ridge with canyon views. Continue down the eroded ridge—watch your footing on log steps—and drop to Koke'e Stream. A very short spur trail goes left to a cascade and pool. The trail continues a few hundred feet to the top ledge of Waipo'o Falls, falling 800 feet into the canyon. *Be Aware:* You don't get a good look at the falls. Check it out from across the canyon at Polihale Picnic Area, TH61.

To Kumuwela Lookout, the trail crosses Koke'e Stream at the falls and then goes up gradually along a grassy slope. You contour to your left across the head of the canyon, dipping in and out. About 1.75 miles from the falls, you reach Kumuwela Lookout. You can see all the way down Waimea Canyon to the ocean, almost an entire cross section of the island. To your left is Po'omau Canyon, which wyes off Waimea Canyon to the northwest and abuts Alakai Swamp. *Be Aware:* Don't try to cross the top of the falls if the water is at all running swiftly. *More Stuff:* From Kumuwela Lookout you can continue about 2.5 miles back to the road near Koke'e Museum, a shorter route if you have someone to do the car shuttle.

BIKE: Mountain bikers can park at the trailhead and take off down **Halemanu Road**. By veering left at the first trailhead sign .75-mile in, and then veering left again after less than .5-mile, you can connect with **Faye Road**. Faye Road leads to Koke'e Park headquarters. Doing this involves escorting the wheels over a short trail that connects the Halemanu Road with Faye Road. You can also ride a spur off Halemanu Road by veering right after the trailhead sign. This spur takes you to the junction with the Black Pipe Trail, which can be ridden in most sections, but be sure to dismount for hikers. To explore this area, you may wish to buy a map at the park headquarters, if you care to know where you are. On the other hand, as long as you stay on rideable roads and avoid trails, the region is small enough so that you will be able to ride yourself out of being lost or disoriented. Halemanu and Koke'e are very good biking areas, with copious trees and wildlife, and roads that dip and turn without monotony.

64. MAKAHA RIDGE ROAD HIKE, BIKE

WHAT'S BEST: See a Napali ridge the easy way.
PARKING: Head up Waimea Canyon on Hwy. 550. Pass mm. 13/550 and Pu'u Hinahina Lookout, and turn makai on paved Makaha Rd., almost to mm. 14/550. Go about 3 mi. on Makaha Rd. and look for a road on left.

HIKE: Makaha Arboretum (3 mi.)

To **Makaha Arboretum**, which has sugi pine trees mixed among a number of native and introduced species, look for Pine Forest Drive on your left as you are making a long, straight descent to the Makaha Ridge. Pine Forest Drive loops back out to Makaha Road about a mile farther down, and the trail to the arboretum spurs off about midway along it—you can also walk in on the second road.

The pine forest here, not tropical at all in its appearance, underscores that climates exist for virtually every growing thing on the Garden Isle. After walking in about .5-mile on Pine Forest Drive, take the road as it drops away from the ridge and then skirts seaward along the rim of Kauhao Valley. A mile after leaving Pine Forest Road, you come to a picnic area. Makaha Ridge isn't always a great lunch spot—during Hurricane Iniki in 1992, winds reached 227 mph, the most powerful ever recorded in Hawai'i.

BIKE: Beginning at the highway, the 4-mile **Makaha Ridge Road** is an easy roll in for cyclists, although you're looking at a 1,500-foot pump on the return leg. Cheaters can have someone drive down and pick them up. The paved road, which does have some flat dips along the way down, ends at a military guard gate, tantalizing close to the ridge's viewpoint. But you can backtrack a short distance up from the gate, jump up on the road's shoulder, and get a view of Makaha Valley, out to sea, and across toward Miloli'i Ridge. A side pedal to **Makaha Arboretum**, as per the hiking description above, is also a pleasant excursion for mountain bikers.

65. MILOLI'I RIDGE HIKE, BIKE

WHAT'S BEST: A long ride or hike to land's end on a little traveled Napali ridge.
PARKING: Take Hwy. 50 to Waimea and turn mauka toward Waimea Canyon on Hwy. 550. Go almost to mm. 14/550 and turn makai on paved Makaha Ridge Rd. Go .3-mi. on Makaha Ridge Rd. and park off road on right at Miloli'i Rd.

HIKE: Miloli'i Ridge (11 mi.)

Miloli'i Ridge road contours parallel to the highway for the first 1.25 miles, twisting through moist forest. It then drops and hooks seaward, beginning the first of its 1,800-feet of descent over a 5.5-mile run. After 2.5 miles—amid a mature koa forest in the Napali-Kona Forest Reserve—you come to a picnic shelter. The shelter is set on a grassy flat with tree-filtered views of Makaha Ridge and Nualolo.

From the picnic area, the road becomes a wide trail, doing the most of its drop over the last 3 miles. You descend an eroded cut-bank, and then the trail goes up and over two knobs that lie along the ridge. During the last 1.5 miles you descend more gradually, through a fresh-scented pine forest. Avoid spur trails and keep right as the trail keeps dropping. Finally, the road ends at a grass patch amid pine trees looking 1,600-plus feet down to Miloli'i Beach, where remnants of a heiau tell of the people who once lived there. Across the way is Nualolo Ridge. From the grass patch, you can walk up the eroded rise to your left, which leads out onto the ridge, with ultra views everywhere. Look for goats scampering about. *Be Aware:* Stay away from crumbling slopes.

BIKE: **Miloli'i Ridge** should be attempted by fit, experienced cyclists. Although not inherently dangerous—beyond the usual ruts, roots, slick mud and road debris—the road is a workout, with several steep segments. Less experienced mountain bikers might consider a hike 'n' bike: Ride to the picnic area, about 2.5 miles in, and walk the rest of the distance.

66.   NUALOLO TRAIL   HIKE

WHAT'S BEST: Hike through the forests of Koke'e and break out to a narrow bench high above the Napali coast.
PARKING: Take Hwy. 50 to Waimea and turn mauka toward Waimea Canyon on Hwy. 550. Pass mm. 15/550 and look for trailhead sign on left, just before entering Kokee State Park headquarters.

HIKE: Nualolo Trail hikes: Kuia Natural Area (.4-mi.); Napali Kona Forest Reserve (5.5 mi.); Nualolo Cliff Trail jct. (7 mi.); Lolo Vista Point (7.5 mi.)

The **Nualolo Trail** descends about 1,500 feet to a precipitous terminus at Lolo Vista Point. Prepare for a challenging day hike with few trail companions, as more hikers are drawn to other trailheads in the region, in spite of Nualolo's considerable charms. *More Stuff:* The beginning of the hike is near a short nature loop next to the Koke'e headquarters that will be of interest to strollers and bird watchers.

From the trailhead, you head up steeply for the first .25-mile, entering the **Kuia Natural Area Reserve**. From the area reserve you drop gradually but steadily through forest with the occasional clearing. Birds love it here. The descent continues, as forests give way to open areas and the surround becomes noticeably drier. The trail swerves, making a left bend and then back to the right again as you descend a broad ridge top. At this point, almost 3 miles from the trailhead, you enter the **Napali-Kona Forest Reserve**, where the relief is steeper to either side of the trail and your route continues straight out the bench.

The trail goes seriously down, coming to the **Nualolo Cliff Trail junction**. Most hikers to Lolo Point will also want to walk out a distance on the Nualolo Cliff Trail to scope the valley and blue-water view, before doubling back to resume the hike. The cliff trail double-back can also be an option to going all the way to Lolo Point. Continuing on the Nualolo Trail from the junction, you'll soon come to a fork in the trail; the left fork is a spur trail, so keep right. The trail drops down an eroded slope and onto a bench above the Nualolo Valley, on your right. You follow the valley rim to a viewpoint with a railing, marked by the USGS as Lolo No. 2. The rugged beach where Nualolo Valley meets the Pacific is Napali Coast State Park, 2,200 feet down and accessible only by boat. *Be Aware:* The earth is crumbly on the valley rim. Stay behind the rail and don't venture near the edge.

More Stuff: The Nualolo Cliff Trail crosses around the rim of Nualolo Valley for 2 miles and connects with the Awa'awapuhi Trail, TH67. The Nualolo Cliff Trail is not for acrophobics, and it is often in poor condition due to erosion. A car-shuttle hike between Nualolo and Awa'awapuhi trails is about 8.5 miles. If you plan this, inquire locally about the condition of the adjoining trail and prepare for a full-on trek.

67. KOKE'E STATE PARK   HIKE, BIKE

> **WHAT'S BEST:** Discover the least-known face of Kaua'i, hidden in a birdland forest of countless varieties of trees, vines and flowering shrubs. Repeat hikers and cyclists flock to these forests.
>
> **PARKING:** Head toward Waimea Canyon on Hwy. 550. Go past mm. 15/550 and keep right at sign to Koke'e Museum and park headquarters. Continue on Hwy. 550 .1-mi. and turn right on Kumuwela Rd., which is marked with a sign to Camp Sloggett. Drive almost .5-mi. to first turnoff to the right and park. Kumuwela is a four-wheel road, which is usually okay for passenger cars at least for the first .5-mile; if you choose to park at the highway, add road mileage to hiking distances.

Notes: The descriptions below are adequate for hiking; but, if you plan on hiking this area extensively, stop by the museum and pick up an inexpensive park map. Plan on spending some time at the Koke'e Museum which serves as an interpretive center, gift shop, gallery and bookstore. Then wade through the roosters to the Koke'e Lodge next door for a bowl of their hearty homemade chili.

HIKE: Halemanu-Koke'e Trail (2.5 mi.); Kumuwela-Waininiua loop (2.5 mi.); Ditch Trail loop (4.5 mi.); Berry Flat loop (2.75 mi.); Alakai Swamp trail-Pihea loop (3.75 mi.)

For the **Halemanu-Koke'e Trail**, walk toward Camp Sloggett—on the first road to the right off Halemanu Road—for .1-mile and look for the trailhead on your right. This is a good choice for birdwatchers and would-be botanists, wishing a self-guided forest tour with easy hiking. Koa and ohia lehua trees dominate the forest. If you have a field guide, some plants to look for are mokihan, maile, pukiawe, halapepe, and ikiuki. Flitting among the branches, and providing the music, you may see i'iwi, apapane, elepio, and amakihi. In ancient times, exotic bird feathers were plucked here—the birds were captured and released.

After 1.2 miles, the trail comes to Halemanu Road, TH63. You can turn around here; or make a longer loop hike by turning right on Halemanu Road. If you choose the loop, follow Halemanu, keeping left, for about .2-mile to road's end, where you take an unnamed trail to the left. Stay on this trail for .2-mile to where you connect with Faye Road. Turn right on Faye, which joins Hwy. 550 in .5-mile, and from there it's another mile back to Koke'e and your car.

For the **Kumuwela-Waininiua loop**, walk to the next right turnoff, which is just past the Camp Sloggett road. Go down the road, crossing Koke'e Stream near several homes. About .25-mile after the stream crossing look for Waininiua trailhead on your left. The Waininiua Trail ascends gently but steadily for almost .5-mile, through koa trees and vines, before reaching Kumuwela Road. Turn right on Kumuwela. After a short distance a spur road leads to your left; this left turn goes to the Ditch Trail and you need to keep right. Continue on Kumuwela Road for 1.25 miles to where Kumuwela Trail comes in from the right, which is the route back to the car. You may wish to take a side-trip here: By continuing down Kumuwela Road for .5-mile to its end, you reach Kumuwela Lookout.

Turning right on Kumuwela Trail, you walk through dense woodlands, with a unfathomable number of trees, vines and shrubs competing in a profusion of greenery. This woodland area, at the beginning of the 1900s was trampled and eroded by feral pigs and goats, with cows thrown in for good measure. In the 1930s, the animals were curtailed and a number of plants introduced. The trail continues for nearly 1 mile, before reaching Kumuwela Road, at its end. Walk Kumuwela Road, past the Waininiua trailhead and back to your car.

For the **Ditch Trail loop**—recommended for experienced hikers only—start out by following the above description for the Kumuwela-Waininiua loop. The Ditch Trail is perhaps the most scenic among the interior Koke'e Trails. Inquire at the park museum or headquarters before taking this trail, however, as it sometimes deteriorates with bad weather. As you complete the Waininiua Trail section, and then turn right on Kumuwela Road, look for another road within .1-mile cutting back to your left. This is Waininiua Road, a .5-mile section that contours around and joins the Ditch Trail. Once at the Ditch Trail, turn left—the right-heading section is often not well-maintained. Turning left takes you both through woodlands and spots affording views of Po'omau Canyon. In about 1.5 miles of tough-walking terrain, the Ditch Trail joins with Mohihi Road. Go left on Mohihi Road, which becomes Kumuwela Road, and continue 1.75 miles back to your car.

The trailhead for **Berry Flat loop** is just under 1 mile in from Hwy. 550, at the first road that forks to your left. You can park at the Camp Sloggett Road, and walk to this trailhead, which adds .75-mile to the Berry Flat hike, making it about 3.5 miles roundtrip. Berry Flat, or Pu'u Kaohelo, is a forested nature trail, featuring koa, ohia, lehua, sugi pine and even a variety of redwood. Start up the road fork, which goes for .2-mile, and locate the trailhead on your left between two residences. The trail wiggles through a thicket of vines and ferns, under a shade canopy. At least two spur trails lead to nowhere; keep right as your contour in a circle for 2 miles, reaching Mohihi Road. Turn right on Mohihi and follow it back about .5-mile to your car.

For the **Alakai Swamp-Pihea loop**, you need to drive in 3.2 miles from Hwy. 550. Although the road in can be driven much of the way by passenger vehicles, it should be avoided in rainy conditions and is recommended for four-wheel drive. Walking in from Hwy. 550 will add 6 miles to hiking distances. *Note:* Alakai Swamp can also be accessed from TH69, Pu'uokila.

From the highway, take Kumuwela Road past the Camp Sloggett Road. About 1.25 miles in, the Mohihi Road comes in from the left; you are now on Mohihi Road. After .25-mile from this junction—about 1.5 miles in from the highway—a sign for four-wheel drive vehicles lets you know the road gets worse from here. From that sign, it's another 1.5 miles to a sign indicating the Alakai Forest Reserve, where you will see a picnic shelter. Check slipperiness of the road before driving in.

From the picnic shelter, walk up a side road about .25-mile to the Alakai Swamp trailhead. The trail from here to the Pihea Trail junction has been greatly improved by sections of boardwalk. You follow a utility road put in during the installation of a phone line in World War II, through a swampy bog, and meet the Pihea Trail after about 1.25 miles. The junction gives you three choices: Your choice is to double back sharply to your right, south on the Pihea Trail as it follows Kawaikoi Stream back to Mohihi Road. Continuing straight at the junction takes you up Pihea Trail as it comes down from the Pu'uokila overlook. Turning right at the junction is a continuation of the Alakai Swamp Trail. Some hikers may wish to continue a distance into the Alakai Swamp on the boardwalk. The Alakai Swamp is what remains of the volcanic caldera that formed Kaua'i.

Alakaʻi Swamp boardwalk

On your return leg, coming south on Pihea Trail down Kawaikoi Stream, you go down a series of switchbacks and come to Kawaikoi Stream. A trail here fords the stream and connects with another trail, the Kawaikoi Stream Trail. Both the Pihea Trail and Kawaikoi Trail head downstream, on opposite banks, .75-mile back to Mohihi Road—take your pick. Once at Mohihi, turn right and walk less than .5-mile back to the swamp picnic shelter. *More Stuff:* Mohihi Road continues for several more miles to Camp 10, with access to Po'omau Canyon Lookout Trail, Kohua Ridge Trail and Mohihi-Waialae Trail. Access to these trails should be in four-wheel drive vehicles. *Be Aware:* For all Koke'e trails bring rain gear and water. Keep your bearings and backtrack if you are unsure of your location.

BIKE: As you may gather from the hiking descriptions, the **Koke'e trails** lend themselves to exploration on a mountain bike. **Kumuwela** and **Mohihi Camp roads**, about 17 miles if you rode them all, are perhaps best seen from the seat of a mountain bike. Many will consider this area more interesting riding than hiking. A mountain bike solves the dilemma of whether to take a rental car off-highway, which is a violation of most rental agreements. Cyclists might consider a bike-and-hike option: The Ditch Trail is a particularly good one, as is the Alakai Swamp Trail. Also recommended for mountain bikers is to ride in about 4.5 miles on Mohihi Camp Road and take the walk to **Po'omau Canyon Lookout**, which is just after the road across Waiakoali Stream. The .5-mile walk takes you over a footbridge, passing Norfolk and sugi pines, to a viewpoint at the head of Po'omau Canyon. You look down to where this canyon joins Waimea Canyon. **Camp 10** is about 6 miles in on Mohihi Road, a slippery ride with stream crossings and a few roots to contend with. You'll pass through a grove of sugi pine, or Japanese cedar, on the way.

68.   AWA'AWAPUHI   HIKE

WHAT'S BEST: This is one of Kaua'i's beauties. Hike through natural tropical gardens to an adrenaline-rush ridge, the jewel of the Napali.
PARKING: Head up Waimea Canyon on Hwy. 550. Pass Koke'e Museum. Park just after mm. 17/550 on left at signed trailhead.

HIKE: Awa'awapuhi (6.5 mi.); Kaluapuhi (2 mi.)

The **Awa'awapuhi Trail** is to tropical hiking what the Golden Gate is to bridges and the Eiffel is to towers: powerfully beautiful and unique. For this reason it gets more hikers than many other trails, but not so many as to feel crowded. The trail drops about 1,500 feet over its 3.25 mile course, meandering for most of its distance through abundant forest and then teetering across grassy spines to overlooks some 2,500 feet above the Napali Coast State Park. *Be Aware:* Prepare for rain and wind, and gear-up for a full-fledged day hike. Don't go beyond the railings at the overlooks.

You begin walking through a good example of native dry forest—although dry for Kaua'i is different from dry in, for example, Nevada. The trail is in the Napali-Kona

Forest Reserve, although the Awa'awapuhi Trail is managed as wilderness due to the rich number of native dryland plant species you see along the way during the last part of the hike. Many of these plants are identified trailside, and park officials have published a guide for the plants which may be available at the museum.

Just under 3 miles into the hike, the Nualolo Cliff Trail joins this trail from your left, which takes you 2 miles across the treacherous head of Nualolo Valley and joins the Nualolo Trail, TH66. You can use this route for an 8.5 mile loop back to your car at Awa'awapuhi, including 2 miles up the road. *Be Aware:* The Nualolo Cliff Trail is not always in the best shape. In-

Awa'awapuhi

quire locally as to its condition before making this loop. The Awa'awapuhi overlooks are less than .5-mile from the Nualolo junction, a breathtaking scamper to two different vantage points. You overlook the Nualolo and Awa'awapuhi valleys, down vertical green escarpments. These valley floors, accessible only by boat and then a scramble up from the shore, are part of the Napali Coast State Park. The remains of a heiau are to be found in Awa'awapuhi Valley, on your right, but not visible from this height. You might want to bring binoculars.

The **Kaluapuhi Trail** begins about .25-mile up Hwy. 550 from the Awa'awapuhi trailhead; look for a red-dirt path heading up on a curve in the road. A plum grove (kaluapuhi) once thrived in Kahuama'a Flat, but don't expect fruit, even in season, since the grove has succumbed to neglect and competition from grasses and berry vines. The one-mile Kaluapuhi Trail makes the most sense for someone walking up from Awa'awapuhi to the Kalalau Overlook, which is only .25-mile up the road from trail's end. *More Stuff:* The Honopu Valley trailhead was closed due to deterioration, even before Hurricane Iniki. But some trailblazers attempt this hike, allured by the "Valley of the Lost People." The so-called trailhead on the left near mm. 17.5, where the road makes a sweeping right bend, near the Kaluapuhi trailhead. Although some unoffical clearing has been done in places, getting lost is a risk. Maybe you'll get lucky and pick a time when some unoffical trail work has been done.

69.   PU'UOKILA   HIKE

> **WHAT'S BEST:** A tropicbird's view of Kalalau Valley, or a walk into a primordial swamp to the edge of the world. (!!!) The lookout view graces magazine covers throughout the world.
> **PARKING:** Head up Waimea Canyon on Hwy. 550. Go past Koke'e State Park and past Kalalau Lookout to end of road at Pu'uokila Lookout. *Note:* The last .75-mile of the road (from the Kalalau Lookout) may *still* be closed although the contract for repairs was scheduled for completion in 2006.

HIKE: Pihea Overlook (2 mi.); Alakai Swamp Trail (3.5 mi.); Kilohana Overlook (7.5 mi.)

At 4,280 feet, the **Pihea Overlook** is the highest point along the rim of the Kalalau Valley. The trail gives you hours of viewing on foot what tour helicopters see for a few seconds. Added to this view is a continuation hike across Alakai Swamp to Kilohana Overlook of Wainiha Valley—making this one of the most remarkable walks you can make anywhere. Starting at the viewpoint, you know you're in for a mud stomp, as a the ragged downslope at the beginning is indicative of the trail's worst parts for the first mile. A hiking pole is recommended. In some places, you'll need all four limbs to negotiate the trail—over sections of steps cut into hard-packed, greasy dirt—though it is not hazardous for the cautious hiker. The Pihea Overlook is on a hands-on spur trail beyond the junction with the Swamp Trail. From the Pihea Overlook, don't forget to turn your back on the ocean and take a survey inland of the Alakai Swamp, especially if you are headed that direction.

To **Kilohana Overlook**, look for a signed junction a mile in from trailhead parking—just after completing a difficult hands-and-feet staircase. You drop down away from the rim, on a trail which at first is muddy and steep. But after a short distance you hit the boardwalk and series of stairs and rails, which make the rest of the walk a relative breeze. After about .75-mile you reach the junction with the trails coming up from Mohihi Road; see TH67.

To the Kilohana Overlook from the junction, go left toward Alakai Swamp. You stairstep down, cross the stream and then lose the boardwalk for a stretch as you climb up from the drainage through dwarf fauna on the other side. At the top you pick up the board-walk again and march right through the 60-square-mile swamp—an open bog of ferns, grasses, shrubbery and dwarf trees spreading out at 4,000 feet above sea level. The caldera from Hawai'i's first eruption has evolved over millions of years to become the

Kalalau Valley from Pihea Trail

highest elevation swamp in the world. From edges of the swamp, including the ridge of Mount Waialeale, are the origins of all rivers and streams on the island.

The boardwalk ends at Kilohana, a small platform on the edge of the Wainiha Pali. From Kilohana you look down from 3,800-foot jungle cliffs rising above a river valley that runs from the north shore near Haena to near the middle of the island at Waialeale. If clouds are in your face, wait awhile since they are fickle and may well give you an opening, if you've been good. Wainiha Valley is a fissured green gorge similar in size to Waimea Canyon, but is rarely seen because it is privately held. See TH4. From the overlook you might hear the river far below. Hanalei Bay is in the center of a north shore view. *Be Aware:* Don't attempt to go beyond the overlook; there is no trail and the terrain is dangerous and impassible. Do not venture into the swamp. You'll be knee deep in mud and have a good chance of getting lost. When rain and fog come in, getting off the boardwalk can be a fatal mistake.

A BRIEF HISTORY OF KAUA'I

Captain James Cook, an Englishman, made landfall in January of 1778 at Waimea Bay, thus "discovering" the "Sandwich Islands." But the Polynesians discovered Kaua'i about 16 centuries before the English, perhaps as early as 100 AD. At that time the cradle of Western culture, Paris, was little more than an encampment on the Seine. The first Polynesians were from the Marquesas, an island group well below the equator, 2,400 miles to the southeast of Kaua'i and due south of California. What caused these Marquesans to take to the sea is not known, but their navigational skills remain a marvel of mythical proportions. The myth extends to the Americas, where some anthropologists suggest that early American peoples, those people known as the Anasazi, who pre-dated other tribal cultures in the Southwest, may have been of Polynesian descent.

The first Polynesians, perhaps coming in a series of migrations over the next several centuries, brought with them domestic animals, plants and seed stock to make a go of it in their new world. They became skilled stone workers, constructing many of the water ditches, agricultural terraces, fish ponds and heiaus—temples—that are in evidence today. Legend say these feats were accomplished by a mythical race of primitive engineers, tiny people, called the Menehunes.

The best guess now is that these Menehunes were actually the Marquesans, smaller in stature than the second wave of Polynesian settlers, who came from Tahiti as much as 1,000 years after the Marquesans. In the Tahitian language, the word for slave, or lower class worker is very close to today's "Menehune," giving credence to the theory that the Marquesans were subjugated and conquered by the Tahitians. The Marquesans who survived the Tahitian migration did so by retreating into river valleys, and, as recently as the late 1800s, the U.S. Census Bureau counted 65 "Menehunes" living in Wainiha Valley.

The Tahitian migrations are thought to have taken place in waves until the 1400s, perhaps including back-and-forth voyages on their double-hulled sailing canoes. Then, for reasons unclear, the migrations ceased and, like their predecessors, these Polynesian were on Kaua'i for good and without outside influence.

The second wave of Polynesians also brought with them domesticated animals, such as pigs, goats and dogs, as well as taro, breadfruit and other plants that were to sustain them over the next 400 years. Over the generations, the Hawaiians developed a way of life based on family communities sharing a self-sufficient plot of land, called an ahupua'a. The ahupua'a was usually a wedge-shaped plot, with an inland point encompassing a river or stream valley, and then fanning out over terraced agricultural lands to a seacoast.

From this ahupua'a, fruits, vegetables, livestock and sea foods—all that was needed to sustain the community—were cultivated by the members of the community, called the ohana. Today's aloha spirit has its roots in the ohana. Working together was a virtue among the Hawaiians, and all turned hands toward productivity. A person who was selfish and without friends did not survive in times of famine or natural calamity.

Hula Dancers

from a far away friend here the mid-Pacific

Angela H. Wright
Waimea Kauai

Aloha Nui
HAWAIIAN ISLANDS

Early Kauaians lived in harmony with their surround for centuries, developing a philosophy called the Huna. The Huna is an evolving belief system that includes both their spiritual views and the accumulation of practical knowledge. Many concepts of the Huna foreshadowed, or paralleled, concepts in Western schools of thought. The Huna—and the islanders' social fabric—was held in check by a system of rules—the kapu—governing behaviors among individuals as well as their interactions with their natural world. Kapu violations of the severest nature were dealt with by swift capital punishment.

The Kauaian culture was transmitted over the generations by the hula—a dance performed by men and women, accompanied by chants and percussion—which kept alive both history and mythology. This ancient dance is alive today. The hula supplanted textbooks, for the Hawaiians had no written word. The Hawaiian alphabet of 12 letters and the spelling of all words were developed by academics.

To the Kauaians, place names, which sound similar and comically run-together to the Western ear, are very precise and descriptive. Each place on this complicated island was described in terms of its attributes and relation with all other places. Each place was part of an ahupua'a, which sustained the ohana, and all this fit together to make Kaua'i.

Hawaiian culture not only survived, it also thrived, and by the time of Captain Cook's arrival in 1778, the population of Hawai'i was about 300,000. Cook, an accomplished navigator and captain, had been leading an exploration of the South Pacific for a dozen years, searching for the theoretical Southern Continent. Ironically, he had been sailing right over it—Oceania, the Polynesian civilization of islands cast about the sea. Giving up on the Southern Continent, Cook set sail northward, this time in search of the illusive Northwest Passage.

Cook was on the furthest edge of the known world when his ships, the *Discovery* and *Resolution*, raised three islands, Oahu, Kaua'i and Ni'ihau. The ships dropped anchor in Waimea, staying not much longer than a vacation—about three weeks—making cursory notes and provisioning before resuming their quest. An officer with Cook was William Bligh, who was to lose the *Bounty* to mutiny, ten years later.

A year later, Cook returned from North America, this time putting in at Kealakehua Bay on the Kona coast of the Big Island. He arrived during the Makahiki—a yearly time of celebration honoring the god of peace and fertility, Lono. His timely landing led local chiefs to proclaim that Cook himself was Lono. Cook's status as deity quickly wore thin, however, as his sea-weary men made increasingly greedy demands for women and food. After a few weeks, Cook and his men sailed from Kealakehua, but a storm damaged a ship's mast and they were forced to return.

Cook's return to Kona was as poorly timed as his arrival had been good. The Makahiki was over. While in harbor, local warriors stole one of Cook's cutters, a small boat. One thing led to another, a confrontation escalated. Cook was clubbed to death on the rocks of the bay, several Hawaiians were shot and Cook's ships skedaddled. Hawai'i was not visited by Western ships again for six years.

Cook's arrival was coincident with the emergence of King Kamehameha the Great, nephew of an ali'i on the Big Island. Kamehameha was an intelligent, large man—over six-foot-six and north of three hundred pounds—whose political skills were matched by those as a warrior. By 1795 Kamehameha I, as he was later called, had unified all the islands under his rule, except for the island of Kaua'i.

Attempts to conquer Kaua'i were thwarted twice—once by the fierce waters on the Kaua'i Channel that separates it from Oahu, and a second time when the invading force was depleted by an illness that had been brought by Europeans. Kauaian warriors kept lookout for the invading ships for a dozen years, but the assault did not happen. Kaua'i did not come under Kamehameha's rule until Kaua'i's last ali'i, Kaumuali'i, voluntarily signed a treaty in 1810. The treaty was due in part to both kings' recognition that outside forces, represented by both American and Russian trading ships, were a part of the near future and it behooved the Hawaiians to be a unified people.

Kamehameha the Great ruled until 1819, during a time when whaling ships and other vessels traded with the Hawaiians to replenish their ships' stocks. The word was out on these abundant islands, and spreading fast. Sandalwood trade also flourished during the early 1800s, when forests of this fragrant wood on Kaua'i were denuded.

Significantly, one year after Kamehameha's death, when his son, Liholiho or Kamehameha II, ascended the throne, the kapu system was abolished and the first New England Protestant missionaries arrived in Waimea. The onset of the missionaries left an American imprint on the islands, and dispelled any last hopes the Russians—who had built two forts on Kauaian soil—had of making Hawai'i a Russian territory.

Kamehameha's sons and grandsons, two of each, ruled the islands until 1872. During this time American influence came not just directly from the missionaries. The Gold Rush in California created a demand for Hawaiian sugar, meat and vegetables, and a decade later, the Civil War increased the demand for sugar, since the Union was cut off from Southern sugar supplies and had no other source to satisfy its sweet tooth. The development of the sugar industry—the first mill on Kaua'i was built in Koloa in 1835 and operated until the late 1990s—also brought in workers from China, Japan and the Philippines to meet the labor demand. On Kaua'i, since then, no ethnic majority has existed, and therefore no minority. The blending of different races sharing an island is also part of the Aloha spirit, compatible with the concept of the ohana.

Another influence stemming from the mid-nineteenth century evident today is land ownership. About 41 percent of Kaua'i's land is owned by six private corporations and families who trace their purchases back to the 1800s. Owning land was not a concept in Polynesian culture. Eliza Sinclair, an ancestor of today's Gay and Robinson Corporation, bought the island of Ni'ihau in 1864 for $10,000.

The end of the Hawaiian monarchy came in 1893, the last year of the reign of its first woman leader—Queen Liliuokalani. Part of the monarchy's downfall was due to the excesses and economic foibles of the two kings after Kamehameha IV, Queen Liliuokalani's predecessors. A power struggle between the queen and her rivals—during which Queen Liliuokalani was betrayed—ended in a bloodless revolution. In 1898, about five hundred years after the Tahitians took over from the Marquesans, the U.S. Congress annexed Hawai'i as a U.S. Territory. In 1900, Sanford B. Dole, a leader among plantation owners and industrialists and one of Queen Liliuokalani's adversaries, became Hawai'i's first governor.

Hawai'i's agriculture trade dominated development in the early 1900s, as more and more workers were brought in to meet demand. Most workers were from Japan, accounting for 40 percent of the island's population in 1930. U.S. Immigration put restrictions on Japanese immigration and workers from other Pacific locales were recruited. Tensions came to a head in 1941 when Pearl Harbor was attacked by Japanese planes. Midway Island, at the north of the Hawaiian Archipelago, became the strategic piece of real estate for American forces to defend.

In 1959, Hawai'i became America's fiftieth state, and thus the far north of Polynesia was linked with the way south of North America. Hawai'i is central to America's interests, both as a military force and an economic player with the Pacific Rim countries—the place where the Far East meets the West. In spite of this international context, visitors to Kaua'i will see that Hawaiian culture has endured. Hawai'i is the only state where the culture of its native peoples has retained such vitality, still the overriding influence on the island.

Driving Tours

Four drives featuring the island's scenic, cultural and historical points of interest, taking you on back roads as well as to major tourist attractions. The four tours together cover the whole island. Use the trailhead descriptions to explore more thoroughly the places mentioned in the tours.

Each tour can be driven from half-day to a day, but to see all the listed attractions takes well over a day—be selective. Some eateries and shops are mentioned in the text. Check *Resource Links* for other recommedned places along the way.

top left going clockwise:
Haena
Hanapepe taro
Waioli Mission House
Wailua Coast
Lihue Lutheran Church
Running Waters Beach

DRIVING TOUR ONE

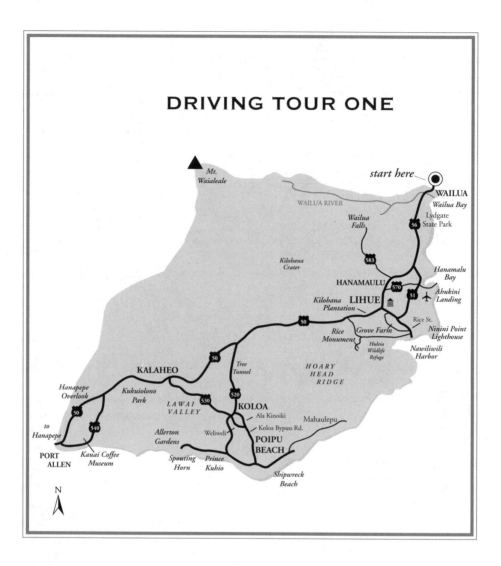

start here

WAILUA
Wailua Bay
Lydgate
State Park

Mt.
Waialeale

WAILUA RIVER

Wailua
Falls

56

583

Kilohana
Crater

Hanamalu
Bay

HANAMAULU

570

Ahukini
Landing

Kilohana
Plantation

LIHUE

51

Rice St.

50

Rice
Monument

Grove Farm

Ninini Point
Lighthouse

Huleia
Wildlife
Refuge

Nawiliwili
Harbor

KALAHEO

50

Tree
Tunnel

HOARY
HEAD
RIDGE

Hanapepe
Overlook

Kukuiolono
Park

530

520

KOLOA

Ala Kinoiki

Mahaulepu

LAWAI
VALLEY

50

to
Hanapepe

540

Weliweli

Koloa Bypass Rd.

Allerton
Gardens

POIPU
BEACH

PORT
ALLEN

Kauai Coffee
Museum

Spouting
Horn

Prince
Kuhio

Shipwreck
Beach

N

TOUR *one*

Waimea Falls, Hanamaulu Bay, Koloa Town, Poipu Beach, Allerton Garden, Spouting Horn, Kalaheo and Kaua'i Coffee plantation. A good tour for a rainy day or for those wishing to see Kaua'i's museums, historical buildings, and seaport.

START DRIVING TOWARD LIHUE ON HWY. 56. TURN RIGHT ON HWY. 583.

Wailua Falls is 4 miles up Hwy. 583, which is Ma'alo Road. Rainbows sometimes appear above the falls, especially in morning light when waters are brimming with storm runoff and mist roils from below. More often, twin cascades make the 80-foot plunge, which you may recognize as one of the shots for the opening of the television program, *Fantasy Island*. Just through the tall cane at the falls cul-de-sac are views of the Kilohana Crater and Waialeale. In ancient times, Kauaian chiefs would dive over the edge to prove their love and courage to chosen sweethearts. Upriver from the falls, is a secret cave—accessible only by diving under the stream and crawling through an underground entrance—where royal maidens were hidden in times of war.

BACKTRACK ON HWY. 583. TURN RIGHT ON HWY. 56.

Just after the turn, on the right you'll see Kapaia Stitchery, a must-stop for those interested in Hawaiian fabrics and quilts.

CONTINUE ON HWY. 56 AND TURN LEFT ON HWY. 570 WHICH IS AHUKINI ROAD. CONTINUE ON AHUKINI TOWARD AIRPORT, VEER LEFT AND TAKE AHUKINI ROAD 2 MILES TO END.

Ahukini Recreation Pier State Park, with its dilapidated labyrinth of a concrete pier, was the major port for the sugar industry until Nawiliwili Harbor was developed. Meaning "altar for many blessings," Ahukini today is where locals fish and talk story. The view inland is of Hanamaulu Bay, once the community of Portuguese cane workers. Above the bay, inland, is Kalepa Ridge, where Kauaian warriors kept a lookout for Kamehameha's invading army in the early 1800s, and U.S. servicemen kept a lookout for invading Japanese in the 1940s.

BACKTRACK ON AHUKINI ROAD AND TURN LEFT ON HWY. 51, KAPULE HWY. GO 1.25 MILE ON HWY. 51 AND TURN RIGHT ON RICE STREET. CONTINUE 1 MILE ON RICE STREET AND PARK NEAR UMI STREET.

Lihue was not much of a settlement until recent Kauaian history, the late 1830s, when Kamehameha III's high chief was ordered to plant cane. Prior to that date, the high chief resided in Waimea and the major routes from there to Wailua bypassed Lihue. The chief chose Lihue—meaning "gooseflesh" or "cold chill"—for its wetter clime.

Now the county seat, Lihue still has a number of buildings dating back to the 1800s—check out Kress Street which is two blocks down from Umi Street. If you're hungry, try the Barbecue Inn for local-style fare, or the Hanamura Saimin Hut. The Kaua'i Museum is the lava rock building on Rice Street one block up from Umi on Eiwa Street. Opened in 1960, the museum features displays on volcanoes,

Kauai Museum, Lihue

Polynesian migrations, missionaries and sugar plantations, among its wealth of material. A 30-minute video presentation gives you an aerial view of Kaua'i. Next door, the County Building, which stood alone when it was built in 1915, is a good place to take a breather under huge shade trees at the park in front of it.

CONTINUE UP RICE STREET PAST MUSEUM. TURN LEFT ON HALEKO ROAD. LOOK FOR LEFT-HAND TURN LANE, THE BLOCK BEFORE YOU GET TO THE STOP LIGHT.

Haleko Road takes you down a gully and through the business end of the Lihue Sugar Mill, founded in 1849 and in operation until 2000. Most of Lihue's shopping areas, including Kukui Grove Shopping Center, were cane fields well into the 1900s.

CONTINUE ON HALEKO ROAD TO NAWILIWILI ROAD, WHICH IS HWY. 58. TURN LEFT ON NAWILIWILI ROAD, HEADING DOWNHILL TOWARD HARBOR.

On the left, almost 1 mile down and just past Aheahe Street, is Grove Farm Homestead Museum. Tours of the George Wilcox estate—the home, cottages and gardens of the Grove Farm sugar plantation, founded in 1864—are by reservation only, although you can take a look at the grounds. To call Grove Farm Homestead, see *Resource Links*.

Grove Farm Homestead

CONTINUE ON NAWILIWILI ROAD FOR ABOUT .75-MILE AND VEER LEFT ON LALA ROAD.

Lala Road, which passes Kaua'i High School, is the back road down to Nawiliwili Harbor. Off this road a five-acre heiau once stood, built by the Menehunes, or first Marquesan settlers.

AT THE BOTTOM OF THE HILL, TURN LEFT, AND GO SHORT DISTANCE AND PARK AT ANCHOR COVE SHOPPING CENTER OR NAWILIWILI BEACH PARK.

Nawiliwili Harbor is the main port for Kaua'i, both for glitzy cruise ships and get-down cargo freighters. Navy ships also port here, often offering tours when they do. During World War II, on New Year's Eve 1941, the harbor was shelled 15 times by a Japanese submarine but sustained only slight damage, since most shells were duds.

The Kaua'i Marriott, a world-class resort sitting above Kalapaki Bay, offers entertainment and Hawaiiana displays, including Prince Kuhio's vintage outrigger, *The Princess*. You can walk or drive out Nawiliwili Jetty for a view of the harbor, looking across the jetty to the Kuki'i Point light sitting at the edge of the golf course, and out to the mouth of the bay to Ninini Point Lighthouse. The pick among the shops at Anchor Cove Shopping Center, is the Seven Seas Trading Post—a banquet for the senses. Sit under the lazy fans at their coffee bar and take in the tasetful array of artwork and gifts worthy of any exotic Pacific port.

CONTINUE, DRIVING AWAY FROM THE BAY ALONG THE HARBOR, ON WA'APA ROAD. TURN LEFT ON WILCOX ROAD, PASS MATSON. TURN LEFT AT THE BOAT HARBOR.

Nawiliwili Small Boat Harbor, a nook in the bay sitting below majestic Hoary Head Ridge, is an anchorage for cruising sailboats—offering an up-close look for those who

have fantasized about this life-style. You can take a short walk out the harbor's jetty to heighten the effect, and also check out the Huleia Stream, a popular kayaking spot.

BACKTRACK AND TURN LEFT AND THEN VEER LEFT ON HALEMALU ROAD.

In a short distance you'll come to the turnout on the left for the Alakoko, or Menehune, Fish Pond, a pool alongside the stream built by the Menehunes more than 1,000 years ago. The Menehunes, several thousand workers, are said to have passed the stones from hand-to-hand from 25 miles away in Makaweli. The turnout also affords a view of the Huleia National Wildlife Refuge. The refuge is closed to people,

Kauai Marriott

Kipu

but you can get a closer look by taking a side-trip down Haiku Road. CONTINUE ON HALEMALU ROAD FOR SEVERAL MILES, TURN LEFT ON KIPU ROAD AND FOLLOW TO END.

At the end of Kipu Road is the Rice Memorial, erected by Japanese workers after the plantation owner's death. The memorial, a good picnic spot, is at the start of Rice's Norfolk pine-lined drive, heading on private property to Hoary Head Ridge. On the way to the Rice Memorial, as the road crosses the creek on a one-lane bridge, you may wish to take a side-trip on a short but rough trail to Kipu Falls, a favorite swimming hole among locals. To get to the falls—a fifteen-foot high cascade filling a large pool—walk .25-mile down the narrow cane road that is on your left across from the bridge sign. Listen for the thunder of water and take a short spur trail on the right. *Note:* This is a place locals hang out; on weekends you might want to let them have it to themselves. Leave your car free of valuables. Heed private property signs.

BACKTRACK ON KIPU ROAD AND TURN LEFT AT JUNCTION WITH HALEMALU ROAD, DRIVING .5-MILE OUT TO HWY. 50. TURN LEFT ON HWY. 50, GO 3 MILES AND TURN LEFT TOWARD POIPU BEACH ON HWY. 520.

Highway 520 is known as the Tree Tunnel, named for the shaded corridor formed by the eucalyptus trees that border the road. The trees were damaged by direct blasts from hurricanes—Iwa in 1982, and Iniki in 1992—but have recovered.

CONTINUE TO KOLOA ON HWY. 520. TURN LEFT AT STOP SIGN

Koloa Town

AND THEN TURN RIGHT ON WELIWELI ROAD. PARK.

Koloa Snack Shop walk-up window

Koloa, which means "long cane," was the bustling center of Kauaʻi from when the first sugar mill was built here in 1835 to the later part of that century. An early mission was established here also, in 1835, by the Gulick family. Today, Koloa's town square and shops make it one of the best places on the island to walk around amid fragments of another time. Grab a cone and get lost in the small historical courtyard or stop at the Snack Shop outdoor counter for a local-style plate lunch of mahi-mahi, some Portugese soup, or a hot-off-the-grill teriburger.

CONTINUE ON WELIWELI ROAD.

Note a right turn for St. Raphael's Catholic Church, a short distance off the road. St. Raphael's is the oldest Catholic Church on Kauaʻi, built in 1854.

CONTINUE ON WELIWELI, FOLLOWING SIGNS FOR POIPU—TURN RIGHT ON ALA KINAIKI, THE BYPASS ROAD.

Hyatt Regency lagoon

Just as you near the bottom of the grade, look to your left for a glimpse of the crater, called Puʻu Wanawana, left by the island's last volcanic activity. Now only a few lava spires stick up from cacti and brush.

TURN LEFT AT STOP SIGN

On your right is the Hyatt Regency Kauaʻi, rated one of the world's best tropical resorts, and definitely worth a walk-through and perhaps a lunch or beverage at the Ilima Terrace restaurant. The resort is situated on Shipwreck Beach.

CONTINUE PAST HYATT ON WELIWELI ROAD. ROAD BECOMES DIRT, BUT GRADED. PASS ROAD TO STABLES, AND FOLLOW SIGNS TO KAWAILOA BAY. IF YOU DON'T

WANT TO DRIVE ON DIRT ROADS, OR WANT TO SPEND TIME ELSEWHERE, SKIP TO BACKTRACK BELOW.

Mahaulepu Beach at Kawailoa Bay was the site of a 13th century battle in which a Kauaian king out-

Koloa Sugar Mill

foxed an invading armada of ships led by a king from the Big Island, who had already subjugated the rest of Hawai'i. This was 400 years before Kamehameha the Great failed twice to invade the island with consolidated forces. Mahaulepu is a sunning beach for the endangered monk seal, the only other mammal besides humans and bats known to have made it ashore in Hawai'i. From Mahaulepu are rugged seascapes and a view of the other side of Hoary Head Ridge—which you drive past on Kipu Road.

For a side-trip from the gated entrance to Kawailoa Bay, go straight on the cane road to the Koloa Mill, on the site of the original mill of 1835. Sugar production ceased in the late 1990s, and tropical foliage is already creeping up the sprawling structure.

Mahaulepu

BACKTRACK TO THE HYATT. CONTINUE TO STOP SIGN ON WELIWELI ROAD AND TURN LEFT ON PE'E ROAD. PE'E ROAD CONNECTS WITH HO'ONE ROAD.

Dozing Monk Seal, Longhouse Beach

Pe'e Road takes you over a bluff, through beachside condos and homes and down to Brennecke's Beach, a popular surfing spot. Next to Brennecke's—past the burger-and-beer joint of the same name—is Poipu Beach County Park. You can walk several sandy coves of Poipu, a sunny beach fronted by resorts and timeshares. Bring along your snorkeling gear.

CONTINUE ON HOʻONE ROAD AND TURN RIGHT AT BEACH PARK ON HOʻOWILI ROAD. THEN TURN LEFT AT STOP SIGN ON POIPU ROAD.

Poipu Beach

Poipu Road bypasses the resorts. To get another look at Poipu on its other end, you can turn in, left, toward the Sheraton on Kapili Road. Kapili Road quickly joins Hoʻonani Road, at the Sheraton. Also worth seeing are the Moir Gardens at the Outrigger Kiahuna Plantation across from the Sheraton. Going away from the Sheraton on Hoʻonani—or to your right as you come down—in about .5-mile you come to Koloa Landing at Whalers Cove. The landing isn't much to look at today, except when you consider that this little cove was in the glory, gory days of whaling the third most-used port in Hawaiʻi, behind only Honolulu and Lahaina on Maui.

CONTINUE ON POIPU ROAD, TURN LEFT TOWARD SPOUTING HORN ON LAWAI ROAD.

In less than a mile on Lawai Road, you come to Prince Kuhio Park, with its monument marking the 1871 birthplace of the prince who was the Territory of Hawaiʻi's congressional delegate until 1922. The park features picnic areas, as well as remains of a home site and heiau.

McBryde Garden

Not far beyond Kuhio Park, on your right, is the visitors center for the National Tropical Botanical Garden. At the center are a gift shop and interpretive displays, and also a self-guided walk of the center's gardens. The center is also where you sign up for tours of Allerton Garden and McBryde Garden. The nearby gardens, once the favorite of Queen Emma, wife of Kamehameha IV, are now devoted to horticultural research and saving tropical plants.

Across the street from the visitors center is Spouting Horn, where wave-pressurized

Allerton Gardens

sea foam shoots geyser-like into the air from a hole in the lava reef. The gushing white water is accompanied by the plaintive groan of air escaping from a vent in the reef.

BACKTRACK ON LAWAI ROAD, TURN LEFT ON POIPU ROAD, OR HWY. 520 AND CONTINUE TO KOLOA. AT KOLOA TURN LEFT ON HWY 530, WHICH IS KOLOA ROAD.

Koloa Road takes you up through pastoral Lawai Valley, flanking the grounds of the tropical gardens. Near Highway 50, look for a shrimp rendering factory down to the left on Lauoho Road, which was the old pineapple cannery. This area is also prime for roadside fruit stands. On the right at Highway 50 is Hawaiian Trading Post, a longtime souvenir shop known for its large collection of museum-quality Ni'ihau shell necklaces.

TURN LEFT ON HIGHWAY 50.

Immediatley on your left is Wawae Road, entrance to the 88 Holy Places of Kobo Daishi, a revered Buddhist shrine. Drive in and park at a gate for the Lawai International Center. The shrines are just beyond the gate, to your right. Each minature shrine is named for a Buddhist saint, and under each are sacred sands brought from the original 88 Holy Places in Japan, which date back a thousand years. The number 88 signifies the 88 sins committed by man, and it is believed that pilgrims worshiping here will be released from the sins. Might as well give it a try. Just past the shrines is another spiritual place. Heads up and turn right near mm. 11/50 at Anuhea Place.

Drive in up the hill to see the low-tech factory that cooks Kukui jams, made from guava and other tropical fruits. Inside (tours are unofficial, so ask someone) is the sacred spot where Jimmy the Jar Man has tightened lids for 25 years. This is not a tourist stop, but it is *tres* Kaua'i.

88 Holy Places of Kobo Daishi

CONTINUE ON HIGHWAY 50, 2 MILES TO KALAHEO. TURN

LEFT AT LIGHT ON **PAPALINA ROAD. CONTINUE** ON **PAPALINA 1 MILE AND TURN RIGHT** ON **PU'U ROAD AND ENTER KUKUIOLONO PARK.**

From the pavilion on the large knoll in Kukuiolono Park is a commanding view of the south and west coasts, as well as of Ni'ihau offshore and the Lawai Valley sweeping below. On the grounds are small Japanese and Hawaiian gardens, as well as a collection of stones carved on by the Menehunes. Kukuiolono—which means "Lono's light," after the god of peace and fertility—was once the site of several heiaus and later the estate of sugar magnate Walter McBryde. McBryde, who is buried here, beautified the grounds in honor of his mother.

BACKTRACK TO **HWY. 50. TURN LEFT** ON **HWY. 50. PASS THROUGH KALAHEO. CONTINUE** ON **HWY. 50,** PASSING THE JUNCTION WITH **HWY. 540,** FOR **2 MILES. STOP** AT **HANAPEPE OVERLOOK.**

Hanapepe Overlook is a preview for the beginning of Tour Four. From the rim of the canyon is a view of the lush river bottom hemmed by red-and-green cliffs. A number of crops have been cultivated in Hanapepe Valley, most recently seed corn which has taken over from sugar cane. The acreage across the highway from the overlook, now a coffee orchard, has a history of its own. In 1824, the last battle on Kaua'i took place here, a failed revolt led by Prince Humehume, the son of Kaua'i's last king—or ali'i. Prince Humehume would not accept his father's treaty with Kamehameha's forces.

CONTINUE DOWN **HWY. 50. TURN LEFT** BEFORE **PORT ALLEN** ON **HWY. 540,** WHICH IS **HALEWILI ROAD. CONTINUE 1.5** MILES ON **HWY. 540** TO **KAUA'I COFFEE MUSEUM** ON RIGHT.

Kukuilono Park entrance, Hanapepe

In addition to offering a free sample of the local brew, Kaua'i Coffee Visitors Center and Museum exhibits plantation artifacts and shows a video detailing coffee production from the tree to the mug. In recent years, McBryde sugar cane fields have been converted to the beans, and Kaua'i now surpasses Kona as the largest coffee grower among the islands. A few sips here and you'll be perky for the rest of the day.

CONTINUE UP HWY. 540 BACK TOWARD HWY. 50 AT KALAHEO.

To your right as you head up Highway 540 is Numila, or "New Mill," with its row of classic sugar shacks. On the coast below Numila, which is private property, are two ancient fishing shrines and Nomilu Pond, a crater filled with brackish green seawater, where the fire goddess Pele is said to have made her last attempt to make a home on Kaua'i before leaving to create mischief on the Big Island. Some say that when eruptions occur on the Big Island, the waters of Nomilu Pond turn warm and sulfur yellow.

TURN RIGHT AT HWY. 50, HEADING BACK TOWARD START OF TOUR.

Just after passing Kipu Road, look on the right for Kaua'i Nursery & Landscaping. Though set up to service landscapers, the nursery's many acres include a huge covered area (great rainy day stop) that is one of Kaua'i's best places to commune with thousands of exotic and native plants and trees. Take your own free botanical tour. The nursery is certified to ship orchids—you won't beat the price.

A little farther on the highway—after passing the community college —you may wish to check out Kilohana Plantation Estate. Built in the 1930s, Kilohana is a 16,000-square-foot Tudor mansion, once home to the island's prominent Wilcox family. Wagon tours are available around the estate's 35 acres of manicured gardens and cane fields. Inside is a restaurant, center for crafts and history exhibits.

Beyond the Kukui Grove Center, on Highway 50—turn left on Ho'omana Road—is Lihue Lutheran Church which was chartered in 1881 by Pastor Hans Isenberg. Plantation houses line the road on the way to the church.

Kilohana Plantation garden

DRIVING TOUR TWO

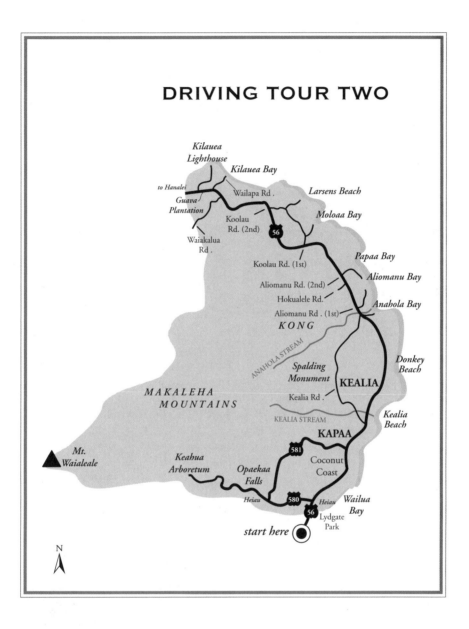

Kilauea
Lighthouse

Kilauea Bay

to Hanalei

Wailapa Rd .

Larsens Beach

Guava
Plantation

Koolau
Rd. (2nd)

56

Moloaa Bay

Waiakalua
Rd .

Koolau Rd. (1st)

Papaa Bay

Aliomanu Rd. (2nd)

Aliomanu Bay

Hokualele Rd .

Aliomanu Rd . (1st)

Anahola Bay

KONG

ANAHOLA STREAM

Spalding
Monument

Donkey
Beach

KEALIA

MAKALEHA
MOUNTAINS

Kealia Rd .

KEALIA STREAM

Kealia
Beach

KAPAA

Mt.
Waialeale

Keahua
Arboretum

581

Opaekaa
Falls

Coconut
Coast

Heiau

580

Heiau

Wailua
Bay

56

Lydgate
Park

start here

N

TOUR  Two

Heiaus of Wailua Bay, Opaeka'a Falls, Keahua Arboretum, Kapa'a Town, Royal Coconut Coast, Sleeping Giant, Kong and Anahola Mountains, Larsens Beach, and Kilauea Lighthouse and Wildlife Refuge. A tour that blends scenery with shops, and beachcombing with resort beaches.

Fern Grotto cruise

START DRIVING TOWARD WAILUA ON HWY. 56. TURN RIGHT ON LEHO DRIVE, BEFORE REACHING WAILUA RIVER. FOLLOW SIGNS TO LYDGATE PARK.

The mouth of the Wailua River, at today's Lydgate Park, is the cradle of Hawaiian civilization, where the royal ali'i built the first of seven sacred heiaus that led from here inland, following the Wailua River up to its source at Mount Waialeale. At a site on the grassy slope up from the river mouth are the remains of Hikina'akala Heiau. Also here are ancient petroglyphs, seen on large black rocks between the heiau and the water. This area was also the site of Hauola City of Refuge, where miscreants and vanquished enemies could escape punishment for having violated the kapu—the system of rules that kept the Hawaiian way of life in check.

CONTINUE, TAKING LEHO ROAD OUT TO HWY. 56. TURN RIGHT ON HWY. 56, AND TURN LEFT IMMEDIATELY TOWARD SMITHS TROPICAL PARADISE.

Across Highway 56 from the resort is the largely intact, but hard-to-find, Malae Heiau. Smiths Tropical Paradise features hula shows and its own (excellent) tropical garden, and nearby are boat rides to Fern Grotto up the Wailua River. A unheralded feature of Smiths is the good view, at Wailua State Park Marina, of the docks, river and Sleeping Giant. Bring a picnic lunch and relax along the riverbank under the umbrella of a cocopalm.

BACKTRACK AND TURN LEFT ON HWY. 56, CROSS RIVER AND TURN

Smith's tropical peacock

Located here are Pohaku Hoʻoanau—Royal Birthstones—on which the afterbirth of royal babies were ceremoniously placed. The attributes of the animal which ate the afterbirth foretold the fortune of the child. This was also the site of the third heiau from the sea, Holoholoku Heiau, said to be used for human sacrifices. Across the street is another king's sacred site—the now-defunct Coco Palms Resort, where Elvis filmed *Blue Hawaii*. Elvis is still remembered for his kindness by aging former staff. The crew of *South Pacific* also stayed here. The Coco Palms will be remembered by many Kauaʻi visitors for

Coco Palms lagoon

its nightly torch-lighting ceremony, enacted to the sound of drum beats and an exotic narration. Native-clad performers ran along the resort's lagoon, lighting the way for an outrigger canoe that followed. The lagoon predates the resort, built for Queen Emma in the 1800s. Behind the resort is the Royal Coconut Grove, for which this area is also well-known. Plans to restore the Coco are in the works.

CONTINUE up Hwy. 580.

In less than 2 miles, look on the left for Poliahu Heiau, formerly the residence of kings—the aliʻi. The Bell Stone, a short walk down a nearby trail, was used to ring in a royal birth. Great views of the river are to be had from this heiau.

Opaekaʻa Falls

CONTINUE up Hwy. 580.

On the right not far from the heiau is Opaekaʻa Falls, only 40 feet in height, but with a thunderous flow, especially during storms. Just beyond the falls on the highway, a steep road veers to the left to Kamokila Village, a recreated folk village showing the ancient Hawaiian way of life. The village, a private concern, was used as a set for the movie *Outbreak*. For a real-deal respite, drive farther up the road to the Kauaʻi Hindu Monastery (turn left near mm. 4.5 on Kaholalele Road).

CONTINUE up Hwy. 580 for 5 miles, passing the junction with Hwy. 581, to END

Keahua Arboretum

OF ROAD AT KEAHUA ARBO-
RETUM. TO BYPASS THE ARBO-
RETUM, TURN RIGHT ON HWY.
581, AND SKIP PARAGRAPH
BELOW.

A spillway marks the end of the road for most rental car drivers, and to take a short walk around the Keahua Forestry Arboretum you may have to get your feet wet. If the water is low, drive across the spillway and park. The nearby University of Hawai'i station has set up an educational walk among native and exotic trees. The arboretum is also the taking-off point for a number of hikes, including one toward the Mount Waialeale basin.

BACKTRACK ON HWY. 580. TURN LEFT ON HWY. 581, WHICH IS KAMALU ROAD.

The wide, green valley above the sea was where royal families made their homes and cultivated crops. This stretch takes you along the mountain-side of the Sleeping Giant, so readily visible from Kapa'a and many places on the island. The Sleeping Giant is part of Nounou Forest Reserve, featuring a wide variety of species planted in the 1930s.

CONTINUE ON HWY. 581 AND TURN RIGHT ON OLOHENA ROAD, WHICH IS A CONTINUATION OF HWY. 581. CONTINUE ON OLOHENA TO KAPA'A. PARK BEFORE REACHING STOPLIGHT.

Funky Kapa'a Town is the capital of local-style living, a seamless blend of Kaua'i's ethnic groups in a beachside community that is part falling-down and part brand new. Kapa'a is conveniently located, but most people live here for the coral-and-coconut coast and the aloha spirit. Kapa'a was once the pineapple center of the island and fell on hard times when the industry subsided in the mid-1900s. Several beach parks border cottages along the coast, and the town's triangular "downtown" section. You'll discover a lot just poking around. Look for tiny Orchid Alley for an intricate

Kapa'a

floral encounter. Hemp kids hang around for the veggie stuff at Mermaids Cafe. To tour the town on two wheels, head for Kauai'i Cycle, a premier bike shop.

CONTINUE to Hwy. 56. TURN LEFT on Hwy. 56, and CONTINUE to Kealia.

In 1877, the hills around Kealia were planted in sugar cane by Captain James Makeʻe. The cane road along the coast from the popular surfer's and stroller's beach also leads to a pier, used when Kapaʻa's pineapple cannery was thriving. Just beyond the pier on the dirt road is Donkey Beach. The wild section of coastal land between Kealia and Anahola is now being converted to large-parcel real estate.

TURN LEFT on Kealia Road, across from main gate at Kealia Beach.

Keep to your right on Kealia Road. On the right you'll see Kealia Kountry Store. You can stop in for lunch in a pleasant surround, but the real treat are the owners, Joe Lopez and Lihue Kinimaka-Lopez. Their families go back to the Hawaiian aliʻi and pineapple plantation days. Next, the road climbs to the left and becomes unpaved, heading toward the two rows of tall

Joe and Lihue, Kealia Kountry Store

Norfolk pines at Spalding Monument. The stone edifice marks the former estate of Colonel Zephaniah Spalding, son-in-law of Makeʻe, who eventually sold most of the properties to Lihue Plantation.

TURN RIGHT at Spalding Monument.

Kong

This portion takes you on an up-close look of Kong, a.k.a. Kalalea, and sometimes mistakenly called Amu or Kikoo, the sharp peak in the Anahola Mountains, a.k.a., Kalalea Mountains or Makaleha Mountains—just plain Kong to most people. On top of Kong is a ruined heiau of three terraces. At the base of Kong was the Hole in the Mountain, which, legends told, was formed when a visiting king from the Big Island threw his spear clean through the ridge. After centuries as a landmark, the opening almost completely caved in during the late 1990s.

CONTINUE DOWN KEALIA ROAD TO HWY. 56. **TURN LEFT** ON HWY. 56 AND **TURN RIGHT** IMMEDIATELY ON ANAHOLA ROAD. CONTINUE .25-MILE ON ANAHOLA ROAD AND VEER LEFT AT BEACH PARK ON KAMANE ROAD.

The valley around Anahola was designated by the Land Act of 1895 as a settlement in which Hawaiians could acquire

Hongwanji Mission

lands on 999-year leases. The Act was augmented in 1956 by the Hawaiian Homelands project, which allowed Hawaiians to finance homes on formerly government-leased sugar cane fields. Anahola today is the locus for Hawaiian political leaders who seek reparations stemming from the annexation of Hawaii by the United States in 1898.

BACKTRACK TO HWY. 56 AND **TURN RIGHT**. CROSS OVER BRIDGE, PASSING STORE AND POST OFFICE AND **TURN RIGHT** ON ALIOMANU ROAD (FIRST). FOLLOW ALIOMANU DOWN TO THE RIVER MOUTH.

Anahola Bay, all of it a beach park, is split in two by the Anahola Stream—you can look across the bay to the other side of the park. Aliomanu Bay is to your left as you face the water. When you get back out to the highway, cross over to see the photogenic Hongwanji Mission. Some of *Jurassic Park* was filmed near here beneath jungled ramparts.

BACKTRACK TO HWY.56 AND **TURN RIGHT**. CONTINUE ON HWY. 56 TO JUST PAST MILE MARKER 14/56 AND **TURN LEFT** ON HOKUALELE ROAD.

This road, a dead end after less than one mile, gets you as close to Kong as you can get in a car. Along the way, you may see self-serve stands for gardenias and other sniffers.

BACKTRACK ON HOKUALELE ROAD TO HWY. 56 AND **TURN LEFT. CONTINUE** ON HWY. 56 AND **TURN RIGHT** ON KO'OLAU ROAD (FIRST), WHICH IS

Moloa'a Bay

PAST MILE MARKER 16/56. AFTER ABOUT 2 MILES ON KO'OLAU, TURN RIGHT ON MOLOA'A ROAD. FOLLOW MOLOA'A ABOUT 1 MILE DOWN TO BAY.

At the highway turnoff to Ko'olau Road is Moloa'a Sunrise Fruit Stand, where you can indulge in one of their ingeniously concocted smoothies while enjoying and open-air look at the mountains. Warning: One stop will lead to another, and so on. Beyond the fruit stand, the paved road takes you down a lush tropical valley to scenic Moloa'a Bay—made only slightly less so by a few houses that crowd the shore. Fans of *Gilligan's*

Moloa'a Sunrise Fruit Stand

Island will like to know the television program was shot here. Moloa'a, meaning "tangled roots," was the island's main region for producing tapa, the paperlike cloth made from mulberry bushes.

Larsen's Beach

BACKTRACK ON MOLOA'A ROAD AND TURN RIGHT ON KO'OLAU ROAD. CONTINUE ON KO'OLAU A LITTLE MORE THAN ONE MILE AND TURN SHARPLY RIGHT AT WHITE BEACH ACCESS POLE.

This road takes you one mile out to Larsens Beach, a pristine coral-reef beach perfect for strolling. You look down on the beach from the parking lot, an easy .25-mile walk. But don't forget to look seaward: whales and dolphins have been known to breach offshore, and seabirds, such as albatrosses and tropicbirds, might be winging about. You won't see any gulls; none live in Hawai'i.

BACKTRACK TO KO'OLAU ROAD, TURN RIGHT, AND CONTINUE TO HWY. 56. TURN RIGHT ON HWY. 56 AND CONTINUE TO MILE MARKER 21/56 AND TURN LEFT ON WAIAKALUA ROAD.

This one-mile dead-end road is part of Kilauea Farms. Many of the island's organic fruit and vegetable growers reside up this pastoral drive, and you may be able to make a juicy purchase along the way. Waiakalua Road gives you a look at the open, grassy upslopes along this part of Kaua'i.

BACKTRACK TO HWY. 56 AND TURN LEFT. CONTINUE ON HWY. 56 AND TURN RIGHT ON WAILAPA ROAD, WHICH IS BEFORE YOU GET TO MILE MARKER 22/56. GO ALMOST .5-MILE AND VEER LEFT, DOWN A DIRT ROAD THAT ENDS AFTER .5-MILE.

Na Aina Kai Botanical Gardens

Kilauea Bay has a large sandy beach and scenic stream, which borders the bluffs of the Kilauea Wildlife Refuge. Slippery Slide, of *South Pacific* fame, is upstream but unreachable from here—and on private property. At the end of Wailapa Road are the fanciful grounds of the Na Aina Kai botanical gardens—a must for green-thumbers and families with kids.

BACKTRACK OUT TO HWY. 56 AND TURN RIGHT. CONTINUE ON HWY. 56, PAST MILE MARKER 23/56, AND TURN LEFT ON KUAWA ROAD.

A short distance in on Kuawa Road is the Guava Kai Plantation, featuring a gift shop within the orchards where you can learn all about guavas—tennis ball-sized berries that have 4 times more vitamin C than oranges—and sample the fruity punch made from them. Also on the grounds is a short nature walk, displaying well-known trees and shrubs, a good place for a botanical primer course.

BACKTRACK TO HWY. 56 AND TURN LEFT. AFTER A SHORT DISTANCE ON HWY. 56 TURN RIGHT TOWARD KILAUEA LIGHTHOUSE ON KOLO ROAD.

Kilauea was shaken by the 1971 closure of the Kilauea Sugar Mill, but has since reinvented itself as a tourist stopover and bedroom community for both the north shore and Kapaʻa. Helping attract tourists is Christ Memorial Episcopal Church—located on Kolo Road as you make the left turn toward the lighthouse on Kilauea Road—a small edifice built of lava rock and featuring detailed stained-glass windows.

Just down Kolo from this church is St. Sylvester's Church, an octagonal building of lava rock, glass and wood, whose walls are adorned with frescoes by Jean Charlot.

TURN LEFT ON KILAUEA ROAD AND CONTINUE TWO MILES TO END, AT LIGHTHOUSE.

Christ Memorial Episcopal Church

On the way to the lighthouse, browsers will want to stop at Kong Lung, a classy gift store featuring island clothing, jewelry and ceramics. The shopping area also features a small art house cinema, natural foods grocery and a bakery cafe. In back, Island Soap & Candle Works is a particularly illuminating stop.

Mokuaeau Island

Kilauea Lighthouse is situated on a bluff that is the northern-most part of the populated Hawaiian Islands. It's within Kilauea Point National Wildlife Refuge. From the tip of the bluff you look down on tiny, wave-washed Mokuaeae Island, usually the resting spot for seabirds. Among the birds soaring and flitting about are Laysan albatrosses, the B-1 bombers of the bird world, able to fly thousands of miles over oceans; great frigatebirds, with wingspans of seven-to-eight feet; tropicbirds, commonly seen soaring the Napali Coast and Waimea Canyon; nene, or Hawaiian goose, the state bird; plovers; red-footed boobies; and wedge-tailed shearwaters, which nest around the visitor's center near the lighthouse. A small admission is charged.

The lighthouse was built in 1913, featuring a French-made, 12-foot high Fresnel lens, the tallest in the world. The lens was replaced by a light beacon in 1974, and four years later the lighthouse was placed on the National Register of Historic Places.

BACKTRACK ON HWY. 56 AND TURN LEFT, RETURNING TO WAILUA. *Note: Hwy. 56 at Kilauea is where Tour Two connects with Tour Three.*

A mile or two past Kapa'a is Kaua'i Village—on your right noted by the green Safeway and whale murals—more interesting than its strip mall exterior suggests. If

you're hungry, try the Asian mix at the Pacific Island Bistro, or the very organic Papaya's, where you can hang with the health food set. Next to Papaya's are two winners: On the right is the Kaua'i Children's Discovery Museum with an inventive gift shop, walk-through exhibits, and day-camp program. Kids dig it. On the left is the Kaua'i Heritage Center of Hawaiian Culture & Arts. Inside are examples of most all the ancient crafts, as well as some of the people who perform them. It's a treasure.

A little farther down the highway from the village on the left is the Coconut Marketplace. Surrounding an inside square (of mostly a concrete motif) are a number of places to find a Kauai souvenir for someone waiting back home or chill out with a creamy double-scooped Lappert's cone. The Marketplace also has free hula shows, where aloha-shirted onlookers are snagged to demonstrate their Polynesian wiggles. Art lovers will want to stop by at Ship Store Galleries, perhaps the island's most prestigious, featuring the work of Fred Tangalin, as well as a host of other local artists.

If leaving Wailua for Lihue, you'll want to keep a mauka eye peeled for Bambulei—it's before reaching the Coco Palms. You drive in a short distance and wind up decades into the past, inside a restored plantation house that is chockablock with vintage clothing, aloha wear, lamps, and antiques, all of it uniting to say, *Bambulei!* (C'mon, say it.) In the same jungled nook is Cafe Coco, an island-hip bistro where local musicians may arrive incognito to serenade the moonlight. The word is out on this once-a-wayside, but you can't keep a good thing secret for long.

Kapa'a footbridge, artist Fred Tangalin, hula at the Marketplace

DRIVING TOUR THREE

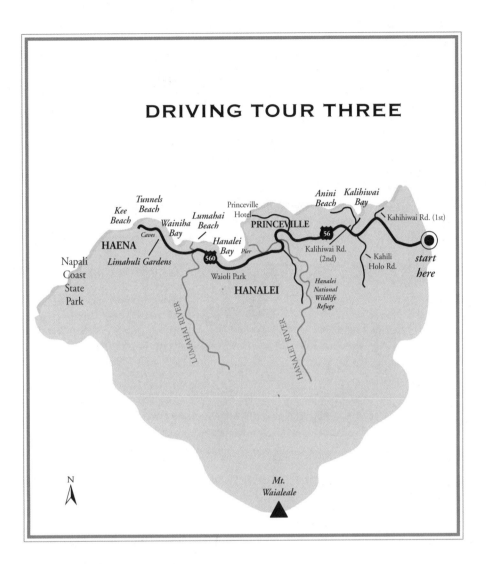

Kee Beach
Tunnels Beach
Wainiha Bay
Lumahai Beach
Princeville Hotel
Anini Beach
Kalihiwai Bay
Kahihiwai Rd. (1st)
Caves
HAENA
Limahuli Gardens
560
Hanalei Bay
Pier
PRINCEVILLE
56
Kalihiwai Rd. (2nd)
Kahili Holo Rd.
start here
Napali Coast State Park
Waioli Park
HANALEI
Hanalei National Wildlife Refuge
LUMAHAI RIVER
HANALEI RIVER
N
Mt. Waialeale

TOUR *Three*

Anini Beach, Kalihiwai Bay, Princeville, Hanalei Town and Wildlife Refuge, caves, hula temple, and all the beaches along the tropical paradise of the north coast. Start early, especially on sunny days, when road's end attracts many visitors.

START ON HWY. 56 IN KILAUEA AND PROCEED TOWARD HANALEI. AFTER MILE MARKER 24/56, TURN LEFT ON KAHILIHOLO ROAD.

Kahiliholo Road takes you a few miles up through the "Beverly Hills of Kaua'i," with lovely rolling gardens separating opulent estates, and some more modest homes. These uplands, a popular horseback riding area, give you a wide-open view of the Kalihiwai Ridge, source of many streams and rivulets that gather to form the Kalihiwai River.

BACKTRACK ON KAHILI-HOLO ROAD TO HWY. 56 AND TURN LEFT. CONTINUE ON HWY. 56, CROSSING BRIDGE, AND TURN RIGHT ON KALIHIWAI ROAD (SEC-OND), ON THE UPHILL PAST MILE MARKER 25/56. VEER RIGHT AT FIRST OPPORTU-NITY AND FOLLOW ROAD ABOUT 1 MILE DOWN TO END.

Kalihiwai Bay is mostly a locals' beach, for picnicking and surfing, both onshore and at the bay's point break. To access the beach park, across the river, you turn on Kalihiwai Road (first), which is just past Kilauea. Kalihiwai Bay was twice devastated by tidal waves, in 1946 and 1957, and now few homes are built near the water. This bay historically was a favorite spot for a hukilau—when people of the ohana would gather and haul in a huge fishing net, reaping a bounty of fish. The harvest was accompanied by song, and all pulled together on the command, "huki!" Hukilaus were common throughout Kaua'i; certain men could tell what fish were running just by viewing the waters from cliffside overlooks.

BACKTRACK ON THE ROAD. TURN RIGHT ON ANINI ROAD TO ANINI BEACH PARK.

Anini Beach, Kalihiwai Bay

Anini Beach

Along Anini Beach is the longest coral reef in Hawai'i. Windsurfers, snorkelers, campers and even polo players enjoy the pleasant park space that borders the two-mile beach. You can spot old-timers on Kaua'i if they call this place "Wanini Beach," its name before the "W" fell off a highway sign that no one bothered to fix.

BACKTRACK OUT TO HWY. 56 AND TURN RIGHT. CONTINUE PAST MILE MARKER 27/56 AND TURN RIGHT ON KA HAKU ROAD, THE MAIN ENTRANCE TO PRINCEVILLE MARKED BY LARGE FOUNTAIN. CONTINUE ON MAIN ROAD FOR TWO MILES TO PRINCEVILLE RESORT.

Both of Princeville's golf courses are championship quality, and the Princeville Resort, with its splashy view of Hanalei Bay, Wainiha Pali and the tip of Bali Hai, is rated among the world's top tropical resorts. Prior to becoming a manicured resort community, Princeville was a cattle ranch, the source of much of the island's beef. Before that, in 1853, the lands were owned by British Resident Minister R.C. Wyllie. Wyllie, who made his fortune in Scotland in 1845, came here to find a new career as King Kamehameha IV's foreign minister, working for 20 years to get Hawai'i recognized a sovereign nation. But Wyllie's personal dream was of a grand plantation on this bluff above Hanalei Bay to be named for Kamehameha's son, Albert—thus the name Princeville. Unfortunately, little Albert died at age four; Wyllie died three years later and the plantation went into debt and was auctioned off in 1867.

Prior to being Wyllie's plantation, the Princeville bluff was the site of Russian Fort Alexander. An interpretive kiosk to the right of the hotel marks the spot, and

Princeville Resort

Pu'u Poa Beach

provides an excellent viewpoint of Hanalei Bay and north coast. The Russians, under the leadership of Dr. Anton Schaffer, retreated here from Fort Elizabeth in Waimea after being banished by Kauaian chiefs. For several days they considered making a stand for the Russian Empire—Schaffer had proclaimed his country would claim Hawai'i at all cost—but they soon realized their predicament and set sail from the islands for good.

BACKTRACK to Hwy. 56 and TURN RIGHT. CONTINUE beyond the Princeville Shopping Center, TURN LEFT INTO the Hanalei overlook.

The valley, like all such valleys with streams or rivers, was an ahupua'a—a division of land that provided the entire needs of a community. From this viewpoint, you can easily imagine how these fertile lands could be cultivated. Taro is the prominent crop today, taking over from rice. Across the street, the shopping center is dedicated mainly to local commerce, but a few of the shops are worthy of a walk through, notably the whimsical Magic Dragon Toy & Art Supply, which is worth making the drive out here.

CONTINUE on Hwy. 56 and cross one-lane bridge over Hanalei River. TURN LEFT IMMEDIATELY after bridge and continue two miles on Ohiki Road. *Note: Hwy. 56 becomes Hwy. 560 after Princeville.*

Waterfowl and shorebirds streak over the taro fields as you drive though Hanalei National Wildlife Refuge. About a mile in on your right is the restored (perhaps unsigned) Haraguchi Rice Mill, a remnant of large-scale rice production that took place alongside the taro from 1912

Hanalei Wildlife Refuge

through the 1950s. During prohibition, bootleggers made a fiery spirit, called okolehao, from ti plants harvested in the hills above the mill.

BACKTRACK OUT TO HWY. 560 AND TURN LEFT. CONTINUE TO HANALEI TOWN.
Note: You may want to drive through to the end of the road and catch town on the rebound.

Mission School of Waioli Huiʻi Church

You could easily spend the day—some people spend years—wandering around Hanalei Town, with its long bay, beachside bungalows, historic buildings, and quirky shops. Hanalei Pier, at Black Pot Beach near the river mouth, was the link to civilization and commerce after it was built in 1912, and later became a set piece for a number of Hollywood movies.

Several churches draw visitors, including St. William's Church, a longhouse-style building with sliding doors as sides, and St. Thomas Episcopal Church, of Asian design. But the town's postcard is green-shingled Waioli Huiʻia Church. Near Waioli church is the Waioli Mission House, built in 1841. The mission was established several years earlier by Bostonians Abner and Lucy Wilcox.

Rising inland from the town are the ridges of Waioli Valley, called the "birthplace of rainbows." Numerous waterfalls appear in the dark green walls after rains. Much of Hanalei's walk-around shopping charm lies at the base of this valley, with the Hanalei Center set in the old elementary school. (Though don't overlook the places on the way into town, especially Ola's for art glass and fine woodworking, and Kayak Kauaʻi, which has lots of outdoor stuff, along with being ground-zero for north shore adventuring.) At the Center, the Hanalei Surf Company is town incarnate, with active staff buzzing to local tunes amid a breaking wave of surf wear and gear. Sand People carries made-on-Kauai products and island-themed ware,

Surfer swap meet, Hanalei Center

but don't spend all your clamshells before heading out back to Yellowfish Trading Company to see its esoteric Hawaiiana and collectibles. In the center of the center is Java Kai, where you can embrace a coffee beverage and vogue with the local hipsters. At Ching Young Village (across the street), you'll find good old Village Variety, crammed with cheap t-shirts, sarongs, and beach towels and Pedal 'n Paddle, the place to go prior to getting wet, muddy, or sandy.

One of Hanalei's ultra-charms is Ki Hoalu Slack Key Guitar—in the Hanalei Community Center—where Doug and Sandy McMaster give low-key concerts and talk story, usually on Friday and Sunday afternoons; see *Resource Links* for contact info. The red-hot tip (don't tell anyone) is that these true masters play each night at sunset on the beach at the Hanalei City Pavilion. Heaven = Slack Key + Hanalei Bay + Sunset. The McMasters are more than generous with their talent and their music can travel back with you on the two CD's they've produced and sell pre-performance.

CONTINUE ON HWY. 560.

Leaving Hanalei, you cross Waioli Stream and pass Waikoko Beach, which forms the far side of the bay. Then around the point is Lumahai Beach and River, after mile marker 5/560. Lumahai is best known for its treacherous combers, able to snatch a stroller from the shore, and for being where Mitzi Gaynor wanted to "wash that man right out of her hair," in *South Pacific*. Prior to that, in the mid-1800s, Lumahai gained a reputation of being a spot where robbers would waylay travelers.

CONTINUE ON HWY. 560.

Lumahai Valley

At mile marker 7/560 is Wainiha—the town, valley and river. Spanning the river are quaint, one-lane bridges. Much of the island's power is generated from the perpetual cascades deep up the Wainiha Valley. The Wainiha Pali—cliffs—rise nearly 4,000 feet from the river valley. They appear to be a ridge, but in actuality the other side of the pali is the Alakai Swamp, resting on a horizontal plane at the same elevation as the top.

The last of the Kaua'i's Menehune, 65 of them, lived in Wainiha, according to a late 19th century U.S. Census. Even prior to the Menehune, the valley, according to legend, was also home to tiny people, refugees from the Lost Continent of Mu. The Hawaiians would try to lure them from the jungle with traps set with tasty foods, but the Mu people were too swift, taking the food and fleeing in the night. Some Hawaiian families currently living in Wainiha trace their heritage back several hundred years.

CONTINUE ON HWY. 560.

Rounding the turn from Wainiha, past mile marker 8/560, you reach Haena Beach Park and Tunnels Beach, popular among campers and surfers, and also a premier snorkeling destination. From the beach are views of Bali Hai Ridge—cor-

Haena Beach

rectly called Makana or "Fire Cliff." In pre-missionary times, specially trained men would hurl flaming logs from the summit to the sea, creating a shower of sparks that Kauaians would come to see, in canoes and on foot, from all parts of the island. The fire fall was not only for entertainment, but also to honor the sacred hula temple that sits below the peak.

On your left just past the spillway on the road is Maniniholo Dry Cave, the end of a lava tube that extends several hundred yards under the cliff and finally, as a narrow opening, pokes out the top of the mountain. Legend tells that this cave was dug by Menehune, who used it to trap demigods who were stealing their fish. Beyond the dry cave, look to the mountains to spot Pohakuokane—the Rock of Kane—a large boulder sitting atop a rounded peak. It is said that when this rock falls, Kaua'i will sink beneath the sea. A sister rock, perched near the beach, was washed away in a tidal wave of 1946.

CONTINUE ON HWY. 560.

On your left past mile 9/560 is Limahuli Garden, a National Tropical Botanical Garden, and one of the few spots on the north shore where you can get into one of the lush valleys.

Haena Beach Park

Limahuli specializes in native plants, providing a historical as well as horticultural experience. The garden tour includes a booklet that alone is worth the price of admission.

On the left just beyond the garden entrance are Waikapalae Wet Cave and, a short hike up beyond the first cave, Waikanaloa Wet Cave. The volcano goddess Pele is said to have dug these caverns, in search of a fiery home for herself and her lover, Lohiau, but, alas, she came up wet, prompting her to flee Kauaʻi and head south through the island chain. In the 19th century, Hawaiian boys would make sport of climbing the walls of the cave and diving 30 feet into its chilling waters.

CONTINUE TO END OF HWY. 560 AT MILE MARKER 10/560.

Alula
Brighamia insignis

An endangered species native to Kauaʻi and Niʻihau presently being reintroduced into the protected wild habitat of Limahuli Garden

The end of the road is better known as the beginning of the Kalalau Trail, a rugged path along 11 miles of the roadless Napali Coast. You can see down the coast from about .5-mile on the difficult trail—or by walking a short distance to your right down Keʻe Beach. In the winter, huge waves explode against the buttresses that stick out to the sea. During calm conditions, during the summer and also frequently in the winter, Keʻe is an excellent snorkeling pool.

A short trail from Keʻe Beach leads to the Kauluolaka Heiau, Lohiau's hula temple. The sacred heiau, the

Approach to Hankapiai Beach, Kalalau Trail

Napali

passionate meeting place for Pele and her lover, Lohiau, is the only dancing platform in Hawai'i dating back to mythological times.

Among Hawaiians studying the ancient dance, this site was the equivalent of the most prestigious university. The best young pupils from Hawai'i came, camping nearby, and were taught the traditions, chants and dances of their ancient heritage. The graduation ceremony included a swim out the channel from Ke'e Beach, said to be guarded by a large shark. The hula temple is in use today—treat it like a church. Just below the dance platform are the remaining ramparts of another heiau, Kaulupaoa Heiau, which guarded the dance platform.

Kaulupaoa Heiau

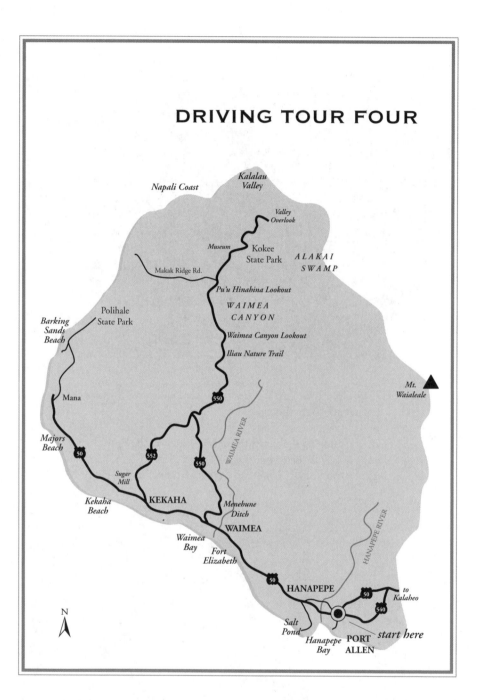

DRIVING TOUR FOUR

Napali Coast

Kalalau
Valley

Valley
Overlook

Museum

Kokee
State Park

*ALAKAI
SWAMP*

Makak Ridge Rd.

Pu'u Hinahina Lookout

*WAIMEA
CANYON*

Polihale
State Park

Barking
Sands
Beach

Waimea Canyon Lookout

Iliau Nature Trail

Mt.
Waialeale

Mana

550

WAIMEA RIVER

Majors
Beach

50

552

550

Sugar
Mill

Kekaha
Beach

KEKAHA

Menehune
Ditch

WAIMEA

Waimea
Bay

Fort
Elizabeth

HANAPEPE RIVER

50

HANAPEPE

50

to
Kalaheo

540

N

Salt
Pond

Hanapepe
Bay

**PORT
ALLEN**

start here

TOUR *four*

Port Allen, Hanapepe and Waimea towns, Waimea Canyon, Kokeʻe State Park, Kalalau Valley overlook, Kekaha Beach and Barking Sands Beach. Take the Waimea Canyon portion on a clear day.

START AT SECOND JUNCTION OF HWYS. 50 AND 540. TURN LEFT TOWARD PORT ALLEN AT MILE MARKER 16/50 ON WAIALO ROAD. CONTINUE .5-MILE DOWN TO DOCK AREA.

Port Allen, on Hanapepe Bay, is Kauaʻi's most active port for sportfishing, sightseeing and whale-watching excursions. Its breakwater and docks provide a glimpse of bustling harbor life, as does the small boat harbor down a road on the right from the larger dock. Napali Coast cruises, which used to begin in Hanalei, now depart from Port Allen. Some cruisers, like HoloHolo Charters, take you offshore of Niʻihau.

BACKTRACK OUT TO HWY. 50 AND TURN LEFT. AFTER A SHORT DISTANCE ON HWY. 50 VEER RIGHT TOWARD HANAPEPE ON HANAPEPE ROAD. PARK AFTER .5-MILE AT SWINGING BRIDGE.

Hanapepe, Kauaʻi's "biggest little town," is known for its bougainvillea and an eclectic assemblage of old-style buildings, some overgrown and some being converted into galleries and shops, all strewn along the banks of the Hanapepe River. You'll want to take a walk across the Swinging Bridge and poke into a gallery or two, including Kauaʻi Fine Arts, which is on your right as you enter town. Hanapepe has a history that befits its Wild West look: In 1924, 20 people died here in a riot between police and striking sugar cane workers. And just up the road is where Prince Humehume, son of Kauaʻi's last king, staged an unsuccessful revolt against the forces of Kamehameha the Great. If you want to get wild these days in Hanapepe, try Art Night (usually Fridays from sundown to maybe 9 p.m.) when the town is all prettied up. A hot dinner ticket is Hanapepe Cafe, which has its own gallery and sits besides one of the town's better art nooks, the Dawn M. Traina Gallery. For local-style eats, head for the Imu Hut, or the old standby, the Green Garden. At the Banana Patch Studio you can watch them make coloful ceramics, and at JJ Ohana you can get a bead on reasonably priced Niʻihau shell jewelry. Guys looking for a quick departure from all this need only to pop into Dr. Ding's Westside Surf Shop.

Hanapepe Town

CONTINUE THROUGH
HANAPEPE, CROSSING THE
RIVER ON ONE-LANE
BRIDGE AND REACHING
HWY. 50. TURN RIGHT ON
HWY. 50.

Salt Pond Beach Park

On the way to Waimea Town are three side trips. The first is immediately after Hanapepe on your left, the turnoff on Hwy. 543 to Salt Pond Beach Park. This is a good snorkeling and picnicking spot you might want to try on the return leg of the tour. The park includes historic salt ponds, dating back to the 1700s—they may look like puddles, but the salt was highly valued by seafaring vessels.

Gay & Robinson Plantation

At mm. 19/50, turn makai on Kaumakani Avenue and you'll be transported immediately to main street of a 19th century sugar mill town—a real one that leads to one of only two active sugar mills in the state of Hawaii. Although you can drive to see the giant Gay & Robinson Plantation facilities, plan on taking a tour if you have any time. You'll see how the plantation is able to compete against cheap world-market labor by using the wealth of island rain runoff, rich Kauaian sunshine, and ingeniously efficient methods. Their yield per acre is the highest in the world. The tour is not a tourist trot; they get you right in there with the workers.

The third side trip, off Highway 50 after mile marker 22/50, is Russian Fort Elizabeth Historical Park. Due to its location, the fort is a popular attraction, but you'll have to use your imagination to see a fort amid the remnants, dating from 1817. The Russians, along with the Americans, established a trading presence on Kaua'i during the early 1800s. But, not long after the fort was built, Kauaian chiefs decided to boot the Russians from the island, distrusting them and feeling the Yankees were the stronger ally.

CONTINUE ON HWY. 50 TO WAIMEA TOWN.

Along the weathered streets of Waimea Town are layers of the past that echo a diverse history. Captain James Cook made the first European landing here in 1778, and for nearly the next century, Waimea was the capital of Kaua'i—a favorite harbor and provisioning port for early whalers and traders. The red-dirt fields around town were well-suited for crops and livestock, in great demand by seafarers. The destructive sandalwood trade of the early 1800s was also centered here.

In the 1820s, the first missionaries landed in Waimea, not branching out to other parts of the island until 1835, and Waimea then was

Captain Cook Monument, Waimea

the major settlement for whites. In 1850, the town was named the port of entry for all foreign ships, on par with Honolulu. Japanese, Chinese and Portuguese grew rice and taro in surrounding fields, their presence evidenced by the churches tucked away on back streets. Today, efforts are underway to bring more visitors here, including plantation tours and the development of guest cottages. On the way out of town are the Waimea Plantation Cottages and the Waimea Sugar Museum. Long before any of this, Waimea was a principal settlement for the Menehunes, who built heiaus and an ambitious water-conveyance ditch, extending 25 miles up the canyon. You can drive one mile up Menehune Road to see a fragment of the ditch.

Kukui trail to Waimea Canyon

CONTINUE THROUGH WAIMEA TOWN ON HWY. 50 AND TURN RIGHT TOWARD WAIMEA CANYON ON HWY. 550, JUST AT THE EDGE OF TOWN.

Views of the canyon begin not long after starting up highway 550, and you could spend many days exploring the trails and viewpoints along the way to the top. On the other hand, for the first-time visitor to the "Grand Canyon of the Pacific," a drive to the top can deliver what seems like weeks' worth of experience in a few hours.

Waimea Canyon is an eroded gorge of the Alakai Swamp—the swamp itself is the transition of a 60-square-mile ancient caldera that was Hawai'i's origin and which lies at almost 4,000 foot elevation on the side of the canyon opposite the road. The canyon is about one-mile wide, ten-miles long, and 3,700-feet deep, with other canyons branching off it. Several developed lookouts adorn the road, part of Waimea Canyon State Park. The first, after mile marker 7/550, is the Kukui Trailhead, which features a short walk, Iliau Nature Loop. After mile marker 10/550 look for Waimea Canyon Lookout and after mile marker 13/550 look for Pu'u

Alakai Swamp

Hinahina Lookout. Note also, as you drive this stretch, on your left are a series of trails that head out onto ridges of the west Napali.

TURN LEFT ON MAKAHA RIDGE ROAD, JUST PAST PU'U HINAHINA LOOKOUT, BEFORE MILE MARKER 14/550.

This road takes you four miles out on Makaha Ridge, where Kaua'i's strongest winds were recorded during Hurricane Iniki—227 mph. Although a military installation prevents you from getting to the very end, you do get looks at steep valleys and ridges to either side on this lesser-known part of the Napali Coast.

BACKTRACK out to Hwy. 550 and
TURN LEFT. CONTINUE to Koke'e
State Park Museum.

Koke'e Museum

The boundary for Koke'e State Park is just
after Makaha Ridge Road, and where
Halemanu Valley Trailhead offers a series of
trails to canyon viewpoints. Koke'e Natural
History Museum, at the edge of the park's
spacious lawn and towering trees, is a
wealth of information about the natural and
cultural history of the area. No trip to the canyon should exclude stop here. Then wade
your way through the wild chickens to the Koke'e Lodge next door, for a restful lunch
and a browse of their giftstore. Short and long trails network the park. Some trails, east
of the park, are forested and others, the Nualolo and Awa'awapuhi west of the park,
lead out to spiny ridges far above the wild shores of Napali Coast State Park. Many
Kauaians have cabins in the Koke'e area, and church and community organizations
maintain camps along the many unpaved roads.

CONTINUE up Hwy. 550

Napali Coast

Two miles beyond Koke'e's
lawn area is Kalalau Lookout,
a viewpoint of the fabled valley, 4,000 feet below steeply
diving, rippling green walls. As
recently as the early 1900s, 500
Hawaiians lived in the valley.
Garden terraces rise above the
beach. Now only adventure-
some backpackers make the 11-
mile hike down the Kalalau
Trail, that begins at Ke'e Beach
on the north shore. Kalalau
means "the straying."

A mile beyond this first lookout is Pu'uokila Lookout, providing another don't-miss view
of the valley. (You may have to
walk this section if they *still*
haven't paved the potholes.)
Listen and watch for goats on
tangled perches of the valley's
bowl. The Pihea Trail begins at

Niʻihau shoreline

this overlook, providing not only a walk along the valley rim, but also entrance to the Alakai Swamp and, at the edge of the swamp, a high-altitude look from the Wainiha Pali down to Hanalei Bay—a hike more than any other that underscores the island's peculiar and spectacular topography.

BACKTRACK DOWN HWY. 550. CONTINUE PAST MILE MARKER 7/550 AND VEER RIGHT ON HWY. 552, WHICH IS KOKEE ROAD, TOWARD KEKAHA.

From Highway 552 to Kekaha are dramatic views of Niʻihau, lying less than 20 miles offshore—the so-called Forbidden Island where only those of the purest Hawaiian blood are allowed to live. The 100-square-mile island remains in the hands of the Robinson family, whose ancestors bought it in 1864 for $10,000. A ferry each month brings Niʻihau residents, who are known for intricate shell necklaces, to Waimea. Niʻihau's two, tiny satellite islands, both uninhabited, also can be seen on the clearest of days—Lehua, a mile to the right, and Kaula, 19 miles to the left of Niʻihau.

The only Japanese fatality on land during the Pearl Harbor attack took place on Niʻihau, on December 8, 1941. After a Japanese pilot had crash-landed, he terrorized the locals with a pistol, searching for the persons who had taken his papers from the wreckage when he had been unconscious. The pilot threatened the wife of one Hawaiian, and the husband charged, taking three shots before he was able to get hold of the pilot and smash him, with one fatal toss, against the lava wall of his house. Since then, there has been a saying in the islands: "Don't shoot a Hawaiian more than twice. The third time he gets mad!" (One of the hero's descendants, Richard Kanahele, works today at Allerton Gardens in Koloa.)

AT THE BOTTOM ON THE GRADE IN KEKAHA, TURN LEFT ON KEKAHA ROAD.

If in need of libation, stop by the Waimea Canyon General Store at the junction. Then drive past the old Kekaha sugar mill, a red-dirt stained, gargantuan structure that washed and chewed tons of cane. The mill ceased operation in 2000.

TURN RIGHT ON PUEO ROAD, OR ANY ROAD THROUGH THE NEIGHBORHOOD. MAKE YOUR WAY SEVERAL BLOCKS BACK OUT TO HWY. 50. TURN RIGHT ON HWY. 50.

You drive along Kekaha Beach, playground for surfers, fishermen, strollers and horseback riders. In a few miles you pass, on the left, the Pacific Missile Range Facility, which

Road to Polihale Beach

allows day use of Majors Beach, by special permit. Although it's hard to imagine, the area inland along this drive, surrounding the now-defunct outpost of Mana, used to be swamplands, created by water seepage from the ridges fanning down from the Alakai Plateau. A canal ran through the lower part of the bog, allowing the Hawaiians to canoe all the way to Kekaha. Water development for cane and seed crops have drastically altered the horticultural landscape. Also on these sloping lands was the Holua slide, a long chute paved with lava rock and padded with pili grass. In February, at the end of the Makahiki—a four-month festival during which work and war were prohibited—young Hawaiian athletes would fashion sleds from logs and ride the slide with abandon.

CONTINUE ON HWY. 50 TO ITS TERMINUS. FOLLOW SIGNS SEVERAL MILES TO POLIHALE. *Note: The road to Polihale is rough and can be muddy.*

The beach at Polihale State Park, including Barking Sands, is part of the longest sand beach in Hawai'i. A massive dune abuts the northwest section of the Napali Coast—the ridges loom over the beach—and fans all the way around Mana Point to Kekaha, although the Naval base makes some of the beach inaccessible. Surfers dare the waves at Polihale, but the only spot for swimmers, except during rare calms, is Queens Pond. Barking Sands, a fine mixture of coral and lava particles, gets its name from the "woofing" sound the sliding dunes make when settling or being trod upon; Legend says these are the barks of an ancient fisherman's beloved pets, directing him ashore after being lost at sea.

Polihale was the heiau on the island from which the etheral spirits of the deceased escaped their mortal coils and went to the next world. Two heiaus are in the area, Kapaula Heiau, inland from the camping area, and Polihale Heiau, also the site of Sacred Springs, located beyond where the beach meets the cliffs.

Polihale

free advice & opinion

SAFETY TIPS THAT CAN SAVE YOUR LIFE
AND RECREATIONAL FACTOIDS OF MARGINAL USE.

HIKING

People have been walking here for centuries: If there is no trail already, you can't get there … That nice green embankment may be tangled grass and air: stay back from drop-offs … Carry an equipped day pack on hikes more than a mile or two … Drink plenty of water … Don't trust rocks with footing: they break free … Use a hiking stick … Never walk downhill with your hands in your pockets … Boink! Be aware of falling coconuts … At hike-to beaches, make sure to memorize where you enter the sand: finding the trail on the return trip can be difficult …

Use hunting trails on weekdays and wear bright colored clothes … If you see hunters, don't hide behind bushes and snort or squeal … Even bloodhounds get lost on Kaua'i: follow the trail, not your nose … Backtrack the moment you get lost or lose the trail … Don't hike alone … Give right-of-way to a 400-pound pig … If the sun rises on a clear Waialeale, head for Waimea Canyon … Bring something warm when hiking Koke'e … Go south and west to look for sun in the winter … You're in the tropics: protect your skin … Drink more water …

Loose rocks fall with waterfalls; don't dawdle beneath one … On black rock beach trails: follow the mud and sand left by the flip-flops of your predecessors … Flash floods happen on sunny days too, when it's raining inland: stay alert in stream beds … A high stream will subside, so wait a couple hours rather than make a dangerous crossing … Know the halfway point of your hike, and plan for enough time to get back … Heed No Trespassing signs … Public right of way on the coast is all land and rocks below the vegetation line, as a rule of thumb … Let someone know if you're taking a long hike … You need a permit to camp anywhere or to sleep on any beach … Hikes on Kaua'i take longer than you expect, due to tough conditions and astounding scenery; add an hour for every four hours you think it will take.

WATER SAFETY

Good judgment beats the most dangerous conditions … Throw a stick in the water before entering to see which way it floats … Float face-down when you first get in to see which way the current takes you … Observe the water for fifteen minutes before getting in … Outgoing current is like a river, carrying out the surf surge: look for blue channels, riffles, and places in a wall of surf offshore where the waves aren't curling: that's where water is going out … Wave for help if you're in trouble … Be extra cautious at remote beaches … High surf means stronger rip current … Stay out of rocky areas with surge … If possible, view swimming place from above to observe current … Waves coming in means current is going out someplace … Water isn't safe just because some tourist like you is in it … Aloha Survival: Locals will be glad to tell you about water safety: ask a surfer or swimmer who knows … Start your swim against a mild current, so you can swim with it when returning ... Get out of a current too strong to swim against ... Swim with fins ... Waves are like thugs: don't turn your back on them ... Every beach is both safe and unsafe, depending on the day ... If you get swept out, go with it and then swim parallel to shore once the current has taken you out and released you ... Don't panic and wear yourself out by swimming against a current you can't beat; it will release you ... Surfers offshore are a safety net, but don't count on them ...

Shore break can break you ... High surf rolls in on nice days from storms unseen far offshore ... Local surfers will be safe in water that is dangerous for you ... Tilted sand means deep water ... But drop-offs can occur on flat beaches, too ... Don't dive into unknown waters ... Swim with a buddy, always ... Go to the opposite side of the island from a high-surf beach: it should be calmer in the lee ... Safest swimming is near a lifeguard ... If you get stung by a jellyfish, put meat tenderizer on the wound ... You don't need to fear the ocean; fear your bad judgment ... When in doubt, stay out ... All beaches are public places: keep your pants on.

BICYCLING

Bust a helmet, not your head ... Lower your seat going downhill ... Dismount for horses and speak so they know this helmeted thing is a person ... Look: It's a vehicle! No, it's a pedestrian! Biking is the best of both worlds ... Most of the backroads on Kaua'i are places rental cars can't go ... Leaving bikes unlocked is a sign of a local ... But why take the chance? ... You can't take bikes on buses ... A bike is the fastest wasy to get through Kapa'a ...

You can continue past gates unless a sign tells you not to ... Respect private property ... Stay on trails to avoid erosion ... Exception: Swerve onto grass on paved paths to avoid pedestrians ... Dismount if you see hunters with dogs ... Never ride down a road you can't get back up ... Hard dirt becomes greasy slick after a few drops of rain ... Add extra lube: rust grows here fast ... Carry an extra tube ... Don't assume cars see you: drivers are looking at scenery.

KAYAKING

It may be raining inland: watch for flash floods ... Don't venture offshore without a local's advice ... Paddling upstream, branches usually stop you before shallow water does ... Remember your way back ... Some of the island's best streams have no people on them ... Ask a local if authorities ever found the anaconda in the Wailua River ... Rivers were Kaua'i's first roads: you'll see the island on them like no other way ...

Don't paddle into mangroves ... Keep open wounds out of stagnate fresh water: bacteria danger.

DRIVING AROUND

Driving is the most dangerous sport ... Wear a seatbelt or get a ticket ... Aloha driving: allow merges and turns ... Speeding tickets are likely souvenirs ... Park it or drive it: rubbernecking is dangerous ... Hanging beads or a shell necklace from your rearview mirror will give your rental a local look ... A box of baby wipes in the glove box provides an instant relief from red-dirt sweat ... Signs that beckon: Dead End, No Outlet ... On weekends, try to leave locals' beaches to the locals ... Littering carries a stiff $1,000 fine.

GEAR

Hiking poles are a third leg and you'll need one ... Bring a waterproof shell jacket ... Spitting in your swim mask will clear fog ... Muddy puddles make for great dye-your-own red dirt shirt dunking ... It's cheaper to rent snorkeling gear for a few days, cheaper to buy for a week or more ... It's cheaper to rent a bicycle for a couple days, cheaper to ship if biking for more than that ... You can rent a bike rack for the rental car ... Or hang the bikes out the trunk ... It's cheaper to rent kayaks and surfboards ... Call rental places first to make sure expert advice comes with the rental ... See *Packlist* for what to bring ... When mountain hiking, bring a plastic bag to put your shoes in after hike ... Clothes are gear: No nudity on any Hawaiian beach ... Attend to skin with antibacterial and fungicide: This is the Garden Island and everything grows here ... Carry water, but if you do use a water pump, use iodine to go along with the filter ... Most-common island footwear: bare feet ... Bring lightweight hiking shoes that you can hose off.

DISCLAIMER

Think of this book as you would any other piece of outdoor gear: It will help you do what you want to do, but it depends solely upon you to supply responsible judgment and common sense. Weather and new rules may alter the condition of trails and beach access; please let us know. The publisher and authors are not responsible for injury, damage, or legal violations that occur when someone is using our books. Furthermore, the publisher and authors hope that none of these bad things happen and that you have a great time.

ALOHA AUTHORS
Excerpts from some better known writers

"*The far end of Kalalau Valley had been well chosen as a refuge. A sea of vegetation laved the landscape, pouring its green billows from wall to wall, dripping from the cliff lips in great vine masses, and flinging a spray of ferns and airy plants into its multitudinous crevices. Koolau had fought with this vegetable sea. The choking jungle, with its riot of blossoms, had been driven back from the bananas, oranges and mangoes that grew wild, and in every open space where the sunshine penetrated papaya trees were burdened with their golden fruit.*"

—Jack London,
Koolau The Leper

"*The Pacific is inconstant and uncertain like the soul of a man. Sometimes it is grey like the English Channel, with a heavy swell, and sometimes it is rough, capped with white crests, and boisterous. When it is calm and blue, the blue is arrogant. The sun shines fiercely from an unclouded sky. The trade wind gets into your blood and you are filled with an impatience for the unknown, and you forget vanished youth with its memories, cruel and sweet, in a restless, intolerable desire for life.*"

—W. Somerset Maugham,
The Pacific

"No alien land in all the world has any deep strong charm for me but that one, no other land could so longingly and beseechingly haunt me, sleeping and waking, through half a lifetime, as that one has done. For me, its balmy airs are always blowing, its summer seas flashing in the sun; the pulsing of its surfbeat is in my ear, I can see its garlanded crags, its leaping cascades, its plumy palms drowsing by the shore. I can hear the splash of its brooks and in my nostrils still lives the breath of flowers that perished twenty years ago."

—Mark Twain,
Roughing It in the Sandwich Islands

"The sea was smooth under the lee of the island; it was warm besides, and Keola has his sailor's knife, so he had no fear of sharks. A little way before him the trees stopped; there was a break in the line of the land like the mouth of a harbor; and the tide, which was then flowing, took him up and carried him through. The next minute he was within, floated there in a wide shallow water, bright with ten thousand stars, and all about him was the ring of land, with its string of palms trees."

—Robert Louis Stevenson,
The Isle of Voices

"I wish I could tell you about the Pacific. The endless ocean. Reefs upon which waves broke into spray, and inner lagoons, lovely beyond description. I wish I could tell you about the sweating jungle, the full moon rising behind an ancient volcano."

—James A. Michner,
Tales of the South Pacific

HAWAIIWOOD

Take a self-guided tour to the locations of some of the more recent among 50-plus major motion pictures that have been filmed in Kauaʻi. The first was *White Heat* in 1934. Locations are listed, starting at the north shore and working around the island. TH = Trailhead, DT = Driving Tour.

Keʻe Beach, TH1 — *Lord of the Flies, Throw Momma From the Train, Thorn Birds*
Haena Beach Park, TH2 — *North*
Kepuhi Point, TH3 — *Body Heat*
Wainiha Beach, TH4 — *Pagan Love Song*
Lumahai Beach, TH5 — *South Pacific*
Lumahai Valley, TH5 — *Uncommon Valor, Dragonfly*
Hanalei Bay, TH7 — *South Pacific, Wackiest Ship in the Army, Miss Sadie Thompson*
Hanalei Valley, TH8 — *Uncommon Valor*
Anini Beach, TH13 — *Honeymoon in Vegas*
Pilaʻa Beach, TH16 — *None But the Brave*
Moloaʻa Bay, TH21 — *Gilligan's Island, Castaway Cowboy*
Papaʻa Bay, TH22 — *Six Days, Seven Nights*
Anahola Mountains/Kong, TH23 — *Raiders of the Lost Ark*
Kamokila Village, DT2 — *Outbreak*
Kapaʻa Town, TH28 — *Honeymoon in Vegas*
Coco Palms, TH33, DT2 — *Blue Hawaii, South Pacific*
Lydgate Park, TH34 — *Blue Hawaii*
Waialeale Basin, TH32 — *Jurassic Park, Flight of the Intruder, Jurassic Park III*
Wailua River, TH33 — *The Hawaiians, Islands in the Stream, Donovan's Reef, Outbreak*
Wailua Falls, TH36 — *Fantasy Island*
Ahukini Landing, TH39 — *Donovan's Reef, Pagan Love Song*
Nawiliwili, TH41 — *Diamond Head, The Lost World: Jurassic Park,*
   Throw Momma from the Train
Kalapaki Beach, TH41 — *Hawaiian Eye*
Huleia Stream, TH41 — *Raiders of the Lost Ark*
Mahaulepu, TH42 — *Six Days, Seven Nights; Islands in the Stream, Hook*
Kukuiula Harbor, TH45 — *The Thorn Birds, Islands in the Stream*
Allerton Garden, TH46 — *Jurassic Park, Acapulco Gold, Last Flight of Noah's Ark,*
   Honeymoon in Vegas
Hanapepe Town, TH51 — *The Thorn Birds, Jurassic Park, George of the Jungle*
Waimea Canyon, TH34 — *Wackiest Ship in the Army, Fantasy Island*
Barking Sands, TH57 — *South Pacific*
Kalalau Valley, DT4, TH1 — *King Kong*

KAUAIAN TIMELINE

5,000,000 BC Lava pokes above water; Kaua'i is born.

200 AD First Polynesians arrive from Marquesas; the Menehunes.

1100 Second Polynesian migration, from Tahiti.

1700 300,000 Hawaiians living on eight islands.

1778 British Captain James Cook arrives at Waimea; Hawai'i is discovered by the rest of the world.

1795 King Kamehameha unifies islands into one kingdom, except Kaua'i. Two attempts to conquer Kaua'i fail.

1810 Kauaian King Kaumuali'i signs peace treaty with Kamehameha.

1816 Russian traders erect fort in Waimea.

1817 Russians driven from the island; their attempt at empire over.

1819 Kamehameha the Great dies.

1820 First New England missionaries arrive in Waimea. Kapu system of laws abolished by Kamehameha II.

1835 First sugar mill, Koloa; worker emigration from China, Japan, Portugal, Philippines and Korea over next decades as sugar becomes king. During Civil War and Gold Rush, Kaua'i becomes major sugar supplier to U.S.

1842 United States recognizes Hawai'i as independent nation.

1864 Eliza Sinclair, ancestor of today's Gay & Robinson Corporation, buys island of Ni'ihau for $10,000.

1874 Rule of Kamehameha's two sons and two grandsons ends.

1893 Queen Liliuokalani betrayed and overthrown; end of monarchy. First hotel opened in Lihue.

1898 United States annexes Hawai'i as territory; Marines occupy Honolulu.

1912 Duke Kahanamoku wins Olympic gold medal. Goes on to win 5 more medals in swimming, ending with silver in 1932.

1930 U.S. restricts Japanese emigration to Hawai'i. Japanese comprise 40 percent of population.

1941 Nawiliwili Harbor shelled during World War II.

1958 *South Pacific* movie released.

1959 Hawai'i becomes 50ᵗʰ state.

1967 One million people visit Hawaiian islands.

1982 Hurricane Iwa.

1992 Hurricane Iniki.

1993 United States formally apologizes for overthrow of Hawaiian kingdom.

2005 Kaua'i still most popular island for outdoor recreation.

A GLOSSARY OF HAWAIIAN WORDS AND PHRASES

The Hawaiian alphabet consists of 12 letters: A, E, I, O, U, H, K, L, M, N, P, W.

The Polynesians transmitted their knowledge and culture through speaking, dance and chants; they had no written language. Missionary scholars in the 1800s derived word spellings from the Polynesian phonetics.

Kaua'i is pronounced: kow-WAH-ee

The apostrophe-like doohickey that goes between double vowels is called an okina. For instance, "a'a" is pronounced, "ah-ah."

Selected Hawaiian place name suffixes and prefixes, to give you an idea of how places were named and interconnected by their attributes:

A'a, rough lava
Ahi, land
Aina, land
Akau, north
Ala, road
Ana, cave
Anu, cool
Hana or *hono*, bay
Hema, south
Hikina, east
Haole, foreigner
Hau, spreading tree
Holo, run
Hono, bay
Hou, new
Hua, fruit, seed
Iki, small
Kaha, place
Kahawai, stream
Kai, sea
Kea or *keo*, white, clear
Koa, rocky, coral
Koko, blood
Komo, enter
Komohana, west
Kua, black

La, sun
Lani, heaven
Lau, leaf
Lena, yellow
Lolo, stupid
Lohi, slow
Lua, crater
Lulu, sheltered
Luna, high
Mala, garden
Malu, shelter
Maka, point
Mana, power or divide
Mano, shark or many
Manu, bird
Mau, moist
Mauka, toward the mountains
Mauna, mountain
Mele, merry or song
Mo'o, water spirit
Moi, king
Moku, island
Nalu, surf, wave
Nani, pretty
Niu, coconut
Nui, large
Ohu, fog

Olo, hill
Omao, green
Oluolu, please
One, sand
Papa, flat
Pau, finished
Pele, goddess of fire
Pono, harmony
Puna, water spring
Pu'u, hill
Tutu, aunt
Ua, rain
Uka, inland
Ula, red
Ulu, breadfruit
Uma, curve
Waa, canoe
Wai, water
Wailele, waterfall
Waimea, reddish waters
Walu, many
Wili, twist

SOME HAWAIIAN WORDS

Ahi, albacore or yellow tuna

Ahupua'a, land and coast segment that supported a community

'Aina, land, earth

Ali'i, king, royalty of highest nobility

Aloha, love, affection, welcome, hello, good-bye

Hale, house or building

Hana, work or activity

Haole, caucasian, originally any foreigner

He'enalu, surfing

Heiau, ancient temple or place of worship

Hoku, star

Huki, pull

Hukilau, hawaiian method of group net-fishing

Hula, the art of hawaiian dance

Ilio, dog

Kahuna, an expert, priest or religious leader

Kai, the ocean

Kama'aina, citizen of long standing,

Kanaka, human being, the Hawaiians

Kane, male

Kapu, prohibited, keep out

Keiki, child

Kona, leeward

La, sun

Lanai, porch or balcony

Lei, necklace made of flowers

Luau, Hawaiian feast

Mahalo, thank you

Mahina, moon

Makahiki, annual harvest and peace festival

Makai, toward the ocean

Mana, power

Mauka, toward the mountains.

Mauna, mountain

Moana, ocean

Mu'umu'u, mother hubbard dress

Ohana, the people of the community

Pali, cliff

Paniolo, hawaiian cowboy

Pele, goddess of volcanoes

Po, night

Poi, dish of mashed taro root

Popoki, cat

Pupu, hors d'oeurve

Spam, a traditional pork dish

Ua, rain

Wahine, female

Wikiwiki, fast, quickly

GREETINGS, TOASTS AND PHRASES

Aloha Nui, A Big Aloha!

Hau'oli La Hanau, Happy Birthday

Hau'oli Makahiki Hou, Happy New Year

Hiki, Okay

Honi Kaua Wikiwiki, Kiss Me Quick

Kamau, Here's To Your Health

Kipa Mai, Welcome

Komo, Enter

Mahalo Nui, Many Thanks

Me Ke Aloha, With Love

Mele Kalikimaka, Merry Christmas

Nani Wahine, To a Beautiful Woman

Okole Maluna, Bottom's Up

PIDGIN EXPRESSIONS

Pidgin is a form of English spoken by kamaʻaina. It is more a dialect and intonation of speech—flowing like a babbling brook—than a collection of phrases. Pidgin's origin is not Polynesian, but rather the rainbow of ethnicity that meld together as Hawaiian. Hang around places where locals shop or surf and you may hear snippets.

ʻAss awri, That's alright

ʻAss why hard, That's why it's hard, life is tough

Auntie, Kids' word for all adult women in the calabash

Boddah you? You like to start something?

Brah, Brother

Bumbye, In the future; by and by, soon

Bummahs, Too bad

Bus laugh, Laugh out loud

Bus nose, Reaction to bad smell

Calabash, Friends and family, extended family

Calabash cousin, Not blood relation, but close friend

Chicken skin, Chills, goosebumps

Coast haole, Caucasian from the Mainland

Cockroach, To steal

Cool head main ting, Keep calm, don't panic

Da Kine, thingamajig, whatever speaker wants it to mean

Eh, Brah, Hey, you

Garans, Guaranteed

Grind, To eat

Grinds, Food

He been go, He went

Hey, Bruddah, Hey, Brother

Howzit?, How are you? Pidgin for Aloha

Huhu, to be upset

I shame, I'm embarrassed

J.O.J., Just off the Jet (tourist)

Junks, small personal things

Lesgo, let's do it

Local style, Hawaiian way of doing things

Lolo, Dumb-dumb

Moke, Local tough guy

Mo' bettah, Better

No boddah, Don't bother

No can, Cannot

No mention, Don't mention it, you're welcome

Not, No can be, You got to be kidding

Moah betta, More better

Plate lunch, Rice, meat or Spam and veggies, a fast counter lunch

Poi dog, Local mix of many breeds, small canine

Shaka, Right on, brah' (hand sign: fist with thumb and pinky out.)

Shave ice, Snow cones

Slack key, Hawaiian folk-blues played on loose-string guitar

Stick, Surfboard

Stink-eye, Dirty look

Stuffs, see Junks

Talk story, Tell stories, conversation

T'anks, Thank you, mahalo

Tita, Local tough girl

Uncle, Kids' word for all adult men in the calabash

Whack 'em, Eat up

Whatevahs, Whatever

Yeah?, Put anywhere in sentence

SURFER'S DICTIONARY

AIR: The invisible stuff that's on top of waves. Also, a gaseous substance necessary for a surfer to surf.

BAD: That which has nothing to do with surfing.

CAR: A disposable device used to transport a surfer and surfboard to the surf.

CRUELTY: Taking a surfer's surfboard.

FEET: Things that allow a surfer to stand on a surfboard.

FOOD: A substance that surfers swallow in order to go surfing.

GOD: An entity that created waves and surfboards.

JOB: An activity by which a surfer acquires money in order to go surfing.

LIFE: Surfing.

KAUAʻI PACKLIST

For two weeks, staying in hotel.

BASICS

Long pants/dress for airplane
2 swimming suits
Hat, sunglasses
Rain-proof shell (pants optional)
Aloha shirt/dress for dress-up
2 pair hiking/riding shorts
1 pair dress shorts
7 T-shirts, one for every two days
1 or 2 lightweight long sleeve tops
(Dri-fit or polyester equivalent)
Waterproof watch

FOOTWEAR

3 pair lightweight hiking socks
1 pair flip-flops, a.k.a., zories, slippers
  (for driving, beach walking, shopping)
1 pair Tevas or beach shoe *(optional, more range for beach or reef walking)*
1 pair lightweight, washable hiking shoes; your mud shoe
1 pair tennis shoes—*can be same as hiking shoe*
1 pair hotel/airport/dress shoes
Optional boat shoes, sandals

KNAPSACK/DAYPACK:

Water, energy food
Flashlight
Swiss Army Knife
First aid, sunscreen
Water treatment tabs or pump
Rain shell
Sunglasses/hat
Mosquito repellant
Camera

GEAR:

Hiking pole *(retractable, bring with you)*
Mask, snorkel, fins *(Bring or rent here. Cheaper to buy if you'll use for more than 5 or 6 days. Cost here about $30.)*
Surfboard *(Ship if you will use more than 5 days; otherwise rent. Contact airlines and outfitters to compare prices.)*
Bicycle helmet
Bicycle *(Ship if use more than 3 days. Contact airlines and outfitters to compare prices.)*
Kayak *(Rent, about $20 per day.)*

FACTSHEET

TEMPERATURES
Average, year around, day and night: 75 degrees

Extremes:	Record High	Record Low
Kilauea	87	50
Lihue	90	50
Poipu	92	40
Kokee	90	29

WIND

Summer:	Trades and Kona winds from south
Winter:	Trade winds generally from north

RAINFALL YEARLY AVERAGE IN INCHES

Waimea Town	28
Poipu	35
Koloa	65
Lihue	38
Kapaʻa	56
Princeville	98
Waialeale	460 (most in the world)

ETHNIC MAKEUP:
Hawaiian: 23%
Filipino: 23%
Japanese: 22%
White: 19%
Other: 13%

MAJOR HURRICANES

		average wind speed m.p.h.	maximum m.p.h.
1950	ʻHiki	68	93
1957	Nina	92	111
1959	Dot	81	103
1982	Iwa	65	117
1992	Iniki	145	227

HIGHEST PEAKS: Kawaikini, 5,243 ft.; Waialeale, 5,148 ft.
MILES OF COASTLINE: 110
SQUARE MILES: 550
AVERAGE DIAMETER, MI.: 28

LAND OWNERSHIP: (397,000 acres)
Six largest corporations: 41 percent
State of Hawaii: 39 percent
Small private landowners: 13 percent
Hawaiian Homelands: 6 percent
Federal government: 1 percent

POPULATION
Locals: 59,000
Visitors (average daily): 16,000
Total: 73,000

SUNSHINE MARKETS

County-licensed outdoor markets offering home-grown produce. Times may vary, call 241-6390 for more information. Bring dollar bills and be on time!

Monday:	Koloa Ballpark, Maluhia Road, Koloa, 12 noon.
Tuesday:	Kalaheo Neighborhood Center, 3:30 p.m. Hanalei-Waikoko, 2:30 p.m.
Wednesday:	Kapaʻa New Town Center, near Armory, 3 p.m.
Thursday:	Kilauea Neighborhood Center, 4:30 p.m. Hanapepe Park, behind fire station, 4:30 p.m.
Friday:	Lihue, Vidinha Stadium, Hoʻolako St., 3 p.m.
Saturday:	Kekaha Neighborhood Center, 9 a.m. Kilauea Plantation Center, 11:30 a.m. Hanalei Town Center, 9:30 a.m.

Kealia Kountry Store, call for time and date, 823-0708

FREE HULA SHOWS

Call to verify times and inquire about other cultural events.

Coconut Marketplace, daily, 822-3641
Kauaʻi Coconut Beach Resort, nightly 7 p.m., 822-3455
Hyatt Regency Kauaʻi Resort, nightly 6 to 8 p.m., also torch-lighting
    ceremony daily at sunset, except Tuesday, 742-1234
Kauaʻi Marriott Resort, Wednesday and Saturday at sunset;
    also torch-lighting ceremony Monday and Thursday, 245-5050
Kukui Grove Shopping Center, Fridays, 6 p.m., 245-7784
Poipu Shopping Village, Tuesday and Thursday, 5:30 p.m., 742-2831
Princeville Hotel, Tuesday, Thursday, Sunday, 6:30 p.m., 826-9644

THE MEANING OF *Aloha*

as adopted by a resolution of the State Legislature:

A is for Akahai. Kindness, to be expressed with tenderness.

L is for Lokahi. Unity, to be expressed with harmony.

O is for Oluolu. Agreeable, to be expressed with pleasantness.

H is for Ha'aha'a. Humility, to be expressed with modesty.

A is for Ahonui. Patience, to be expressed with perseverance.

The meaning of ALOHA not yet considered by the State Legislature:

A is for Attire. It's hard to be uptight or uppity in a place where nobody wears pantyhose or neckties, and "dressing up" is colorful prints and flip-flops.

L is for Latitude. In the temperate tropics, with a lack of snow and boiling heat, everyone stays mellow.

O is for a Circle. On an island there's no point in rushing just to get where you've already been. Even the dogs don't chase their tails here.

H is for Healthy. With papayas, bananas, guava, mangos and spam, everyone enjoys the serenity of a healthy diet.

A is for Alone. The opposite of island fever is island euphoria; everyone is alone and isolated in the ocean, pitching in together to help out their neighbors. You don't outrun a bad reputation on a small island.

The Hawaiian word keiki (KAY-key) means both 'child' and also the green shoot of a new banana plant. Bananas are plants, not trees, and each year a new generation must be nurtured to maturity—just like children. By caring for each generation, the arts and skills of village life flourished for centuries on this beautiful, but isolated, island of Kaua'i. Your kids can see many of these arts practiced today. They can also do a lot of other fun stuff that will create life-long memories and bring the family together. The suggestions below will help you plan a day of family fun. Remember that trailhead numbers close together numerically will also be close geographically.

TH = trailhead. DT = driving tour. Activities are listed by ascending trailhead number. See *Resource Links* for telephone numbers.

KEIKI SWIMMING
Ke'e Beach, TH1, page 32
A reef-protected oval pool rests under the jagged Napali ridges. High surf, mainly in winter, makes for strong current.
Pu'u Poa Beach, TH9, page 43
Blue channels lead into coral beds. Set below the Princeville Resort. Can be shallow when the tide is out.

Baby Beach, Kapa'a, TH28, page 77
This wading pool is popular among new moms. Beach cottage neighborhood setting.
Lydgate Park, TH34, page 99
Snorkeling is a sure thing year around at this big man-made lagoon.
Poipi Beach Park, TH44, page 120
A sand spit creates protected swim spots and Hawaiian sun graces this popular beach park, even when clouds frown elsewhere.

Waterhouse Beach, TH45, page 123
You'll have to look for this toddlers' beach, tucked away near Prince Kuhio Park. Bigger kids will like the snorkeling at Longhouse Beach.

Salt Pond Beach Park, TH52, page 140
West Kaua'i's best swimming beach. To the far right of the beach is a smaller splash area.

Queens Pond, TH57, page 151
Families with a sense of adventure will like this calm spot along the long Polihale Beach. High surf often makes conditions very unsafe. Bring your own shade and water to these open sand dunes.

FAMILY NATURE WALKS

Limahuli National Tropical Botanical Garden, TH1, page 32
You might expect dinosaurs to stride down the green ridges and onto the garden terraces. Native and endangered plants abound, many unique to Kaua'i.

Okolehao Trail, TH8, page 40
Big views of Hanalei Valley and Bay are the payoff on this forested ridge hike. It's a bit of a workout, but you'll feel like you've been somewhere.

Sleeping Giant, TH30, page 81
You get a fantastic view of interior Kaua'i and the Coconut Coast from the top of the Giant (Nounou Mountain.) The Norfolk Pine forest on the way up will have everyone's interest. Kids will get a sense of accomplishment.

Keahua Arboretum, TH32, page 84
You've got many options at the arboretum, all beginning where the Wailua River crosses a spillway in the jungle. The Kuilau Ridge is green fantasy land—but make sure to stay on the trail on the steep parts.

Smiths Tropical Paradise, TH33, page 95
The little ones may shriek like the peacocks that float down from the treetops. Bridges span the lagoons of Kauai's best-value gardens and arboretum.

Kukui Trails-Iliau Loop, TH58, page 152
Make this commanding overlook your first stop on the way up Waimea Canyon. Bigger kids in active families can make the trek to the bottom of the canyon.

Nualolo Nature Trail, TH66, page 163
With all the trails and overlooks around Koke'e State Park, many families might miss this woodland, bird-lover's stroll.

BEACH PICNICS

Haena Beach Park, TH2, page 33
Stop by on the way back from Ke'e Beach. Surfers and a play stream add interest to this developed park. The cool caves are across the road.

Pine Trees Beach, TH7, page 37
Large ironwood trees cast shade on a few tables, about midway around Hanalei Bay. Surfers and joggers pass by. (Access via Ama'ama Road, down from the City Pavilion on Weke Road.)

Anini Beach, TH13, page 49
Drop down to this long coral-reef park. Large trees shade camping and picnic areas. A polo field and windsurfers add to the charm.

Kilauea Bay-Kahili Beach, TH18, page 54
No facilities here, but you can take sand seats where Kilauea Stream emerges from a tropical valley at a big sand beach. The drive down is a mini-adventure.

Anahola Bay, TH23, page 67
The road to the beach curves down through a leafy canopy. This side of the bay is rustic, but you can get comfy along the sandy river bank.

Poipu Beach Park, TH44, page 119
You may have company at the pavilions, since sun and safe swimming make this Kaua'i's most-popular beach park.

Prince Kuhio Park, TH45, page 122
The scant-sand beaches nearby are great for snorkeling, but this is the place for a quiet family repast.

Salt Pond Beach Park, TH52, page 140
Palms shade the grassy shores, and swimming is normally safe. Pull off here if cruising West Kaua'i—the locals do.

Lucy Wright Beach Park, TH54, page 144
Water quality is not the greatest, as this is where the Waimea River enters the Pacific, but you can show the kids where Captain Cook landed and take a stroll down the beach to a long fishing pier.

SHORT WALKS TO BIG PLACES

Hula Platform, Ke'e Beach, TH1, page 30
The Kalalau Trail is well-known, but the short walk to the scenic terraces above crashing waves packs a punch. Tread lightly at this sacred Hawaiian site.

Hanalei Pier, TH7, page 37
Watch fishermen haul 'em in and surfers whiz by. The covered pier at Black Pot Beach is a short walk down past the surfer cars to where the Hanalei River enters the bay.

Aliomanu Beach, Anahola, TH22, page 66
Easily reached, this hike-to beach holds the promise of treasure found—shells, coral bits, or maybe a message in a bottle.
Kukui Point Light, TH41, page 107
A path curves from the posh grounds of the Marriott to the entrance to Nawiliwili Harbor. Pick a sunset when a cruise ship is leaving the harbor.

Mahaulepu, Poipu, TH42, page 115
A bumpy ride out sets the tone for a walk along sculpted bluffs and wild waves. You may see a Monk Seal (don't get closer than 100 feet if you do).
Kukuiolono Park, Kalaheo, TH48, page 127
A high green knoll provides a respite. Wild chickens flit about formal gardens and a path skirts the golf course to a pavilion with a big view.
Pihea Overlook-Alakai Swamp, Waimea Canyon, TH69, page 170
All the thrilling overlooks of the canyon on the way up are a prelude to the panorama of the Kalalau Valley. A trail skirts the rim. Trekking families can pile on the adventure by taking the boardwalk trail across the Alakai Swamp.

EASY & ENTERTAINING & EDUCATIONAL
Kilauea Lighthouse, Kilauea, TH17, page 52
Free binoculars aid in the bird-and-whale watching at this dramatic northerly spot.
Kauaʻi Children's Discovery Museum, Kapaʻa, DT2, page 197
Day-camp programs and walk-through exhibits delight the kids.
Lydgate Park Play Bridge, TH34, page 99
The ocean snorkeling pool here is the big draw, but you've also got Kamalani Playground and—just down the bike path—the awesome new Play Bridge.

National Tropical Gardens-Spouting Horn, Koloa, TH46, page 124
Kaua'i's sea geyser gets the oohs and ahhs, but the garden visitors center across the street is an escape into remarkable flora.

Menehune Ditch Bridge, Waimea, TH54, page 144
Everyone over four will get a kick out of the suspension bridge that spans the river.

Koke'e Natural History Museum, Koke'e, TH67, page 164
Caps off a visit to the to Waimea Canyon. Hurricane and natural history exhibits are eye-openers.

Kauai Museum, page 180
The story of the island unfolds through photos and displays. Giftshop gets an A+.

GUIDED ADVENTURES
—see resource links for phone numbers

Get a View from Above
You won't believe the sights from the sky. Several helicopters tour the island; You can't go wrong with Air Kaua'i.

Princeville Ranch Zipline
It's a perfectly safe thrill: Fly over the jungle gorge of a huge private ranch.

Paddle Kalapaki Lagoon
Exotic birds join you on the luscious lagoon paddle on the expansive upper grounds of the Marriott Resort. True Blue, outfitters at Kalapaki Beach, will set you up.

Fern Grotto Boat Ride
Kaua'i's classic since the 1950s. Family hula and ukulele performers enliven the ride up the river to the massive, dripping cave—a natural cathedral.

Pedal the Coconut Coast
A beach path winds along the coast from Kealia to the Wailua River, including colorful Kapa'a Town. Kaua'i cycle is one place to rent wheels (or embark on a guided tour if you'd prefer).

Float through the Hanalei Wildlife Refuge
The lazy Hanalei River leads from the surf, through taro fields, and into Hanalei Valley. Several kayak places are in town.

Learn to Surf
Beginners may like Poipu, but many think Hanalei Bay is the best beginner's beach in the Hawaiian Islands. You can learn from one of the greats, Titus Kinimaka, or take your pick from many other skilled boarders. Hanalei Surf Company has advice to go with their gear.

Wailua River Paddle
The first Hawaiian kings chose to make their home along these banks. Wailua River Kayaks leads a tour to Secret Falls, which includes a short hike.

Na Aina Kai Botanical Gardens
Newly opened children's garden. A world of greenery where kids can be delightfully lost.

FUN PLACES TO EAT
Duke's Canoe Club, Kalapaki
Surfboards and other memorabilia adorn this special occasion resort restaurant right on Kalapaki Beach. Duke Kahanamoku was a surfing legend and Olympic medalist.
Wailua Marina Restaurant
Enjoy local-style eats with a river view, after a river boat cruise or before taking in an evening hula show.
Hamura Saimin Stand, Lihue
Enough noodles to reach the moon and back have been served up at the counter in Lihue's old-town. Spills okay, the counter is Formica. Chopsticks optional.
Koke'e Lodge
Stop in at the old building after a visit to Waimea Canyon and watch the chickens and roosters flit about outside plate glass windows that frame a green expanse of the park.
Moloa'a Sunrise Fruit Stand, Anahola (first Ko'olau Road)
You won't believe that their creamy smoothies are brimming with nutrition. You sit at an outside counter with a view of the Anahola Mountains. The sandwiches draw the working guys from miles around.

JoJo's Shave Ice, Waimea
One of these sweet coolers (a traditional Hawaiian treat) might save the day if the family got ornery after a little too much sun at Polihale. You step inside a funky joint that will part of the fun.
Hanalei Dolphin, Hanalei
Tables are set along the river for lunch, making birds and kayakers part of the show. Their kids' menu is tops.

HULA SHOWS
With chants and dancing to syncopated percussion, the hula tells the story of Polynesian culture. Kids and parents alike will be captivated. Performances vary from keiki dance clubs and resort performers to Hawaiian cultural groups from Ni'ihau and Kaua'i. A listing for free performances is on page 229. Smith's Tropical Garden also holds a Polynesian dance extravaganza, and traditional luaus also come with entertainment. (Princeville Resort and the Sheraton in Kapa'a are two popular feast sites.) Many performances include impromptu lessons by kids volunteering from the audience.

Resource links

Princeville Ranch Adventure zipline

OUTFITTERS

Each outfitter is listed once, under primary activity; ancillary services also noted for each outfitter.

Note: All area codes in Kauai are 808.

HIKING

Most of the trails in Kaua'i, both coastal paths and mountain routes, were laid down centuries ago by native Hawaiians. In addition to these historic paths are forest reserve trails and four-wheel drive roads. Trails usually follow ridgelines up to higher elevations, since steep relief and thick flora doesn't allow for switchbacks. Treks in this book are for day hikers, but backpacking trailheads are included.

Island Enchantment, 823-0705, *tours; also snorkeling*
Kayak Kaua'i, Hanalei, 800-437-3507, 826-9844
Kaua'i Nature Tours, Poipu, 742-8305, 888-233-8365, *natural history and ecology*
Princeville Ranch Adventures, 826-7669, *guided tours, equipment included. 2,500-acre ranch, also has cross-valley zipline rides and kayak tours. Waterfall-and-swim hike an all-timer.*

SNORKELING, SCUBA & CRUISES

Kaua'i has 110 miles of coastline, with waters supporting 650 different kinds of fish. Generally speaking, calmer waters and better snorkeling will be found during the winter months on south and east side beaches. During the summer months, calmer waters will generally be on north and west shore. East and west shore beaches are the least predictable. However, on any given day, any beach can be calm—or turbulent—throughout the year.

BEACHES WITH FULL OR PART-TIME LIFEGUARDS:
Wailua Bay, Lydgate Park, Anahola Beach Park, Poipu Beach, Hanalei, Kealia, Haena, and Salt Pond Beach Park.

Blue Doplphin Charters, Port Allen, 335-5553
Fathom Five Divers, Koloa, 800-972-3078, *lessons and rentals*
HoloHolo Charters, Port Allen, 800-848-6130, 335-0815, *daily excursions, boat tours to Ni'ihau, Napali*
Kalapaki Beach Boys (True Blue), Kalapaki Beach, 246-6333, *rentals, tours, lessons; also surfing, windsurfing, kayak, hiking*

Kayak Kaua'i, Hanalei, 800-437-3507, 826-9844
Liko Kaua'i Cruises, Waimea, 338-0333
Napali Explorer, Waimea, 877-335-9909, 338-9999
Sea Sport Divers, Poipu, 742-9303, *tours, lessons*
Smiths Fern Grotto Cruise, Wailua, 821-6892
Snorkel Bob's, Kapa'a, 823-9433; Koloa, 742-2206, *rentals*

BICYCLING

With miles of forest reserve roads and trails, resort bike paths, disused cane roads and quiet rural roads, Kaua'i is made for biking. Many towns, resort areas and rural neighborhoods are best seen from a bike. On the down side, highway bike lanes could be better, and it's too bad buses aren't equipped to take cyclists over one or two highway stretches that are unsafe. Rentals are about $20 a day. You may want to inquire with your air carrier about shipping cost and compare with outfitters listed below.

Kaua'i Cycle and Tour, Kapa'a, 821-2115, *rentals, tours, sales, service*
Pedal 'n Paddle, Hanalei, 826-9069, *rentals; also kayaks, snorkeling,*
        boogie boards, camping
Bicycle John, Lihue, 245-7579, *sales, service*
Bicycle Downhill, Waimea, 742-7421, *tours, Waimea Canyon*
Bike Doktor, Hanalei, 826-7799, *rentals, sales, service*

KAYAKING

Kaua'i has the only navigable waters in Hawaii, including six rivers and as many streams that are wide enough to be called rivers in most states. Rivers and streams can rise fast after storms, but more often river kayaking on the island is on quiet lagoons that curve inland. Coral reefs and bays also provide dozens of places for sea kayaking, under calm conditions.

Aloha Canoes and Kayaks, Nawiliwili, 246-6804, *tours, rentals*
Kayak Kaua'i, Hanalei, 826-9844, 800-437-3507
        tours, rentals; also bikes, snorkeling, surfboards, camping
Napali Kayak Tours, Hanalei, 826-6900, *specialize in coast camping*
Outfitters Kaua'i, Nawiliwili and Poipu, 742-9667, *tours; also bicycles*
Princeville Ranch Adventures, also hikes and zipline, 826-7669
True Blue, Kalapaki-Nawiliwi, *Family lagoon paddles, paddle-hike tours, 246-6333*
Wailua River Kayak, Wailua, 822-5795, 639-6332
        rentals and paddle-hike tours to Secret Falls on Wailua River.
        Smaller groups and special requests.

SURFING AND WINDSURFING

Surfing originated here, and is called the sport of kings, since Hawaiian royalty began riding the waves centuries ago. Winter months usually bring the biggest surf to north shore and west side beaches. During the summer, look for the biggest surf on the south and east sides of the island.

Hanalei Surf Company, 826-9000, *rentals, lesson referrals, and the island's best surf shop; also snorkeling*
Kaua'i Beach Boys, Kalapaki-Nawiliwili, 246-6333
Kayak Kaua'i, Hanalei, 800-437-3507, 826-9844
Learn To Surf, 826-7612, *lessons, rentals, island-wide*
Nukomoi Surf Company, Poipu, 742-8019, *rentals, lessons, surf shop*
Tamba Surf Company, Kapa'a, 823-6942, *rentals, surf shop, lessos*
Titus Kinimaka, 822-0408, 652-1436, *one of Hawaii's greatest surfers; will teach from novice on up; often sets up truck at Hanalei Pier.*
Lewis Russell, 828-0339
Dr. Ding's Westside Surf Shop, Hanapepe, 335-3805, *custom boards*

AIR KAUAI 800-972-4666, 246-4666, 647-4646

Beautiful Kaua'i's has been 5 million years in the making, nuanced by numerous river valleys, seacliffs, and ragged ridges, all of it adorned with a tangle of life that would put Darwin in a tizzy. The sure way to see how it all folds together is by helicopter—the best bang for your buck when it comes to tours. Kaua'i has several operators. Air Kaua'i is the most experienced and recommended. Their choppers are totally deluxe, featuring larger windows and a speaker system that puts you in a relaxed trance. Novice riders appreciate the gentle ride and the fact that they take the time to shut down the engine and rotor blades as passengers board and exit. Get ready. Gliding into a Napali valley, beside a Waimea Canyon waterfall, and up the face of Mount Waialeale are awesome, inspiring experiences.

HORSEBACK RIDING

CJM Country Stables, Poipu, 742-6096
Esprit De Corps Riding Academy, Kapa'a, 822-4688
Princeville Ranch Stables, 826-6777
Silver Falls Ranch, Kilauea, 828-6718

GOLF

Kaua'i Lagoons Golf Club, Kalapaki Bay, 800-634-6400
Grove Farm Golf Course at Puakea, 245-8756
Kiahuna Golf Club, Poipu, 742-9595
Kukuiolono Golf Course, Kalaheo, 332-9151
Poipu Bay Resort Golf Course, 800-858-6300
Princeville Golf Club, 800-826-1105
Wailua Golf Club, 241-6666

CAMPING PERMITS AND INFORMATION

Try to call for permits a month ahead of your trip. Camping is by permit only in established campsites. Backpacking in the tropics is challenging, even for experienced hikers; be prepared. Car camping in Koke'e and forest reserves is often at unimproved sites; get specifics from agencies listed below. Beach park camping is on small sites on lawn areas near parking, pavilions and restrooms. Plan for rain: Consider bringing a car-camping tent rather than a backpack tent.

Koke'e, Polihale and Haena State Parks, 274-3444,274-3446, 335-8405
Kalalau Trail, Napali Coast, 245-4444, 274-3445
> *Backpacking. Department of Land and Natural Resources, State Parks*

Koke'e Forest Reserves, including Waimea Canyon, 274-3433
> *Department of Land and Natural Resources, Forestry & Wildlife*

County Beach Park Camping, 241-4463, 241-4460
> *County of Kaua'i. Including these beach parks: Haena, Anini, Hanamaulu, Salt Pond, Lydgate, Kekaha, and Lucy Wright; see Trailhead Maps.*

MAPS

Kaua'i Trailblazer's maps and descriptions are all you need for recreating on the island. However, you may want a supplemental map. Generally speaking, the trick to hiking in Kaua'i—whether coastal or inland—is knowing where to go and finding the trailhead; and then following the trail, not a map.

Border's Books and Music, 246-0862, 245-3041 *carries most maps*
Full Color Topographic Map of Kaua'i, The Garden Isle.
> *Best overall for use with this book; indexed place names, widely available, inexpensive. By University of Hawaii Press.*

Northwestern Kaua'i Recreation Map, 800-828-MAPS
> *Best by far for Kalalau Trail, very good for Koke'e area; only includes half of island. By Earthwalk Press*

Na Ala Hele State Recreation Map, 274-3433
> *Very good for state park and forest reserve trails. Mile markers on map don't match highway. By State Department of Land and Natural Resources.*

Basically Books, 800-903-6277. *Bookstore on Big Island that does credit card phone orders; handles USGS and other maps.*

The Ready Mapbook of Kaua'i, 935-0092. *Handy companion street atlas.*

Koke'e Trails, 335-9975. *Inexpensive map for hiking woodland trails of Koke'e State Park. Available at museum at the park.*

USGS Topographic Maps, 888-ASK-USGS. *Because of jungle growth, steep relief and other factors, topo maps are not as useful in hiking Kaua'i as other places. They do not show roads and familiar place names, as a rule.*

MUSEUMS AND HISTORICAL ATTRACTIONS
Gay & Robinson Sugar Plantation Tours, Waimea, 335-2824
Grove Farm Homestead, Lihue, 245-3202
Kaua'i Coffee Company Visitors Center, Port Allen, 800-545-8605, 335-5497
Kaua'i Children's Discovery Museum, Kapa'a, 823-8222
Kaua'i Festivals, listings for island-wide events, 241-6390
Kaua'i Hindu Monastery, Kapa'a, 822-3012, 822-3152
Kaua'i Museum, Lihue, 245-6931
Kaua'i Village Heritage Museum, Kapa'a, 821-2070
Kilohana Plantation, Lihue, 245-5608
Koke'e Natural History Museum, Kokee, 335-9975
Waioli Mission House, Hanalei, 245-3202

GARDENS AND OUTDOOR ATTRACTIONS
Allerton/McBryde National Tropical Botanical Gardens, 742-2623, 742-2433
Fort Elizabeth State Park, Waimea, 245-4444
Gay & Robinson Sugar Plantation Tours, Waimea, 335-2824
Guava Kai Plantation, Kilauea, 828-6121
Kamokila Hawaiian Village, Wailua, 823-0559
Kaua'i Nursery & Landscaping, Lihue, 888-345-7747, 245-7747
Kaua'i Products Fair, Kapa'a, 246-0988
Kilauea Point National Wildlife Refuge, 828-1413, 828-0383, 246-2860
Kukui Jam factory, Kalaheo, 332-9333
Limahuli National Tropical Botanical Garden, Haena, 826-1053
Moir Gardens, Kiahuna Plantation, Poipu, 742-6411
Na Aina Kai Botanical Gardens, Kilauea, 828-0525
Orchid Alley, Kapa'a, 822-0486
Smith's Tropical Paradise, Wailua, 821-6895
Smith's Fern Grotto Cruise, Wailua, 821-6892

CULTURAL & CONSERVATION CONTACTS
Aloha Festivals, *ask for Kauai info,* 589-1771
Cloud Nine (lomi-lomi massage), 635-4475
Kahea, The Hawaiian Environmental Alliance, 524-8220
Kaua'i Heritage Center of Hawaiian Culture & Arts, 821-2070
Ki Hoalu Slack Key Guitar, 826-1469
Garden Island Arts Council, Lihue 246-4561
Ka'ie'ie Foundation, perpetuating Hawaiian culture, 821-2070
Kateo Club International, dance, 338-0265
Kaua'i Coconut Beach, kahiko hula (ancient dance), 822-3455
Susan Maika, fitness consultant, 651-4365

HAWAIIANA SHOPS & GALLERIES

Banana Patch Studio, Hanapepe, 335-5944

Bambulei, Wailua, chic antiques, 823-8641

Dawn M. Traina Gallery, Hanapepe, 335-3993

Hanapepe Art Center, 335-3442

Hawaii Express Flowers & Gifts, Lihue 888-345-7747, 245-7747

Hawaiian Trading Post, Lawai, 332-7404

Hilo Hattie's, Lihue, 245-4724

Hula Moon, Hanalei, 826-9965

Island Soap & Candle, Kilauea, 828-1955. Koloa, 742-1945

Island Mermaid Creations, Kilauea, *sculpture by Amy C. Vanderhoop* 828-6360

JJ Ohana, Hanapepe, 335-0366

Kapaia Stitchery, Hanamaulu, 245-2281

Kaua'i Fine Arts, Hanapepe, 335-3778

Kaua'i Fruit & Flower Co., Lihue, 245-1814

Kaua'i Heritage Center Of Hawaiian Culture & Arts, Kapa'a, 821-2070

Kaua'i Museum Gift Shop, Lihue, 246-2470

Kaua'i Products Store, Kukui Grove, 246-6753

Kilohana Galleries, Lihue 245-9352

Kong Lung, Kilauea, 828-1822

Magic Dragon Toy & Art, Princeville, 826-9144

Larry's Music Center, ukeleles, guitars, Kapa'a, 822-4181

Ola's, Hanalei, 826-6937

Sand People, Hanalei 826-1008; Poipu, 742-2888

Seven Seas Trading Company, Anchor, Cove, Nawiliwili, 632-2200

Ship Shore Galleries, Coconut Marketplace, 800-877-1948, 822-7758

Waimea Canyon General Store, Kekaha, 337-9569

Whalers General Store, Poipu, 742-9431 Coconut Marketplace, 822-9921

Yellowfish Trading Company, Hanalei, 826-1227

LOCAL INFORMATION

Chamber of Commerce, 245-7363

County of Kaua'i Transportation (public buses), 241-6410

Hawai'i Visitor and Conventions Bureau, 800-464-2924

Kaua'i Film Commission, Lihue, 241-6386

Kaua'i Visitors Bureau, 245-3971, 800-262-1400

Matson Shipping, 800-628-7661, 245-6701

Mayor's Office, 241-6300

Public Libraries, Lihue, 241-3222

Weather, 245-6001

Wind and Surf Conditions, 245-3564, 245-6001

Hawaiian Waters report, 245-3564, 335-3720

Where to eat

A calabash of island-style eats, ranging from take-out plates to Pacific Rim gourmet. Some have views and all have Kauai character. Not all serve dinner; call ahead to ask about menu specifics, prices, and ambience. All are recommended; special selections are boldfaced. Area codes are 808.

(C) Cheap or take-out
     (under $10)
(M) Moderate, family
     ($10-$20)
(P) Pricey, special occasion
     (over $20)

KILAUEA
PRINCEVILLE
HANALEI

Bar Acuda, Hanalei	(M) 826-7081
Bubba's Hanalei	(C) 826-7839
Cafe Hanalei,	
Princeville Hotel	(P) 826-2760
Hanalei Dolphin	(M-P) 826-6113
Hanalei Gourmet	(C-M) 826-2524
Hanalei Mixed Plate	(C) 826-7888
Java Kai, Hanalei	(C)826-6717
Kilauea Bakery-Pau Pizza	(M) 828-2020
Moloaʻa Sunrise	(C) 822-1441
Ono Char Burger, Anahola	(C) 822-9181
Polynesian Cafe, Hanalei	(C) 826-1999
Postcards Café, Hanalei	(M) 826-1191
Tahiti Nui, Hanalei	(M) 826-6277

KAPAʻA
COCONUT COAST

Aloha Diner	(C) 822-3851
Balle Vietnamese	(M) 823-6060
Bubba's, Kapaʻa	(C) 823-0069
Bull Shed, Kapaʻa	(M-P) 822-3791
Caffe Coco, Wailua	(C-M) 822-7990
Coconuts Grill	(C-M) 823-8777
Kealia Kountry Store	(C) 823-0708
Lemongrass Grill, Kapaʻa	(M) 821-2888
Mermaids Café, Kapaʻa	(C) 821-2026
Ono Family Restaurant	(C) 822-1710
Pacific Island Bistro, Wailua	(M) 822-0092
Papaya's, Wailua	(C) 823-0190
Restaurant Kintaro	(M) 822-3341
The Eggbert's, Kapaʻa	(M) 822-3787
Wailua Marina	(C-M) 822-4311

LIHUE
NAWILIWILI

Barbecue Inn	(C-M) 245-2921
Cafe Portofino, Marriots	(P) 245-2121
Dani's Restaurant	(C-M) 245-4991
Duke's Canoe Club,	
Kalapaki	(M-P) 246-9599
The Fish Express	(C-M) 245-9918
fresh seafood, gourmet picnic	
Garden Island Barbecue	(C) 245-8868
Hamura Saimin Stand	(C) 245-3271
Hanamaulu Restaurant	(C-M) 245-2511
JJ's Broiler, Kalapaki	(M) 246-4422
Rob's Good Times Grill	(C-M) 246-0311

KOLOA
POIPU

Beach House	(P) 742-1424
Casablanca, Poipu	(M-P) 742-2929
Cornerstone Deli, Lawai	(C) 332-0815
Dali Deli & Cafe, Koloa,	(C) 742-8824
Gaylord's, Kilohana Plantation	(P) 245-9593
Ilima Terrace	
Hyatt Regency	(M-P) 742-1234
Island Teriyaki, Koloa	(C) 742-9988
Poipu Tropical Burgers	(C-P) 742-1808
Roy's Poipu Bar & Grill	(M-P) 742-5000
Sueoka's Snack Shop, Koloa	(C) 742-1112
Keoki's Paradise, Poipu	(M) 742-7534
Plantation Garden, Poipu	(M-P) 742-2121

HANAPEPE
WAIMEA

Grinds Cafe, Port Allen	(C) 335-6027
Hanapepe Cafe	(M-P) 335-5011
Imu Hut Café	
Hanapepe	(C) 335-0200
Jo Jo's Clubhouse, Waimea	
	(C) 635-7615
Koke'e Lodge, Koke'e	
try their homemade chili	
	(C-M) 335-6061
Waimea Brewing Co.	
	(M) 338-9733
Wrangler's Steakhouse, Waimea	
	(M) 338-1218

Where To stay

Hyatt Regency

Give these places a call to inquire about amenities and location. Be sure to ask if you're getting the lowest rate, including weekly offerings. Calling is also a good way to find out which places have Aloha. Also contact Kaua'i Visitors Bureau, 800-464-2924. For island-wide referrals, try **Hawaii's Best Bed & Breakfast** at 800-262-9912.

Area code is 808 unless otherwise provided. All listings are recommended; special selections are boldfaced.

TYPE
(**Rustic**) Cabins, hostels
(**B&B**) Bed & Breakfasts, cottages, homes
(**Condos**) Condominium complex
(**Hotel**) Mid-range, mid-size hotels and motels
(**Resort**) High-end, larger, luxury
(**Agent**) Real estate broker for private residences

(**C**) Cheap ($60 to $100)   (**M**) Moderate (low-$100 to $200)   (**P**) Pricey ($200 & up)

NORTH SHORE — KILAUEA, PRINCEVILLE, HANALEI

Jagged green ridges, secret beaches, and waving palms on the North Shore will fulfill everyone's fantasy about what a tropical vacation should be. Hanalei is hip, funky, and beautiful, with walk-around sightseeing. Princeville is manicured condos and two hotels, set on a bluff and buffeted by golf courses and hike-to beaches. Anini Beach is a quieter, more remote beach community, and Kilauea has more of a pastoral feel. During the winter months, storms hit this shore, along with larger surf. During the summer, blue lagoons await. The North Shore is also a long haul to visit other parts of the island. Oceanfront Realty has excellent service and a line on a wide range of places.

Aloha Sunrise Inn, Kilauea (cottages)	(**M**) 888-828-1008, 828-1100
Anini Aloha Properties (Agent)	(**M-P**) 800-323-4450
Jungle Cabana, Wainiha (cottage)	(**M**) 888-886-4969
Hanalei Bay Resort, Princeville (Resort)	(**M-P**) 800-922-7866
Hanalei Colony Resort, Haena (Hotel)	(**P**) 800-628-3004
Hanalei North Shore Properties (Agent)	(**M-P**) 800-488-3336
Oceanfront Realty (Agent)	(**C-P**) 800-222-5541, 826-6585
Princeville Resort (Resort)	(**P**) 800-782-9488, 826-9644

COCONUT COAST — KAPA'A, WAILUA

With palm groves and coral reef at the shore and mountainous forest reserves inland, the Coconut Coast is a place to visit, no matter where your room is on the island. Weather is decent year around, and the central location makes the rest of Kauai easily accessible. Wailua is where the ancient kings first settled Hawaii, so they must've known something. Cottages in rural neighborhoods await inland.

Aloha BeachResort (Resort), Wailua	**(M-P)** 888-823-5111
Alohilani (B&B)	**(C)** 800-533-9316
B&B Kauai (Agent)	**(C-M)** 823-0128
Garden Island Properties (Agent)	**(C-P)** 800-801-0378
Islander on the Beach (Hotel)	**(C-M)** 800-847-7417
Kaua'i International Hostel, Kapa'a (Rustic)	**(C)** 823-6142
Makana Crest (B&B)	**(C)** 245-6500
Island Rentals (Agent)	**(C-M)** 822-4899
Plantation Hale (Condos)	**(M)** 800-775-4253
Pono Kai (Condos)	**(M-P)** 800-535-0085
Rainbow's End (B&B cottage)	**(C-M)** 961-3833, 966-4663
Sleeping Giant Realty (Agent)	**(C-M)** 800-247-8831
Treehouse, Kapa'a (B&B cottage)	**(C)** 822-7681

LIHUE AND NAWILIWILI

Lihue is the county seat and business district, meaning fewer tourists stay here. But the place is hardly urban, and you can find cheap rooms with quirky neighborhood restaurants and shops nearby. Some of the condos in Nawiliwili, are working-class. All of the island is doable from this central location.

Garden Island Inn (Hotel)
    (C-M) 800-648-0154
Hilton Kauai Beach Resort, Nukoli`i
    (P) 888-805-3843
Kauai Palms Hotel
    (C) 246-0908

Treehouse, Kapa'a

(**C**) Cheap ($60 to low-$100)   (**M**) Moderate (mid-$100 to $200)   (**P**) Pricey (mid-$200 & up)

POIPU AND KOLOA

Beach potatoes will like sunny Poipu, particularly in the winter when surf is lowest and the weather is approaching from the other side of the island. (Surf's up in the summer here.) Although resorts create their own gardens, the environs are arid, with low scrub on the coast, giving way to indigenous forests inland. Good snorkeling and scenic coast walking is to be had, along with ready access to Waimea Canyon, west Kauai, and Allerton Garden. Hanalei is a long haul, but reachable on a day trip. Rates vary from mid-range condos—which tend to be spaced fairly close—to the luxury rooms at the fabulous Hyatt Regency. In Kola and inland communities, you can find low- to -mid-priced cottages in garden settings.

Gloria's Spouting Horn (B&B)	(**P**) 742-6995
Grantham Resorts (Agent)	(**M-P**) 800-742-1412
Hale O Kapeka, Poipu B&B)	(**M**) 742-6806
Hyatt Regency Kauai (Resort)	(**P**) 800-233-1234
Kahili Mountain Park (Rustic)	(**C**) 742-9921 *some restrictions, go to www.kahilipark.org for current info*
Kiahuna Plantation (Condos)	(**M**) 800-367-8020
Koloa Landing Cottages (B&B)	(**C-M**) 800-779-8773
Kuhio Shores (Condos)	(**C-M**) 800-367-8022
Lawai Beach (Condos)	(**M-P**) 800-367-8020
Nihi Kai Villas (Condos)	(**M**) 800-367-8020
Poipu Crater Resort (Condos)	(**C**) 800-367-8020
Poipu Kai Resort (Condos)	(**C-P**) 800-367-8020
Poipu Shores (Condos)	(**M-P**) 800-367-8020
Sheraton Kauai (Resort)	(**P**) 888-847-0208
Suite Paradise (Agent)	(**C-P**) 800-367-8020
Whalers Cove (Condos)	(**P**) 800-367-8020

WEST SIDE — WAIMEA, KOKE'E, KALAHEO

The West Side is basically non-tourist, although during the day rental cars parade to Waimea Canyon and Barking Sands Beach. This is the arid side of Kauai, which means sun most-often graces its long, long beaches. Hanapepe and Waimea are home to many native Hawaiians, and draw visitors looking for old-style rural settings spaced within endless open expanses of blue water. Poipu is close by, but the North Shore is a long day trip. You won't find many places to stay, but deals are available. Koke'e State Park is a few thousand feet up, so prepare for cool weather if that's your choice.

Camp Sloggett, Koke'e (Rustic, also campsites)	(**C**) 245-5959
Kauai Tree Houses, Kalaheo (B&B)	(**C**) 635-3945, 332-9045
Koke'e Lodge Cabins (Rustic)	(**C**) 335-6061
Waimea Plantation Cottages (Resort)	(**P**) 800-922-7860, 338-1625

surfin'
da web

INFORMATIONAL:

www.aloha.net/~kokee
www.aloha-hawaii.com
www.alternative-hawaii.com
www.andhawaii.com
www.e-kauai.com
www.gohawaii.com
www.royalelephant.com
www.hawaii.com
www.hawaii.gov/dlnr/dsp/kauai.com
www.hawaii-nation.org
www.hawaiitrails.org
www.hawaiweathertoday.com
www.pacificislandbooks.com
www.kauaibeachpress.com
www.kauaicc.hawaii.edu
www.kauaigov.org
www.kauai-hawaii.com/parks
www.hawaii-stuff.com
www.kauaimonkseal.com
www.kauainews.com
www.kauaivisitorsbureau.org
www.kauaiworld.com (weather)
www.mele.com
www.ntbg.com
www.oleo.hawaii.edu
www.planet-hawaii.com
www.nativebooks.com
www.thisweek.com
www.trailblazertravelbooks.com
www.101things.com

ACTIVITIES & SERVICES:

www.alohaair.com
www.bikehawaii.com
www.booklines.com
www.campingkauai.com
www.cjmstables.com
www.scuba.about.com
www.kauaiseatours.com
www.hawaiianair.com
www.hulasource.com
www.islandbookshelf.com
www.kauaifrit.com
www.kauaiwedding.com
www.kayakkauai.com
www.kilaueatheater.com
www.outfitterskauai.com
www.rainbowphoto.com
www.sailing-hawaii.com
www.uhpress.hawaii.edu
www.waimeatheater.com

ACCOMMODATIONS:

www.wheretostay.com
www.oceanfrontrealty.com
www.bestplaces.com
www.bnb-kauai.com
www.hanaleisurf.com
www.hanalei-vacations.com
www.kauai-bedandbreakfast.com
www.kauaivacationrentals.com
www.poipubeach.org
www.seatours.com
www.staykauai.com
www.suiteparadise.com
www.travel-kauai.com

index

Notes

FOR PUBLISHER-DIRECT SAVINGS TO INDIVIDUALS AND GROUPS, AND
FOR BOOK TRADE ORDERS, PLEASE CONTACT:

DIAMOND VALLEY COMPANY
89 Lower Manzanita Drive
Markleeville, CA 96120

Phone-fax: 530-694-2740
www.trailblazertravelbooks.com
trailblazer@gbis.com

All titles are also available through major book distributors, stores, and websites.
Please contact the publisher with comments and suggestions.
We value your readership.

DIAMOND VALLEY COMPANY'S
TRAILBLAZER TRAVEL BOOK SERIES:

ALPINE SIERRA TRAILBLAZER
Where to Hike, Ski, Bike, Pack, Paddle,
Fish from Lake Tahoe to Yosemite
ISBN 0-9670072-6-7
*"A must-have guide. The best and most
attractive guidebook for the Sierra.
With you every step of the way."*
— Tahoe Action

KAUAI TRAILBLAZER
Where to Hike, Snorkel,
Bike, Paddle, Surf
ISBN 0-9670072-1-6
*Number one, world-wide among
adventure guides. — Barnesandnoble.com*

GOLDEN GATE TRAILBLAZER
Where to Hike, Walk, Bike
in San Francisco and Marin
ISBN 0-9670072-7-5
"Makes you want to strap on your boots and go!"
— Sunset Magazine

MAUI TRAILBLAZER
Where to Hike, Snorkel,
Paddle, Surf, Drive
ISBN 0-9670072-4-0
"The best of them all."
— Maui Weekly

HAWAII THE BIG ISLAND TRAILBLAZER
Where to Hike, Snorkel, Bike, Surf, Drive
ISBN 0-9670072-5-9
*Top three world-wide among adventure
guides. — Barnesandnoble.com*

OAHU TRAILBLAZER
Where to Hike, Snorkel, Surf
from Honolulu to the North Shore
ISBN 0-9670072-8-3
*"Marvelously flexible. If you aren't sure what
you're looking for, the Best of Oahu list outlines
top attractions, hikes, snorkeling and surfing,
organized to suit your mood and the day."*
— San Francisco Chronicle